Praise for *A Guide to Early Printed Books and M...*

"This is an absolutely essential book. We f
English printed books and manuscripts, bu
through every aspect of the making and circu
binding to reading. Mark Bland meets an urgent need."

Peter Stallybrass, University of Pennsylvania

"Bland's emphasis on the human element of textual production makes this introduction to bibliography attractively readable, where often the subject can seem arid to beginners, but it also is rooted in his conviction that the study of texts must always be grounded in an awareness of the people who contributed to every aspect of their creation."

Chartered Institute of Library and Information Professionals

"Showing an extensive knowledge of the scholarship in his field [Bland] provides an objective assessment, often correcting false reasoning and offering a sound explanation of the facts. . . . I believe that Mark Bland's *Guide* would be of help to anyone interested in the discipline."

European Review of History

"Bland offers a clear and comprehensive guide to bibliography, and it is appropriate that it is most likely to come into its own as part of the work of making meaning, wedged open beneath a researcher's elbow."

The Review of English Studies

"This book is indeed a very practical, clear and valuable guide to books and manuscripts of the sixteenth and seventeenth centuries. . . . The book is well illustrated and Bland makes good use of the images, especially in his exemplary discussion in Chapter Two about how to use watermark evidence."

Script and Print

"Wide-ranging and commendably concise, this handbook provides an up-to-date and practical guide to bibliographical concepts, methods and terminology. . . . This book will equip students, perhaps encountering sixteenth- and seventeenth-century texts for the first time, in their early printed or manuscript form (as distinct from modern editions), to approach bibliographical description and analysis without fear or confusion and, for those wishing to pursue the subject more widely, it will serve admirably as an introduction."

Routledge ABES

"A gateway to some of the major works of bibliography."

Library and Information History

"Bland's *Guide* is distinguished by intelligent and comprehensive coverage, by his extensive knowledge of current scholarship in the field, and by his personal research and rethinking."

The Library

Of related interest

A Companion to the History of the Book
Edited by Simon Eliot and Jonathan Rose

A Concise Companion to Shakespeare and the Text
Edited by Andrew Murphy

Elizabethan and Jacobean England
Edited by Arthur F. Kinney

A GUIDE TO

EARLY PRINTED BOOKS

AND

MANUSCRIPTS

❧

MARK BLAND

A John Wiley & Sons, Ltd., Publication

This paperback edition first published 2013
© 2013 Mark Bland
Edition history: Blackwell Publishing Ltd (hardback, 2010)

Blackwell Publishing was acquired by John Wiley & Sons in February 2007. Blackwell's
publishing program has been merged with Wiley's global Scientific, Technical, and Medical
business to form Wiley-Blackwell.

Registered Office
John Wiley & Sons Ltd, The Atrium, Southern Gate, Chichester, West Sussex, PO19 8SQ, UK

Editorial Offices
350 Main Street, Malden, MA 02148-5020, USA
9600 Garsington Road, Oxford, OX4 2DQ, UK
The Atrium, Southern Gate, Chichester, West Sussex, PO19 8SQ, UK

For details of our global editorial offices, for customer services, and for information about
how to apply for permission to reuse the copyright material in this book please see our
website at www.wiley.com/wiley-blackwell.

The right of Mark Bland to be identified as the author of this work has been asserted in
accordance with the UK Copyright, Designs and Patents Act 1988.

Library of Congress Cataloging-in-Publication Data
Bland, Mark.
   A guide to early printed books & manuscripts/Mark Bland.
      p. cm.
   Includes bibliographical references and index.
   ISBN 978-1-4051-2412-6 (cloth) – 978-1-118-49215-4 (pbk.)
   1. Bibliography, Critical.   2. Early printed books–16th century–Bibliography–Methodology.
3. Early printed books–17th century–Bibliography–Methodology.   4. Manuscripts,
European–History–16th century.   5. Manuscripts, European–History–17th century.
6. Codicology.   7. Transmission of texts–Europe–History–16th century.   8. Transmission
of texts–Europe–History–17th century   I. Title.
   Z1001.B64 2010
   010′.42–dc22
                                                                              2009029981

A catalogue record for this book is available from the British Library.

Cover image: Opera Francisci baronis de Verulamio, Francis Bacon, 1623. By permission of
Bodleian Library, University of Oxford.
Cover design by Design Deluxe

Set in 10/12pt Jannon Text Moderne Pro by Graphicraft Limited, Hong Kong. This typeface was
designed by František Storm of the Storm Type Foundry, based on a design first published by
the engraver Jean Jannon in 1621.

Printed in Malaysia by Ho Printing (M) Sdn Bhd

1   2013

To the memories

of

Don McKenzie
(1931–99)

&

Julia Briggs
(1943–2007)

and for my parents

Fred & Phillippa

Contents

Illustrative Materials

I would like to thank the Bodleian Library, the British Library, the National Library of Scotland, the National Library of Wales, Trinity College, Dublin, the Houghton Library, Harvard University, the Beinecke Library, Yale University, and the Huntington Library for permission to publish these materials.

Acknowledgments

THIS book began with a light-hearted remark: late in 2003, over coffee with Tiffany Stern, I suggested for some amusement that we write a book on literary methodology; she, to my surprise, suggested that I write a book about the practice of bibliography as it pertains to early printed books and manuscripts. On our way back to the Bodleian, she urged me to think about it more seriously. A few days later, I saw Andrew McNeillie, who at that time was still at Blackwell. I mentioned the conversation to him; at an astonishing speed, he agreed, a proposal was written, readers' reports came in, and a contract was issued. Alas, I must confess, progress since then has been rather slower than anticipated. To Tiffany and Andrew, unintended godparents of this book, who were there at its inception, I owe my heartfelt thanks.

I dislike extended litanies of obligation, but there are some debts that need to be acknowledged, both professional and personal. If I was to mention every library, record office, and archive I have visited, the list would be very long, so I hope it is sufficient to say to those who have helped me, in ways both minor and more extensively, that my debt is deeply felt. Similarly, I have had conversations, not all of which can be remembered, that made me reflect on an idea or issue that was on my mind at the time: for every suggestion that was made to me, or anything I had to explain, I owe those who were interested my gratitude.

There are some libraries, and their staff, to whom I owe a more particular debt. The Alexander Turnbull Library was the first nursery of my studies, and it has been a pleasure to engage with its collections, and to benefit from the gift as it was first intended and conceived. Similarly, at Duke Humfrey's, the staff have unfailingly catered to my requests for almost 20 years, and have quietly taught me more than they realized. Similarly, the staff of the relevant collections at Cambridge University Library, Trinity College, Cambridge, the National Library of Scotland, the Houghton Library at Harvard, the Beinecke Library at Yale, the Newberry Library and the University of Chicago, the Folger Shakespeare Library and Library of Congress, the Harry Ransom Center at the University of Texas, and the Huntington Library have helped with my understanding of these matters in ways that are largely beyond recall, although the debts are no less real. To my employer, De Montfort University, I am grateful for the patience and support that have been shown. To Emma Bennett, and the production staff at Blackwell, I hope this book has justified the wait: they have been enormously tolerant.

A number of colleagues and friends have been kind beyond duty or friendship, and have provided me with both support and advice: to David McKitterick, Laurie Maguire, John Pitcher, Tiffany Stern, Andrew McNeillie, Paul Eggert, Steven May, Peter Lindenbaum, Marta Werner, Randall McLeod, Stephen Orgel, and Gary Day, I am indebted for the support and kindness they have shown. On a more personal level, I would like to thank Marcus Quiren, Karl Davies, Tim Myatt, Jeff and Jessica Staniland, Tim Brown and Gael Webster, Felicity Gifford, Tim O'Brien, Olika Kortiyeva, Neil Sewell-Rutter and Emilia Markot: at one stage or another of this journey, they have all made things possible.

To Peter Shillingsburg, the debt is both more serious and specific: to him I owe the wisdom of his company, his engagement with everything that I have done in recent years, his sometimes acerbic but always astute comments on what I have written, his patience with my foibles, his discussions of textual scholarship and bibliographical history beyond the call of professional kindness, his generosity and companionship, and his profound sense of decency. I could not have asked for a better colleague, or friend, in my first four years at De Montfort.

Bright lights cast deep shadows. It was on my return from London to New Zealand in 1979 that I found myself, aged 17, at Victoria University sitting alongside Mary McCallum in the second row on the left-hand side of Easterfield 006. In the course of the next hour, my life changed, although it took longer perhaps to realize the full significance of what that class had meant. Over the next few years, I was privileged to be taught by Don McKenzie on several occasions and, in 1983, he not only supervised my 'dissertation' on the late plays of Jonson; Alexandra Lutyens, Jan Moore, and I were the last students to take his literary scholarship class before he left for Oxford. A few years later, he was my supervisor in Oxford, and I last saw him in the Bodleian a day or two before I went out to New Zealand in 1999, three weeks before his death. This book would have been immensely better for his oversight and advice: I hope it does some justice to the debt I owe him.

Julia Briggs had been at Oxford with Don, and when I moved to De Montfort we shared an office together for several years: at idle hours, our conversation would often turn to the debt we both felt towards his inspiration and kindness. Julia had a knack of reminding me of my better instincts: whatever Don had left brick, she made marble.

The debt to my parents ought not to require any further explanation: I have been graced by their support, generosity, and love.

Oxford
10 May 2009

1 A Guide for the Perplexed

THIS is a book about how to look at written and printed words, not as texts, but as processes of communication in which meaning is made through the relationship between signs, structures, and materials. It has been written to complement the use of Gaskell, and to expand on those areas that were not covered in his book.[1] In the following pages, the intention is both to explain the methods and processes that are used to describe and study early printed books and manuscripts, and to situate that understanding in a scholarly context in order that the insights so derived might be fruitfully employed. The focus will shift from broader narratives about the methods and ideas employed in bibliographical study to specific details and examples that serve to make a more general point. The illustrations have been chosen, where possible, with an eye to freshness. The hope is that those who wish to read this will be able to look at a book or manuscript and study the way in which it was made, the processes through which it may have evolved, and its history as reflected through the archival records as well as the evidence of its use.

I

When we look at the handwriting of someone that we do not know, we form an impression of their personality from their 'character'. We may not do so consciously, but we sense handwriting to be unique and revealing. We perceive whether the script is open or tight; whether the forms are regular and disciplined, or whether majuscules and miniscules are mixed together. We notice whether the hand slopes in one direction, or whether there is a lack of consistency. The size of the letters may be large, small, or so cramped as to require magnification (and perhaps psychoanalysis) to be read. There is an immediate sense of whether a hand looks 'normal', even highly educated; or whether it shows the tremor and difficulty of age. Sometimes a script will reveal illiteracy (that the person has difficulty co-ordinating the letter forms), or it may convey a visceral sense of some deeper kind of personal disturbance. At a glance, we make all these assessments, and usually know whether it was written by a man or a woman, and perhaps the approximate age of the person concerned (owing to a period style, or immaturity), without reading a word.

Except amongst forensic specialists and palaeographers, no-one trains a person to read handwriting: rather, it is a judgment that is made from

---

[1] P. Gaskell, *A New Introduction to Bibliography* (Oxford, 1972; rev. edn. 1974).

experience: difference alerts us either to patterns that have been seen before, or to strangeness. Looking at early printed books and manuscripts requires the same kind of visual, tactile, and historical discrimination: memory, comparative analysis, and sensory perception are fundamental skills that are as much applied as they are theoretical. If the thoughts 'I have seen that elsewhere' or 'that looks odd' occur when handling a document, then the instinct should not be ignored. All early modern documents were subject to variation from one copy to another: there is, even for the same printed edition, no such thing as a duplicate copy in *all* its physical and textual details. As McKitterick remarks, books 'ostensibly offering shared knowledge on the basis of standardised text and image, in fact provided only partial standardisation'.[2]

To understand why some things may be unusual, it is necessary to have a feeling for what is conventional, and the only way to do this is to handle the original items, and a lot of them: microfilm or digital images may provide easy access and magnification, but they obscure information about the internal structure of a document; they impede descriptive methods, and they do not (beyond the image supplied) afford details about provenance or use, or give any indication about paper or bindings. To the scholar who has not seen a physical copy, they may be misleading about dimensions as well as type, and they cannot be structurally examined to determine what changes, if any, have been made. Textually, digital and print facsimile resources facilitate rapid access to an image of the original, but the limitations of simulacra need to be understood.

It is always helpful to look at multiple copies (if possible), to take detailed notes (including physical dimensions and shelfmarks—or call numbers as they are sometimes known), and to be aware not only of the history of the document, but of the libraries in which copies are found. It is not unusual to find that one copy of a printed book may have details about its earliest price or date of publication; another, a gift binding; a third may have marginalia, or an interesting provenance: cumulatively, copy-specific details build up a more complex picture than that which any one volume might present. Further, all copies (whether manuscript or printed) will differ from one another owing to either the practices of a particular intermediary, or as a result of proof correction.

Very deliberately, the emphasis in this *Guide* is on both manuscript and print, which are viewed as parts of a larger whole rather than as being separate fields of study. There are certain technical terms, methods of description, and conventions that are used. Thus a *printer* was fallible

---

[2] D. J. McKitterick, *Print, Manuscript and the Search for Order, 1450–1830* (Cambridge, 2003), 80.

flesh and blood, not a machine linked to a computer, whilst a book that is *slightly foxed* is not in a state of (inanimate) confusion but has paper that is discoloured owing to the conditions in which it has been kept. Other words, such as *felt* and *revise* have a specific technical meaning.[3]

When we look at books as books, we are conscious of more than simply shape, colour, and weight. Imagine, for instance, that on the table is a copy of an early eighteenth-century poem, printed in folio and set in large type with obvious spaces between the lines. If a literary person was asked 'What is the most obvious thing about what you are looking at?', their first reply might be something like 'It is a poem.' To the extent that a poem involves the layout of type on a page in a way that distinguishes it from prose, the answer would have some cunning, but to distinguish the text as 'a poem' is to invite a literary reading of the words as *words*. The most obvious thing about the page (before anything had been 'read') is, in fact, the size of the type and the space between the lines, and that is the step that is often overlooked: large type and extra space meant more paper was used, more paper meant more expense, and someone had to pay the bill—quite possibly not the printer, or publisher. The difference between looking at a page and seeing 'a poem', or seeing a relationship between type, paper, and space is the difference between 'being literary', and thinking like a bibliographer. The physical aspects of a text are always determined by the economics of book production ('Who paid for this?' is a useful question, if one not always possible to answer), as well as the materials and methods combined to create the document.

There is a second point to the example as well, and it has to do with the relationship between form and meaning. To recognize that the text is 'a poem' is to recognize something about its form, its conventions, and its readership.[4] In the first instance, the text does not matter. If, to make the point clear, we were to discover that the text was, in fact, a prayer, we would want to know why the conventions of one textual form had been applied to another; and we would want to know who made that decision, why, and whether the text was, in some way, verse. What the text actually said would still be of secondary importance, and would only come into play once we had understood the way in which the formal criteria had been reapplied. Over time, this is how the conventions of textual design evolve: slight adjustments are made to the formal aspects of presentation

---

[3] An important general reference work for such terms is J. Carter, *ABC for Book Collectors* (London, 1952; last revised, 1973; many subsequent editions); see also, P. Beal, *A Dictionary of English Manuscript Terminology 1450–2000* (Oxford, 2008).

[4] See, N. Barker, *Things Not Revealed* (London, 2001, in offprint): these Panizzi Lectures were given out at the end of the final lecture but have yet to be finally published.

that cumulatively affect the appearance of the page in quite radical ways. Furthermore, texts get presented in new ways to reflect the changing history of their use: an early edition of Shakespeare was printed according to the conventions of seventeenth-century casual reading; a modern edition is usually designed for the classroom with its accompanying introduction, illustrations, notes, and list of textual variants.

An awareness of how the formal aspects of books affect their transmission, and of how the material evidence speaks not of the text but of its own history, lies behind the assertion by Greg that 'with these signs [the bibliographer] is concerned merely as arbitrary marks; their meaning is no business of his', although he allowed that 'we all involuntarily pay attention to the sense of the texts we are studying'.[5] In more recent times, Greg's comment has been ridiculed, and his obvious literary interests pointed up, but that criticism is mistaken in its understanding of the distinction that he was trying to make. Greg believed 'that bibliography necessarily includes, as its most distinctive branch, the study of textual transmission',[6] and he argued for the need to take account of physical processes when establishing the history of a text.

One of the most obvious ways to trace the evolution of a text is to study its typography, or its manuscript equivalent, script. The history of letterforms, and the way in which they are laid out on a page reflect social conventions as well as individual choice. This is why it is possible, simply by looking at a document, to estimate when it was made to within a period of five or ten years. Bindings similarly reveal periods and tastes, as do the apparently incidental features of format, ornament stocks, and the use of ruled borders. Each of these elements has required a conscious decision by someone at some time, and for this reason it is as necessary to see the text as to read it. Indeed, sometimes it helps not to read the text at all—certainly it helps to read the text only after these other aspects of the book have been taken into consideration.

Bibliography is a historical and analytical discipline concerned with literature in the broadest meaning of that word. Hence, it is an appreciation of literary texts and historical facts that usually shapes a desire to recover more accurately the history of a text through the processes of its making and the ways in which it was read.[7] The point,

---

[5] W. W. Greg, 'Bibliography—An Apologia', (Oxford, 1966), 247, 248.

[6] Greg, 'Bibliography—An Apologia' 259.

[7] Greg was unashamedly frank about this connection, to his later detriment at the hands of scholars who ought to have admitted as much: 'At any rate I freely confess that my own interest in bibliography is by no means purely bibliographical. It is literary. . . . It was the results of bibliography that I wanted but my search led me to the far greater discovery of the importance of the subject itself': 'What Is Bibliography?', *Collected Papers*, 82.

however, is that in order to understand printed books and manuscripts, the approach to literary documents cannot be limited to 'high' literature. A printing-house produced more than play quartos or sermons, a scrivener copied more than verse (in fact, more often a scrivener copied political and financial documents), whilst those private individuals who copied poems also wrote letters and wrote or copied other documents. Unless the full range of evidence is taken into account, crucial details will be overlooked that may affect our understanding of such basic matters as attribution, date, or the identity of the person responsible for copying or producing a document. Almost certainly, a limited perspective will deny to any text its proper *context*, and thus obscure the purpose that it first served. There is nothing difficult about being thorough; the problem with thoroughness is that not all the evidence will survive, and that it is time-consuming and, sometimes, wearying.

Perhaps the most basic concept that needs to be borne in mind when studying early books and manuscripts is that repetition reveals process, identity, and expectation; difference describes history. The information so derived may be of two kinds: physical or cultural. For instance, the shift from black-letter to roman, the setting of text within rules and the subsequent disappearance of such rules, the shift from sidenotes to footnotes,[8] and from single-volume folio collections to multi-volume octavo sets, are all defining moments in the evolution of the early printed book, but they can only be perceived to be so because of their difference from past practices. Individual traits may equally be recognized: both Bacon and Jonson preferred (and had access to) fine Italian and Spanish paper rather than the coarser but more commonly available imports from northern France. Whilst the vanity of Margaret Cavendish is revealed in her choice of double pica type for the printing her books—a size larger than even the *Works* of King James, and matched as a text font in the period only by royal proclamations and other broadsides of that ilk. Some authors paid to have their books printed, or paid for special work to be done, but Cavendish is the first clear example among English authors of someone who simply had her work printed in a type of a very large size.

II

As a discipline, bibliography has always allowed itself a very broad scope, even if at times the practice has been rather narrower. All bibliographers, or historians of the book, are interested in the methods

---

[8] See, A. T. Grafton, *The Footnote: A Curious History* (Princeton NJ, 1997).

and mechanisms of human communication and record. Yet defining what this involves succinctly, and how it differs from other disciplines that are broadly interested in the same texts and materials, has provoked considerable debate. In their respective ways, such issues as the role of memory in the transmission of the past, and the instabilities of the digital archive, extend the discipline beyond what is written, printed, or inscribed on a durable surface.[9] With some prescience, almost a century ago, Sir Walter Greg defined the subject as the study of 'the transmission of all symbolic representation of speech or other ordered sound or even of logical thought', and he described what he called 'critical bibliography' as 'the science of the material transmission of literary texts'—the word 'literary' having the meaning 'written' rather than narrowly 'of aesthetic interest' although, even by Greg, this is how it came to be applied.[10]

In some ways, Greg was his own worst enemy. When he first set out his ideas, he was careful not to limit the scope of the subject to printed books (a restriction that he termed 'a very foolish one'); but, in practice, the study of manuscripts, and of memorial, and inscribed texts remained limited to those scholars who had to establish a relationship between non-printed texts in order to study a particular author (Donne is the obvious early modern example). The study of English printed books and early printing-houses, on the other hand, was largely driven by the editing of Shakespeare and the Renaissance drama. Continental book production, and the editing of humanist authors became a separate area of interest, as did the novels and verse of the eighteenth, nineteenth, and early twentieth centuries. Gaskell sought to find some common ground between these various fields of research; but, as a consequence, the focus of his account is deliberately on the production and description of printed books.[11] By the 1970s, medieval and early modern manuscript studies had become, almost, separate disciplines unto themselves.

The important moment of change in bibliographical studies, though delayed in its reception, was laid out in the 1957 Lyell Lectures of the great typographer Stanley Morison (best known for the design of Times Roman). These lectures, which are magnificent for their sheer generosity of scope and richness of detail, went largely unnoticed through the 1960s,

[9] See, in particular, D. F. McKenzie, 'What's Past Is Prologue: The Bibliographical Society and the History of the Book', *Making Meaning: 'Printers of the Mind' and Other Essays* (Amherst MA, 2002), 259–75; also, P. L. Shillingsburg, *From Gutenberg to Google: Electronic Representations of Literary Texts* (Cambridge, 2006).

[10] Greg, 'What Is Bibliography?', 75–88 esp. 78 and 83; Greg's paper was first published in *The Library* in 1914.

[11] Gaskell, *New Introduction*, 1.

as they were not published until 1972.[12] Whilst some have criticized aspects of Morison's argument,[13] the lectures exemplify in their scale of vision the principle that was established on the first page of the introduction: it is not only, he observed, that without bibliography 'the accurate description of anything written, engraved, or printed for the purpose of being read cannot be complete' (something that is necessary for the comparison and analysis of artefacts as witnesses to the texts they record), and thus 'It is the task . . . of the bibliographer to control documentation'; he claimed that the 'grammatically or philologically accurate transcription of a set of alphabetical signs may not always exhaust the suggestions of the text'. What then followed was a statement that Morison modestly suggested was 'for the future':

> The bibliographer may be able, by his study of the physical form of an inscription, manuscript, book, newspaper, or other medium of record, to reveal considerations that appertain to the history of something distinct from religion, politics, and literature, namely: the history of the use of the intellect. So far, that is, as intellect has made its record in script, inscription, or type.[14]

In New Zealand, the first person to borrow Morison's *Politics and Script*, on its arrival at Victoria University of Wellington Library, was D. F. McKenzie.[15] During the 1960s, McKenzie used his detailed knowledge of the Cambridge University Press at the end of the seventeenth-century to overturn prevailing assumptions about early modern printing-houses, most notably in the landmark article 'Printers of the Mind'.[16] Morison offered McKenzie the next step in his argument, one that shifted the study of printing-houses in a positive direction towards an engagement with all the methods of textual transmission in their full complexity.

---

[12] S. A. Morison, *Politics and Script: Aspects of Authority and Freedom in the Development of Græco-Latin Script from the Sixth Century B.C. to the Twentieth Century A.D.*, ed. N. J. Barker (Oxford, 1972). An important related study is M. B. Parkes, *Pause and Effect: An Introduction to the History of Punctuation in the West* (Aldershot, 1993).

[13] For instance, A. Petrucci, 'Symbolic Aspects of Written Evidence', *Writers and Readers in Medieval Italy: Studies in the History of Written Culture*, ed. and trans. C. M. Radding (New Haven CT, 1995), 103–31.

[14] Morison, *Politics and Script*, 1. The comment is also a critique of Greg's claim that the 'real aim and value' of type is that 'it enables us to assign an undated and unlocated book to a particular place and date' (Greg, 'Bibliography—An Apologia', 242).

[15] Shelfmark Z40 M861 P: The issue card has been removed, but the date stamp remains.

[16] First published, D. F. McKenzie, 'Printers of the Mind: Some Notes on Bibliographical Theories and Printing-House Practices', *Studies in Bibliography*, 22 (1969), 1–76; reprinted: *Making Meaning*, 13–85.

Starting from his Sandars Lectures in 1976, then at Wolfenbüttel the following year, again in his presidential address to the Bibliographical Society in 1982, and finally in the inaugural Panizzi Lectures at the British Library in 1985, McKenzie outlined an agenda that moved bibliography away from Greg's positivism towards 'a sociology of texts'.[17] In doing so, he sought to reassert the view of Greg and Morison that the discipline involved more than the study of printed books, and that a text was more than words. He was less concerned to critique Greg's intention, than to address the ways in which Greg had emphasized text over artefact.

McKenzie's career demonstrates that he understood the sociology of texts to be a product of the archaeology of texts as documents. He had perceived both that the material forms of documents might reveal (in Morison's phrase) 'the history of the use of the human intellect', and that they revealed, as French scholarship described, the history of a society as manifest in its uses of texts as a means of record. It is this dual insight that can serve to show that printed books and manuscripts are always witnesses to a history that is separate from the texts that they preserve. As he put it in the Panizzi Lectures: 'In its ubiquity and variety of evidence, bibliography as a sociology of texts has an unrivalled power to resurrect authors in their own time, and their readers at any time.'[18] That view has subsequently been developed in various ways, most notably for early modern studies by such scholars as Roger Chartier, Mirjam Foot, Harold Love, David McKitterick, Randall McLeod, and Henry Woudhuysen.[19]

The most potent aspect of McKenzie's reformulation of the discipline (and this is something that has not always been properly understood) was that he reunited the study of books and manuscripts as artefacts with a broader awareness of the history of books and texts in their malleable and unstable forms. Further, he suggested that bibliography would have to deal with the role of memory in the transmission of texts, especially in non-literate societies, as well as more recent technologies such as film, music, and digital encryption. Language, he remarked, 'knows no social

---

[17] D. F. McKenzie, *The London Book-Trade in the Later Seventeenth Century* (typescript 1976, on deposit at selected libraries); 'Typography and Meaning: The Case of William Congreve', *Making Meaning*, 198–236.

[18] D. F. McKenzie, *Bibliography and the Sociology of Texts* (London, 1986), 19. See note 4 regarding Panizzi Lectures.

[19] For instance, R. Chartier, *The Order of Books* (Oxford, 1994); —, *Publishing Drama in Early Modern Europe* (London, 1998); M. M. Foot, *The History of Bookbinding as a Mirror of Society* (London, 1998); H. Love, *Scribal Publication in Seventeenth Century England* (Oxford, 1993); —, *Attributing Authorship: An Introduction* (Cambridge, 2002); —, *English Clandestine Satire 1660–1702* (Oxford, 2004); McKitterick, *Print, Manuscript and the Search for Order*; for McLeod see footnote 46; H. R. Woudhuysen, *Sir Philip Sidney and the Circulation of Manuscripts 1580–1640* (Oxford, 1996).

or educational boundaries, but saturates society in all its complexity, it serves indifferently the canonical and the marginal, the classical and the vulgar, the serious and the trivial'.[20] It is the fusion of the social and the material that can be used to show that printed books and manuscripts are always witnesses to something other than the texts that they preserve.

In effect, McKenzie reminded bibliographers and editors that books are complex textual and social documents. Greg, and many others before him, had emphasized that authors revise, and compositors and scribes alter what is before them; in the theatre, actors transform texts through performance; and readers assume meanings that are pertinent to their understanding. None of this was new; what was different was McKenzie's preference for pragmatism, and his engagement with rich detail of textual and physical evidence as a guiding principle, as well as his emphasis on embracing the complexity of forms and meanings over the desire for simplification. Unravelling what a text might be, and how it has changed in time, requires an engagement with all the facets of its representation.

The expansive view of bibliography put forward by McKenzie insisted that the analytical methods account for the complexity of the historical evidence. At the same time, he recognized that analytical methods could be employed in new ways to answer different questions in order that the discipline embrace all aspects of how a text communicates its history, aesthetics, context, and meaning. The result, as he perceived it, was a renewed sensitivity to 'the book as an expressive form'.[21] It is an approach that recognizes the ways in which books and manuscripts are not only textually meaningful, but have involved human agency (and therefore decisions) at every point of their creation and use.

Literary criticism reads the otherness of a document: the words that represent an author or editor. Few read the page for what it is: a physical composition of paper, illustration, and script or type. The art of bibliography is to let the page speak, not of its otherness, but of itself: so that it may account for all the variety of influences that gave it form. It requires that we be able to look at and describe a manuscript or printed text and read the signs of its making and, then, to explain how that information can be usefully employed in order to study the transmission and history of literary documents.

If we were to reformulate the idea of what bibliography is, not as we would now describe it, but as someone from the sixteenth or seventeenth-

---

[20] D. F. McKenzie, 'Our Textual Definition of the Future: A New English Imperialism?', *Making Meaning*, 276–81 (277).

[21] D. F. McKenzie, *Bibliography and the Sociology of Texts*: 'The Book as an Expressive Form' is the title of the first lecture, and the phrase appears again in p. 24.

century might have approached it, then we might get closer to what Greg, Morison, and McKenzie meant by suggesting that it is *the art of reading well*: by which is meant *the art of reading all the circumstances of a text and its history, including all the ways in which it has been designed, documented, preserved, and used.* Gaskell explained how a book was put together; the emphasis here is with how to look at, and into, the object in hand and read it well: that is how to look into a book or manuscript and see not only an association of words, but what the various signs tell us of its history and existence. In this chapter, the emphasis is on how to approach the subject; later chapters will proceed step by step through the various kinds of evidence and what they represent.

III

This book has been written with reference to late sixteenth- and early–mid-seventeenth-century documents because they most precisely illustrate the ideas and concepts under discussion. With care, most of what follows can be applied a little more expansively, but the further one strays from the central period, the more likely it will be that other factors (mechanical, commercial, social, and material) need to be taken into account. Broadly speaking, the early modern period might be held to cover the history of Europe from the Black Death to the French Revolution.[22] This book, however, would lose focus and utility if it were to address every nuance of so wide a spectrum of evidence. Rather, the period covered is one in which the printed book-trade had accepted a broad range of conventions (such as the title-page),[23] and in which the production of manuscripts was still a vibrant aspect of private, political, and commercial life. The two forms of textual production were mutually influential and much is to be gained by treating them in conjunction with one another.

For students of the fifteenth or eighteenth centuries, this book will provide an introduction to most of the important concepts, but it needs to be stressed that there are real differences in the methods of production and the contexts of use during these periods that give shape to the evolution of the book in the two centuries between. Even during the sixteenth and seventeenth centuries, the book was not a stable concept—textually, physically, or socially. What is apparent is that certain technical

---

[22] The earliest use of 'early modern' in a book title would appear to be: W. Wulf (ed.), *Rosa Anglica, seu Rosa Medicinæ, Johannis Anglici. An Early Modern Irish Translation of a Section of the Mediæval Medical Text-book of John of Gaddesden* (London, 1929).

[23] For the origins of the title-page: M. M. Smith, *The Title-Page: Its Early Development 1460–1510* (London, 2000).

and historical developments gave shape and impetus to that process. For a few paragraphs, therefore, something needs to be said about the nature of the book during these outlying periods in order to contextualize the discussion that follows and supply guidance to those readers whose interests lie at the margins of its principal concern.

With the end of the Roman empire, commercial book production, as it had been known in the ancient world, came to an end. This was not the result of a single catastrophic event, although the Fall of Rome hastened the decline, but one that had been anticipated in the changing uses of texts during late antiquity.[24] There is much debate amongst scholars as to how literacy and book production evolved, as the decline in literacy amongst the secular elite was by no means universal or consistent.[25] For the next 700 years, however, most book production happened within religious communities. Outside of that environment, literacy was most necessary for political administration.[26]

During the medieval period, six developments that were necessary preconditions for the emergence of the early modern book and book-trade took place. First, and early on, the appearance of the page was modified by the introduction of space within the text; a practice that led to the gradual development of word separation (ancient texts were written in continuous script).[27] Second, at much the same time, scribes began to develop a variety of marks for punctuation and a system for their use. These two developments were concerned with legibility and the clarification of meaning, but they also represent a shift in perception from the texts being primarily oral performances to being written documents. The importance of punctuation is that it facilitates silent reading, suggesting not only logical structure but the inflection of speech: it thus enables a reader to understand the text without having to recite the text

---

[24] W. V. Harris, *Ancient Literacy* (Cambridge MA, 1989), 285–322; G. Cavallo, 'Between *Volumen* and Codex: Reading in the Roman World', *A History of Reading in the West*, ed. G. Cavallo and R. Chartier (Cambridge, 1999), 64–89.

[25] N. Everett, *Literacy in Lombard Italy, c.568–774* (Cambridge, 2003); A. Petrucci, 'The Lombard Problem', *Writers and Readers in Medieval Italy*, 43–58; M. B. Parkes, 'Reading, Copying and Interpreting a Text in the Early Middle Ages', *A History of Reading in the West*, 90–102.

[26] R. McKitterick, *The Carolingians and the Written Word* (Cambridge, 1989), 211–70; S. Kelly, 'Anglo-Saxon Lay Society and The Written Word', *The Uses of Literacy in Early Mediæval Europe*, ed. R. McKitterick (Cambridge, 1990), 36–62; R. Collins, 'Literacy and the Laity in Early Mediaeval Spain', 109–33 in the same volume; M. B. Parkes, 'The Literacy and the Laity', *Scribes, Scripts and Readers: Studies in the Communication, Presentation and Dissemination of Medieval Texts* (London, 1991), 275–97.

[27] P. Saenger, *Space between Words: The Origins of Silent Reading* (Stanford CA, 1997); Parkes, *Pause and Effect*, 20–9.

from memory. Word separation has a further function in relation to the advent of print, for the manipulation of space is necessary in order that each line be the same length as all the others: without it, the text could not be set as an exact rectangle (this is also true for verse and the ends of paragraphs where the apparent irregularity disguises the use of quads and other forms of spacing that justify the text to the right margin).

Third, from the Carolingian period on, there was an attempt to copy some of the classical texts from antiquity. This not only preserved works that might otherwise have been lost (and which served as copy for the early printed editions of these authors); it meant that Carolingian miniscule served as the model for humanistic script, and thus 'roman' type.[28] Fourth, the rise of the universities in the twelfth and thirteenth centuries, together with the formation of stable legal and political institutions, created a demand for scribal services and thus a commercial book-trade that was independent of the practices of the Church.[29]

Fifth and sixth, the universities' interest in Aristotle, and the Arabic versions of his works, led to developments in optics and the introduction of paper to the West. Optics was important because it led to the introduction of spectacles, and because magnification ultimately enabled the kind of detailed work required for the cutting of type punches;[30] whilst the shift to paper provided a resource that freed book production from its dependency on treated animal skins as a writing surface.[31]

The reappearance of commercial manuscript production was an important moment in the development of the book-trade, but other forces were also shaping a new kind of document. The links that were established between the universities, the bureaucracies, and the trade encouraged the production of multiple copies and thus the specialization of tasks and the organization of work on a booklet system within the scriptoria. Illustration was a separate skill in its own right, as was binding. The books produced in this way were essentially specialized products that were intended for the political and administrative elite.[32] Inevitably, methods of commercial manuscript production in the fourteenth and the

---

[28] Morison, *Politics and Script*, 265–93.
[29] The history of these developments in Paris is discussed in detail by M. A. Rouse and R. H. Rouse, *Illiterati et uxorati, Manuscripts and Their Makers: Commercial Book Producers in Medieval Paris 1200–1500*, 2 vols. (London, 2000).
[30] J. Dreyfus, 'The Invention of Spectacles and the Advent of Printing', *The Library*, VI: 10 (1988), 93–106; reprinted, *Into Print: Selected Essays on Printing History, Typography and Book Production* (London, 1994), 298–310.
[31] G. Pollard, 'Notes on the Size of the Sheet', *The Library*, IV: 22 (1941), 122–34; J. M. Bloom, *Paper before Print: The History and Impact of Paper in the Islamic World* (New Haven CT, 2001).
[32] Rouse and Rouse, *Manuscripts and Their Makers*, 235–60.

first half of the fifteenth-century influenced practices in the book-trade after the arrival of the printing-press.[33]

The earliest printed books were, in their manufacture, distribution, and use, conceived of as being similar to manuscripts except that they were produced in multiple copies that were to be hand-finished according to the requirements of individual clients. They were not thought of as texts produced by a different technology. Not surprisingly, the supply of books was far greater than the auxiliary trades could cope with,[34] and many purchasers spared themselves the cost of initials and borders, leaving their copies unadorned; or, conspicuously, they spent their money on the binding rather than extra internal illustration. Fifteenth-century printed books remained artisan products. If this is true for the history of book production, it is true as well for how books were used: most readers did not distinguish between manuscript and print as inherently different sources for a text: both are to be found bound together, and many sammelbände (single volumes that bound together multiple items) were only separated after the seventeenth-century.[35]

Further, manuscript production remained a viable alternative to print: not all texts were required in several hundred copies, and those that were commercially produced in manuscript were often intended for a select audience, to meet a private need, or for a specific patron: these items suited scribal work, and perhaps could be given the extra touches that purchasers of printed copies increasingly spared themselves. Equally, the practice of copying texts, even from printed sources, was deeply engrained. Manuscripts depend on replication for survival; the printed book-trade depends on old books being worn out, on new fashions, and on older texts being packaged in new ways.[36] Those two views of book production remained in tension throughout the early modern period.

We perhaps can understand more about fifteenth-century attitudes towards manuscript and print by looking at a book called *Lumen Anime*. This is a preacher's manual, or commonplace book, of natural and moral philosophy, that gathers together quotations on relevant themes from authors as diverse as Aristotle, Theophrastus, the elder Pliny, Ptolemy, Solinus, Ambrose, Augustine, Jerome, Isidore, Hugh of St Victor, and Avicenna. It is broadly organized in three parts beginning with the birth

---

[33] McKitterick, *Print, Manuscript and the Search for Order*, 30–48.
[34] McKitterick, *Print, Manuscript and the Search for Order*, 34–41. For the crisis in publishing during 1472–3, see: M. J. C. Lowry, *Power, Print, and Profit: Nicholas Jenson and the Rise of Venetian Publishing in Renaissance Europe* (Oxford, 1991), 107–11.
[35] McKitterick, *Print, Manuscript and the Search for Order*, 48–52.
[36] McKenzie, 'Speech—Manuscript—Print', *Making Meaning*, 250.

of Christ, and other theological material, before going on to such worldly matters as abstinence, abjection, adulation, wealth, guilt, love, humility, health, silence, and pride. It then proceeds to the two longer parts: the first, concerned with the natural world of plants, animals, and trees; and the second, in more depth, with moral and philosophical problems. It was composed by Berenger of Landorra, Archbishop of Compostella, between 1317 and his death in 1330. By 1332, a copy of the manuscript had reached Austria, where it was revised, modified, and expanded by an otherwise unknown monk, Gregory of Vorau.[37]

Gregory's version of *Lumen Anime* was immensely popular in the fifteenth-century as a reference work and, despite its Dominican origins, found its natural home and use in the Benedictine orders of Central Europe. There are some 195 surviving manuscripts and fragments, as well as four fifteenth- and one sixteenth-century printed editions. Of the 195 manuscripts, 35 date from the fourteenth-century and the remainder from the fifteenth-century, most from the period of 'print'. Yet only two of these manuscripts derive from the printed editions, and only two of the manuscripts are to be found outside of Central Europe. The printed editions, on the other hand, despite being produced in thousands of copies, are extremely rare (they were read and used until they fell apart). As a form for preserving the text, manuscript was still preferred to print.

It is important to realize, as the *Lumen Anime* demonstrates, that print did not eradicate the making of manuscript books, or the skills of the trade; nor, for all its prolific ability, was the radical part of Gutenburg's invention the *printing-press*, rather it was the creation of *movable type*. The ability to produce identical copies of each letter that could be combined with other letters, as well as punctuation and space, in a rigid structure was the breakthrough that drove the rapid expansion in printed book production, but it did not, at first, replace the skills of scribes. The press was merely the most efficient mechanism that could be adapted (from viticulture) for the purpose of making an impression on a sheet of paper.

Gradually, the economics of the printed trade began to impose its own logic upon the appearance of the page. The problems posed by extra illustration were resolved through initial letters, ornament stocks, and woodcut (later copperplate) images. By the end of the fifteenth-century, many other aspects that came to shape the early modern printed book were in place as well: title-pages, imprints, prefatory material, indices, and errata lists being the most obvious. From the 1490s on, the technical

---

[37] M. A. and R. H. Rouse, 'The Texts Called *Lumen Anime*', *Archivum Fratrum Praedicatorum*, 41 (Rome, 1971), 5–113; N. R. Ker, *Records of All Souls College Library, 1437–1600* (Oxford, 1971), 27.

aspects of the printed book changed little during the hand-press period. What does change is the appearance of the text, the contexts in which books were produced and used, and the material that was printed. To these evolving circumstances, the manuscript trade adapted itself and continued, for the next two centuries, as a vibrant commercial activity.[38]

The rapid expansion of the book-trade; the humanist emphasis on education, combined with population growth and increased paper production across Europe to meet rising demand; the need to control the flow of information and the expansion of the government bureaucracy; the changing structure of literacy that by the end of the sixteenth-century included women on a scale not seen before; and the ideological and spiritual impact of the Reformation and Counter-Reformation; all these factors coalesced to drive a demand for printed books and manuscripts on a scale that transformed access to, and the use of, the written word. Yet the trade was beset by overcapacity which the rapid rise in the supply of second-hand books only compounded. One consequence was trade protection and self-regulation, another was the subversion of authority.

The sixteenth and seventeenth centuries were more literate, and semi-literate groups and communities enjoyed greater access to texts, than is sometimes assumed.[39] The pulpit, the theatre, and the ballad are three obvious ways in which the spoken (or sung) and the written (or printed) coalesced. The ways in which early modern society engaged with texts are equally significant. Manuscript and print are found side by side in the marginalia of many books, whilst the practice of copying texts in manuscript certainly enabled the circulation of information in ways that the press was unable to match owing to its regulation and control. Poetry, in particular, flourished through manuscript circulation and both Donne's and Jonson's poems continued to be mediated in this way even after the publication of their printed texts; that activity, however, represents but a small part of the commercial trade, much of which was related to politics.

By the end of the seventeenth-century, the arrangements that had sustained the book-trade during the previous two centuries were under pressure. In England, the end of licensing in 1695 and the lifting of restrictions on the number of printers and presses affected not only the economics of printed books, but the commercial manuscript trade. Over the next 40 years, as the trade spread from London and the universities,

---

[38] P. Beal, *In Praise of Scribes: Manuscripts and Their Makers in Seventeenth Century England* (Oxford, 1998), 1–30.

[39] See, A. Fox, *Oral and Literate Culture in England 1500–1700* (Oxford, 2000); K. Thomas, 'The Meaning of Literacy in Early Modern England', *The Written Word: Literacy in Transition*, ed. G. Baumann (Oxford, 1986), 97–131.

the number of printers multiplied and the unit cost of book production fell, whilst the manuscript trade concentrated on legal and financial services. As producers of books, scriveners ceased to be able to compete because they could not match the economies of an unprotected trade. By 1740, the printed trade had reached critical mass. Over the next 60 years, the difference between the costs of production (which fell) and retail price (which rose) widened substantially.[40] These increased profit margins, reinforced by the spread of substantial private libraries as forms of conspicuous consumption, enabled the trade to accumulate significant capital resources from their profits. At the same time, private manuscript activity found new impetus in letters as a social art, in diaries and journals—the public and private spheres of the book separated.

This disjunction of the private and the public had several important corollaries for the eighteenth-century book. First, the end of licensing occurred at the same time as new presses increased the size of the platen and thus the area of a sheet of paper that a printer could impress. Very rapidly, the formats of books changed with royal octavo (c.29 × 20 cm) becoming the new standard for the trade. Indicatively, Jonson's 1692 *Workes* was printed as a single volume in double columns on crown folio; the 1716 bookseller's edition of his *Works* was six volumes of royal octavo, and much more amenable to the hand.[41] Second, copperplate engraving was more often a grace-note to a well-designed text. Third, people started collecting manuscripts, not as a research and reference collection (as Cotton had), but as objects of antiquarian interest (as did Harley and Rawlinson). Fourth, the book-trade became more discreet about its mistakes, no longer inviting readers to 'emend with their pen'. Fifth, interest increased in the early history of printing and trade practice: Moxon was the first English manual in 1683, but from the mid-eighteenth-century there were several more.[42] Sixth, as the price of new books increased, the antiquarian trade flourished with the formation of private libraries like those of Malone and Heber. Books were still personalized by their individual owners, but the trade was more effacing in its direct engagement with the text. Books were less often personalized *for* readers, and instead were personalized *by* them to reflect not only knowledge, but taste. The social dynamics of the book had fundamentally changed.

---

[40] These comments are indebted to James Raven: of course, the price multiple for every book varies and it is very difficult to make broad generalizations; what is apparent is the trend of expanding margins and hence capital formation.

[41] McKenzie, 'Typography and Meaning', 228.

[42] J. Moxon, *Mechanick Exercises on the Whole Art of Printing (1683–4)*, ed. H. Davis and H. Carter, 2nd edn. (Oxford, 1962); McKitterick, *Print, Manuscript and the Search for Order*, 166–86.

By the early nineteenth-century, the results of mechanization made further change inevitable. Paper, presswork, and finally typesetting and binding were all subject to new methods of production that increased the uniformity of appearance, despite the greater diversity of material in print. These developments, of course, belong to the machine-press period, but the results of that modernization have shaped understandings of the book as textually and physically consistent, at least until recently. In dealing with the early modern book, one needs to recognize its composite and partial forms as a witness to the past: not only is uniformity not the norm, it is nonexistent. Print did not replace manuscript: the two existed in conjunction with each other as complementary forms of mediation.[43]

IV

In 'The Trout and the Milk', the late Hugh Amory explored the history of a strange object found at a Connecticut burial site: it was a leaf from a duo-decimo seventeenth-century Bible that had fused with the paw of a bear, to which it had been tied and then wrapped in cloth.[44] In an exemplary manner, Amory identified the edition of the Bible from which the leaf was taken, and established the date as being c.1680; and he compared the date to the history of the local Pequot communities and the European colonists. The text had been included in a talismanic medicinal bundle for a young girl, as part of a ritual to preserve the memory of the dead, to present the soul to the world to come, and to protect it from further harm.[45] Amory demonstrated that the item had been made some 20 years before literacy spread through the Pequot community. He also pointed out that such Bibles were not really read by the Europeans either: the type was too small, and their use was much more symbolic than textual (an object carried as a mark of piety). The Pequots had recognized the regard in which the early Puritans held scripture, and they understood its symbolic associations. Adding a leaf from a Bible was like adding an extra charm or incantation; it was a gesture that expressed an accommodation with, and recognition of, the alien culture that had arrived in their midst.

What is significant about 'The Trout and the Milk' is the way in which Amory deftly links bibliographical evidence with ethnography and social

---

[43] Cf. E. L. Eisenstein, *The Printing-Press as an Agent of Change*, 2 vols. (Cambridge, 1979).

[44] H. Amory, 'The Trout and the Milk: An Ethnobibliographical Talk', *Harvard Library Bulletin*, NS 7 (1996), 50–65.

[45] See, in particular, A. Petrucci, *Writing the Dead: Death and Writing Strategies in the Western Tradition* (Stanford CA, 1998).

history, and demonstrates the connection between material evidence and broader social narratives. Bibliography and book history involve more than abstract narratives about books in society, and the history of reading: these are but aspects of the discipline that take their life from the artefacts and documents that bear witness to how they have been made and used.

Randall McLeod, in particular, has been interested in the ways in which books and manuscripts contain signs that are other than the text, or that are not immediately visible to the eye.[46] One article, 'Obliterature' recovers a text of Donne's 'To His Mistress Going to Bed' that has been painted over with an ink wash to suppress it. Another article, 'Where Angels Fear to Read', investigates the use of load-bearing type in the first edition of Castiglione's *Il Cortegiano* (Venice, 1528). McLeod is able to map patterns within the production process from the blind impressions left by type that had been used to stabilize the forme during the impression of the sheet. The reason for the use of load-bearing type might be technical, but what the article demonstrates, in a rather charming way, is that there is more than one possible 'reading' of the physical book as he explores that other narrative about its production processes.

When a book or manuscript, as sometimes happens, is only regarded as a 'text', it can sometimes be forgotten, or at least overlooked that, as objects, books exist in time, in relation to one another, and that their parts exist in relation to their whole. Thus, the bibliographical study of printed and manuscript materials cannot be separated from the history of their creation and use. Any narrative that fails to recognize this complexity, the variety of such relationships, the instabilities of texts, and the differences between artefacts as witnesses to the history of a work or text, will fail to recognize the communicative power of books and manuscripts (rather than words) as witnesses to the past.

The failure to appreciate the significance of books as artefacts is not only an intellectual problem. The fact that they have a history that is separate to their texts has been ignored and this has led to the destruction of material evidence as bindings have been replaced, sammelbände broken up, and manuscript annotations washed away. Further, modern library management (looking for economies where they do not exist) has misunderstood the nature and limitations of new digital resources, often

---

[46] For instance, some recent articles include: R. McLeod, 'Altvm Sapere: Parole d'homme et verbe divin: Les chronologies de la Bible hébraïque in-quarto de Robert Estienne', in B. E. Schwarzbach (ed.), *La Bible imprimée dans l'Europe moderne* (Paris, 1999), 83–141; 'Where Angels Fear to Read', in J. Bray, M. Handley, and A. C. Henry (eds.), *Ma'king the Text: The Presentation of Meaning on the Literary Page* (Aldershot, 2000), 144–92; 'Obliterature', *English Manuscript Studies*, 12 (2005), 83–138.

to the detriment of the collections in their care. At the heart of this mis-management is the idea that a book is but a text; which is, as if to say, that a Greek vase is the decoration and not the pot, or that a painting is but the image. No art gallery would destroy a Titian because they could preserve a digital image of it on the wall, but that is precisely what librarians have done with some of the materials in their care, especially newspapers.[47]

If librarians and scholars have employed a simplified notion of 'text' that separates words from their material record, and manuscript from print, then it is not surprising that the definition of the text has continued to be closely aligned with concepts of authorship rather than with the history of the documents that preserve them. It is, for instance, comparatively rare for library catalogues to identify printed books with significant manuscript marginalia, and thus identify texts with visible traces of having been read.[48] Books of this kind are not only authorial texts, but complex records of how these texts have been used in society; cumulatively, that information can be highly revealing—a study of multiple copies of the Estienne Aeschylus (Paris, 1557), for instance, would demonstrate an extensive history of annotation, and scholarship.[49]

If marginalia represent one aspect of bibliographical information that extends the potential complexity of documents, then the work of such scholars as Mirjam Foot reveals that bindings are not absolutely dead things either. They serve not only as indices of taste, but had commercial imperatives, and in their differences they serve as social and personal witnesses to the history and uses of a text.[50] Gift bindings, in particular, are an expression of patronage relationships and friendships that are signified through their choice of material and decorative embellishment: they range from simple gilt vellum to elaborately worked finishes.

---

[47] In particular, see N. Baker, *Double Fold: Libraries and the Assault on Paper* (New York, 2001); also, M. B. Bland, 'Memory—Witness—Use: Books and the Circulation of Learning', *Turnbull Library Record*, 33 (2000), 11–34; McKenzie, 'Our Textual Definition of the Future', 276–81; McKitterick, *Print, Manuscript and the Search for Order*, 17–21. It may be objected that Greek vases are works of art, and newspapers are not; however, most vases and cups were not conceived as works of art but to serve specific social purposes, whilst often newspapers were published with more literary care than many other ephemeral texts.

[48] The Adv. shelfmark at Cambridge identifies books with marginalia, but is not inclusive; at Oxford, the Auct. shelfmark (opened in 1789 and closed in 1940) includes incunabula, *editio princeps*, and other volumes with significant scholarly marginalia. More recently, Bernard Rosenthal gave the Beinecke Library at Yale a collection of early printed books with extensive marginalia: see B. M. Rosenthal, *The Rosenthal Collection of Printed Books with Manuscript Annotations* (New Haven CT, 1997).

[49] Such observations are not exclusive to the Aeschylus, although the Estienne edition is a useful example of a history of annotation that is largely overlooked by both classicists and early modern scholars.

[50] For instance, M. M. Foot, *Bookbinders at Work: Their Roles and Methods* (London, 2006).

Binding, like engraved illustration, and the typographic layout of the page, involves aesthetic and practical decisions that made Greg distinctly uncomfortable: hence his impulse to separate the language and grammar of a text from its formal structures. What Greg got right was his insistence that the processes of transmission and production could be interrogated for what they reveal about the history of a document; what he failed to recognize was that the criteria that shaped these narratives were always as much aesthetic as textual. Writers, editors, printers, and scribes balance considerations of materials, appearance, price, and use, to appeal to their customers, employers, or readers. The problem was that Greg overstated his case because the implicit target of his criticism was the literary scholar and aesthete George Saintsbury, who selected his 'copy-texts' according to what pleased him without regard to the history of the documents.[51] Greg, on the other hand, wanted some logical rigour brought to the methodology of bibliography and textual criticism. Thus, viewing aesthetics as subjective, rather than as an integral aspect of composition and production, he rejected Housman's view of aesthetic discrimination in the resolution of textual cruces as 'meta-critical' and so exposed himself to later criticisms that he did not anticipate.[52] As McKitterick comments:

> Greg's own primary interests, and his failure to recognise the potential interpretative energy inherent in a more generous view of bibliography, have proved to be more influential than his almost incidental ignorance of later manuscripts or engraved illustration.[53]

Greg's interests inevitably drove later discussions of the discipline, so it is worth recalling that he 'would have our studies be catholic', just as McKenzie would have them be 'secular'.[54] This book starts from the point of view that all aspects of a text and its material forms are germane to understanding its history, and that an understanding of aesthetics, and its relationship with the technical limitations of textual production as well as commercial imperatives, is inseparable from that historical process of analysis. Aesthetics exists in the design of books, just as taste does in the consumption of them: the making of meaning is never static.

---

[51] 'Bibliography—An Apologia' was delivered in March 1932, and published in *The Library* that September. Saintsbury died in January 1933: *Oxford D. N. B.*, 48, 669–71. In targeting Housman, a much greater scholar, Greg could avoid criticizing a revered and elderly man. See also, Saintsbury's *Minor Caroline Poets*, 3 vols. (Oxford, 1925).

[52] Greg, 'Bibliography—An Apologia', 253.

[53] McKitterick, *Print, Manuscript and the Search for Order*, 78.

[54] Greg, 'Bibliography—An Apologia', 244; McKenzie, *Bibliography and the Sociology of Texts*, 28.

Aesthetics tells us that not all editions of printed texts are 'ideal' and that the idea that any are is deeply suspect. Aesthetics instructs editors that they have a duty of care in establishing the relationships between different kinds of evidence and how they seek to reconcile the issues that documents and their contexts create: every decision is a kind of epitaph. Aesthetics alerts us to the significance of meta-textual detail, including paper, script or type, and bindings, and its relationship to the meaning of a document, as well as its history and use. Aesthetics exposes the tension between the limitations of technology and commerce, both then and now, and the complexity of the evidence that survives. What is so dangerous about Greg's denial of the role of aesthetics in the historical analysis of these objects and their texts is the dissociation of sensibility it involves. Those who came after Greg, charged with a new discourse and sometimes a lack of intellectual rigour, made that denial a commonplace of literary scholarship; yet without an understanding of the role of aesthetics in the making of these materials, we know not what we do.

When we take a book in hand, we feel its weight, look at the binding and the type, note the texture of the paper, smell its age, perhaps hunger to read it, all before we hear or read the text on the page. 'Some *Bookes*', wrote Bacon, 'are to be Tasted, Others to be Swallowed, and Some Few to be Chewed and Digested.'[55] What was read was also written, and not always set in type. Savile, in print, called it 'this scribbling age'; Daniel remarked on 'the presse of writings'; Selden wrote of what 'speaks in Print'; and Florio 'could not chuse but apply my self in some sort to the season'.[56] All experienced a world of books, tracts, and documents, manuscript and printed, not as an abstract *culture*, but as a physical and historical fact that impelled them to engage with its almost oppressive diversity and indiscriminate prolixity. Milton, privileging the author, remarked that 'books are not absolutely dead things'; yet imagine a library where every book is not 'a dead thing', but rather its own true witness, archivist, and reporter of its history: the rest is silence.

[55] F. Bacon, 'Of Studies', *The Essayes or Counsels, Civill and Morall*, ed. M. Kiernan (Oxford, 1985), 153.
[56] H. Savile, *The ende of Nero and beginning of Galba* (STC 23642, 1591), ¶2ʳ; M. de Montaigne, *Essayes*, trans. J. Florio (STC 18041, 1603), ¶1ʳ; J Selden, *Titles of honor*, STC 22177, 1614, a2ᵛ–a3ʳ; J. Florio, *Florios second frvtes* (STC 11097, 1591), A2ʳ⁻ᵛ.

2 Paper and Related Materials

WE are now several decades into a technological revolution that has, amongst other things, enabled texts to be written and searched without paper. In most libraries, card indexes, annotated volumes, and pasted slips have been replaced with online catalogues. Electronic mail has not only substituted for, but significantly increased the volume of written correspondence. Newspapers and other media make their texts available in electronic form and update their sites regularly, in much the same way as there were once (and sometimes still are) 'early' and 'late' editions of the news. Most texts are now prepared on a keyboard and preserved in digital form. Narratives need no longer be sequentially organized. For some, this change heralds the end of the 'book' and the arrival of a 'paperless society', yet books and paper have been sturdily resistant to their imaginary impending doom. Recent technologies have only partly substituted for manuscript and print—perhaps manuscript more than print; otherwise, the creation and distribution of digital texts (which are regularly printed out) has involved an expansion of the mechanisms of communication and record. The global paper and publishing industries are rather evolving than in crisis and decline.

In truth, the technologies of communication have evolved in ways that only make access to texts more varied: at no stage has one form of communication completely replaced another. The 'paperless society' was that which had no form of record beyond human memory and the deliberate use of repetition and motifs to preserve narratives. As Plato observed, writing does not enable memory, it enables forgetfulness because the substance of what is written down is preserved beyond the life of any one individual and, therefore, no individual need remember all the details.[1] Modern forms of oral record (such as film and tape, as well as their subsequent mutations including digital encryption) are simply other surfaces on which we preserve text, sound, and sometimes action (sophisticated forms of 'paper', as it were, that require particular technologies for their reading), in order that we do not depend on the ritualized transmission of the spoken word.

It is important to recognize and account for the role of memory in the transmission of early modern texts,[2] however much we depend on the written and material record. We do not know what part Shakespeare acted in *Sejanus*, how he spoke, what his gestures were, or the lack of

---

[1] Plato, *Phaedrus*: see B. Jowett (ed.), *The Dialogues of Plato*, 4th edn., 4 vols. (Oxford, 1953), III.185. For a more extended comment upon this: Bland, 'Memory—Witness—Use', 11–34.
[2] Fox, *Oral and Literate Culture in England, 1500–1700*, 214–27 and 262–81.

them, although at least several hundred people knew this at the time of performance and, some, for many years after; nor can we recover an original performance of Dowland's lute music although we have texts of the music: we do know this of Bogart in *Casablanca*, and of Casals performing the Bach cello suites, although Bogart and Casals died before most people now alive were born. Thus, for the early modern period, it is in paper, parchment, and stone that we capture the texts both imaginary and factual, some transitory and ephemeral (such as plays), some intended for preservation (such as birth and death), that survive beyond the memory of that society as a partial record of its existence. Nor is it possible to fully understand those texts, and their meaning, if we do not understand the surfaces upon which they were inscribed and why they were preserved in their particular ways.

Parchment, Stone, and Paper

Paper was a comparatively late arrival as a surface for the preservation of texts. In the ancient world, papyrus was the lightweight durable writing surface; however, its structure required that it be rolled, and from the late first-century it began to be replaced by the parchment codex.[3] Parchment is animal skin (goat, calf, sheep, and rabbit were all used) that has been washed in slaked lime (calcium carbonate), de-haired, stretched, rubbed smooth, and trimmed: the process takes several weeks to complete.[4] The resulting skins are light and durable; however, it was also expensive if employed for longer texts. Parchment was therefore a premium surface for book production. Hence, in his final letter to Timothy, when St Paul asks for his cloak from Troas, he added that he would like his books, 'and above all the parchments'.[5] What is new here is the emphasis that Paul gives to the artefact: the indication that the material on which a text was written was an important part of its identity as a document.

There were several advantages to the parchment codex. First, it could be folded, stitched, and bound. Second, it was economical with space. Third, it offered a more stable surface for illustration: a roll could only be illustrated with inks, as paint and gold would have fractured and peeled. Hence, it was inevitable that the codex would gain in both utility and sumptuousness, and that the perceived value of the text would determine the elaborateness of the decoration. For St Jerome, at least, this was a perversion of the scripture, and he complained that 'parchments are dyed

---

[3] See, C. H. Roberts and T. C. Skeat, *The Birth of the Codex* (Oxford, 1983).
[4] D. V. Thomson, 'Medieval Parchment Making', *The Library*, IV: 16 (1935), 113–17.
[5] 2 *Timothy*, 4.13.

purple, gold is melted into lettering, manuscripts are dressed up in jewels, while Christ lies at the door naked and dying'.[6] His asceticism was not shared by others, as late medieval books of hours lavishly illustrate.

Parchment continued in use during the early modern period for special copies of books, for the formal parish registers of births, deaths, and marriages, for wills and land deeds, and for other documents such as funeral placards. Most of these artefacts provide clear signs of when and why they were created. With printed books, parchment was only used for exceptional, highly important presentation copies; otherwise, the book-trade would have devastated the livestock of Europe. Thus, if paper first gained acceptance as a low-cost, durable alternative for non-premium book production, it later became an absolute necessity for all but the most important copies of texts or documents, with goatskin, sheepskin, and calf reserved as materials for binding.

The history of stone as a surface for texts goes back to the origins of written language: it was used for law, death, rituals, commemorations, dedications, ceremonies, decrees and injunctions, commerce, accounts, boundaries, calendars, and, inevitably, graffiti.[7] Stone has always been utilized for inscriptions that are supposed to withstand nature and time, which is why the Romans chose it to mark distances. Other materials such as tree bark and wood have been written on in various ways as well; cuneiform texts were preserved on clay tablets, and since ancient Greece, script has often appeared on pottery; more recently, it has been etched in glass and plastics, and on metal. Texts have also been included within pictorial space since antiquity. What needs to be borne in mind out of this diversity is that, in the early modern period, paper was but one of many possible surfaces for a text. In particular, whilst parchment had replaced some of the earlier functions of stone so that the latter was mainly used for gravestones and commemoration, both parchment and stone continued to be selected for literary texts of high authority, especially when these related to the commemoration of the dead.

Since its introduction to the West, via Spain then Italy, paper has been (until recently) preferred for the preservation and transmission of texts intended for multiple users, as well as for private communication.[8] The cellulose fibres of paper withstand folding, and make it uniquely

---

[6] 'Inficitur membrana colore purpureo, aurum liquescit in litteras, gemmis codices vestiuntur, et nudus ante fores aerum Christus emoritur': St Jerome, *Selected Letters*, ed. F. A. Wright (Cambridge MA, 1933), XXII: 32, 130–3.

[7] As a starting point, see, A. Petrucci, *Public Lettering: Script, Power, and Culture*, trans. L. Lappin (Chicago, 1993).

[8] Paper was first made in Spain c.1150 AD. For its earlier history: J. M. Bloom, *Paper before Print: The History and Impact of Paper In the Islamic World* (New Haven CT, 2001).

adaptable to the codex (book) form, although it can be rolled if desired. It is durable and more compact than the alternatives. It can be produced in volume and quickly. It requires little preparation for writing or the press and is, in small quantities, easily transportable. As a general principle, if a text produced after c.1450 (until the 1980s) is not written on paper then this needs to be understood in relation to the physical characteristics of the document and its context.

The manufacture and distribution of paper has a long and complex history, and one almost as diverse as its use.[9] For modern 'white' paper, both laid and wove, there are various grades, materials used in the making, sizes, coatings, thicknesses, weights, shades, chemical balances, and degrees of absorbency. There are different methods of manufacture. Smell, texture, and optical brightness vary from one type of paper to another, and prices for apparently similar sheets can differ markedly. We would recognize a newspaper, a glossy magazine, and a scholarly book as being so without any text having been printed upon it. The paper and its format (how it is folded) are part of the way a text communicates its meaning; and they relate directly to the kind of reading that is being engaged in. The relationship between the reflectivity (the brightness) to the design of the type, or the formal composition of a script, is what helps determine legibility and intelligibility, against which cost must be considered: for instance, small type printed in gold on black paper is very difficult to read; likewise a railway timetable that used opaque non-reflective paper and a seriffed font would lack the clarity desired.

Modern paper is mass produced and production methods seek to minimize differences between one sheet, or one batch, and another; in effect, the paper either effaces or standardizes the history within it, whilst the primary differences between types and grades of paper are generally apparent on the surface and to the touch. Paper like this can be weighed and have its thickness and reflectivity measured, but little would usually be achieved by creating a detailed photographic image of its internal fibrous structure. What distinguishes modern paper is the variety of its uniformity, and its varieties of uniformity.

In contrast with modern methods, early modern papermaking was a craft where the workmen made one or two sheets at a time on wire moulds: thus, the record of each and every mould is to be found within the paper, in the differences of chainlines and, usually, watermarks. In an absolute sense, there were fewer sizes and grades of paper than modern methods of manufacture allow; yet the material record is, in

---

[9] See D. Hunter, *Papermaking: The History and Technique of an Ancient Craft* (New York, 1947). The URL for the International Association of Paper Historians is www.paperhistory.org.

many ways, more complex, as the tray is the unit of production and identification. A watermark can encode the place of origin, the mill that made the paper, on what tray it was made, and when it was made. Owing to wear and tear, the trays were regularly repaired, or replaced with similar but not identical substitutes (each was hand-made). These subtle changes in the watermarks and chainlines constitute a material record that can be measured, photographed, and analyzed against datable documents.[10]

The reason for the presence of watermarks in paper has nothing to do with their subsequent bibliographical usefulness, rather the purpose they served was practical and commercial in the same way as, in ancient Rome, brick-makers stamped their name and place of production upon their output. The Romans did this to identify the bricks made in shared contexts by different makers in the same location and sold on to a single purchaser: the result is that both the sources and dispersion of the bricks can be mapped.[11] Similarly, papermakers in the hand-press period had to identify what they sold to the merchants. Later, the marks sometimes served to assess excise, and taxes were levied accordingly.

The jug, or pot, to be found in paper from northern France, is the most familiar watermark in sixteenth- and seventeenth-century English

---

[10] Some primary resources include C. M. Briquet, *Les filigranes: Dictionnaire Historique des Marques du Papier dès leur apparition vers 1282 jusqu'en 1600*, ed. A. H. Stevenson, 4 vols. (Amsterdam, 1968); W. A. Churchill, *Watermarks in Paper in Holland, England, France, etc., in the XVII and XVIII Centuries and Their Interconnection* (Amsterdam, 1935), and the *Monumenta Chartæ Papyraceæ Historiam Illustrantia*. Unfortunately, these catalogues are not sufficient for accurate analytical work, but they do suggest the complexity of the evidence. See also, J. Bidwell, 'The Study of Paper as Evidence, Artefact, and Commodity', *The Book Encompassed: Studies in Twentieth-Century Bibliography*, ed. P. Davison (Cambridge, 1992), 69–82; Gaskell, *New Introduction*, 57–77 (especially 60–6); E. A. Heawood, 'Paper Used in England after 1600', *The Library*, IV, 11 (1931), 274; P. Needham, 'Allan H. Stevenson and the Bibliographical Uses of Paper', *Studies in Bibliography*, 47 (1994), 23–64; A. H. Stevenson, 'Paper as Bibliographical Evidence', *The Library*, V, 17 (1962), 197–212; Stevenson, *The Problem of the Missale Speciale* (London, 1967), 26–99; Stevenson (ed.), *Briquet's Opuscula: The Complete Works of Dr. C. M. Briquet without Les Filigranes* (Hilversum, 1955), xxxiv–xliii; G. T. Tanselle, 'The Bibliographical Description of Paper', *Studies in Bibliography*, 24 (1972), 27–67; W. A. Weiss, 'Watermark Evidence and Inference: New Style Dates of Edmund Spenser's *Complaints* and *Daphnaïda*', *Studies in Bibliography*, 52 (1999), 129–54; W. P. Williams, 'Paper as Evidence: The Utility of the Study of Paper for Seventeenth Century English Literary Scholarship', in S. Spector (ed.), *Essays in Paper Analysis* (Washington DC, 1987), 191–9; D. Woodward, *Catalogue of Watermarks in Italian Printed Maps ca.1540–1600* (Florence, 1996). For those with German, there is also P. F. Tschudin, *Gründzuge der Papiergeschichte* (Stuttgart, 2002).

[11] See, for instance, K. Greene, *The Archaeology of the Roman Economy* (London, 1986); T. Helen, *Organisation of Roman Brick Production in the First and Second Centuries AD: An Interpretation of Roman Brick Stamps* (Helsinki, 1975).

books and manuscripts, to the extent that it was for many years the ordinary stock of the publishing trade, and a standard grade of writing paper.[12] Thus, when a printed book is not on pot this may be of interest: it could be a matter of scale (a large folio might be printed on crown), or the difference might represent a social or political statement, and a financial investment. All paper with the pot mark is c.305 × 400 mm untrimmed, which is why most folio books from the period are c.290–95 × 190 mm, and the typical quarto volume is c.190 × 140 mm after having been cropped during binding. From the eighteenth-century, larger presses and paper sizes changed the shapes of books.[13] The pot watermark could have a half crescent with five baubles above, or a small bunch of grapes; there is usually one handle, sometimes two, the initials of the maker, and perhaps a letter to indicate the place of origin. The chainlines are generally spaced between 18 and 21 mm apart (and, at most, c.27 mm), and the pots vary in size, although c.75 × 35 mm is common. Such permutations allow for an extraordinary variety of specific detail.

With a printed book of some size, it is normal to find at least two stocks of paper and often more (remembering that every stock will have twin marks from related moulds), because concurrent activity depleted and replenished the paper supply. Where special copies were produced for patrons and friends, the same settings of type might also be printed off on two different stocks of paper: one large or fine (often crown) for presentation copies; the other ordinary (usually pot) for the remaining copies intended for commercial sale. Printers always had stocks of paper on hand, and whilst new supplies were brought in for new books according to the size of the edition and the number of sheets per copy (a ream per sheet giving an edition size of c.480–500 copies after wastage), older paper would generally get used first, so that the stock was replenished rather than being specifically allocated for each book. Hence, a special job can be identified by the homogeneity of its paper stock and its difference from the rest of the output at that time. With manuscripts, multiple paper stocks from different sources typically indicate that the document was built up in different stages.

A book like the first edition of Sidney's *Arcadia* clearly shows the changes in paper stocks during its production: the first, with the initials EO is found until gathering V, when it is mixed with another stock that has the initials SR (figure 2.1). A third paper, with the initials AA, was used

---

[12] See, J. Bidwell, 'French Paper in English Books': J. Barnard and D. F. McKenzie (eds.), *The Cambridge History of the Book in Britain, IV: 1557–1695* (Cambridge, 2004), 583–601.
[13] D. F. Foxon, *Pope and the Early Eighteenth-Century Book Trade*, rev. and ed. J. McLaverty (Oxford, 1991), 19–21 and 52–4 details Pope's concern with the qualities and sizes of paper.

from gathering 2E onwards. The shapes of the pots are quite distinct, with the width between the chainlines differing quite markedly as well.

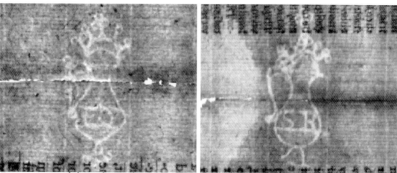

Figure 2.1   Sir Philip Sidney, *The Countesse of Pembroke's Arcadia* (STC 22539–39a; 1590), L4–5 & 2A3–6. Backlit photographs of EO and SR pot watermarks (personal collection, reduced).

With images like these, it is possible to compare the paper of other books printed by Windet during 1588–90 with the *Arcadia*. Together with information relating to entry and publication dates, as well as ornament and type damage, watermarks help to map the history of the book in the printing-house. Whilst any reconstruction cannot be exact, the paper will indicate those concurrent materials that are relevant to the history of a particular volume. All early modern printed books must be assumed to have been in concurrent production with other material unless there is overwhelming evidence to the contrary.

Watermark analysis requires precision. The technical aspects of this can discourage scholars from attempting detailed reconstructions of the available data and often drawings are used. A drawing is a starting point for collecting related images, and is always helpful if combined with accurate measurements; it will not serve to distinguish one nearly similar tray from another; that, only photography and beta-radiography can do: thus, many paper studies lack the precision and detail to facilitate the scholarship that they imply is possible. With photographic images, we can begin to reconstruct the history of when paper from a given batch was most commonly used. Of course, only a few sheets from a batch can be traced; nevertheless, examples can be identified and recorded to establish useful concentrations of relevant data, and to identify where comparative material is to be found.[14] This is possible because all hand-made paper preserves the information of its making and history.

[14] For a useful collection of essays, see D. W. Mosser, M. Saffle, and E. W. Sullivan II (eds.), *Puzzles in Paper: Concepts in Historical Watermarks* (New Castle DE and London, 2000).

The Paper Trade

Much archival work on the early paper trade remains to be done.[15] The centres of production have been studied, however less is known about the commercial aspects of the business. We know how much paper was imported into Britain in the late sixteenth and seventeenth centuries, where it came from, the physical aspects of how it was sold, in what sizes, and for how much. Prior to the late seventeenth-century, however, we have very little real feeling for the distribution networks, the identity of all but a few wholesalers, or the geography of going and buying a quire or ream from a stationer (particularly if the retailer was not a member of the Stationers' Company, and not in London); nor do we know the extent to which printers, publishers, and other booksellers relied on paper sales as a significant part of their commercial turnover.

Paper was produced in almost all of Western Europe, except Britain, by the mid-fifteenth-century, where sporadic attempts to achieve an economically viable business began soon after.[16] The best-known mill was set up by John Spilman near Dartford, Kent, in 1588. This provided the ordinary paper for Jonson's *Sejanus* (large paper copies were also printed), but there is no evidence of this paper being employed for other printed books, and its appearance in manuscripts is rare.[17] The domestic mills were not, it must be emphasised, a major source of supply for the white paper trade until the later seventeenth-century (they did make brown wrapping paper, but how much we do not know). Rather, the different sources for the paper used in English books and manuscripts is revealed by watermarks from the Low Countries, northern France, Burgundy, Switzerland, Italy, and, during the first decade, Spain.

The fact that Britain relied on imported paper for almost all of its writing and printing needs before the end of the seventeenth-century allows the growth of the trade to be mapped from the records in a way that would not be possible for domestic production. The population, in

---

[15] See footnote 10 for the primary sources. An exemplary recent article is C. Fahy, 'Paper Making in Seventeenth-Century Genoa: The Account of Giovanni Domenico Peri (1651)', *Studies in Bibliography*, 56 (2007, for 2003–4), 243–59.

[16] See, A. Stevenson, 'Tudor Roses from John Tate', *Studies in Bibliography*, 20 (1967), 15–34.

[17] For instance, Sir William Cornwallis, the essayist, to John Donne: MS Tanner 306, ff.237–8. Also, T. Churchyard, *A sparke of frendship and warme goodwill. Whereunto is ioined a description of a paper mill, of late set vp* (STC 5257; 1588); T. O. Calhoun and T. L. Gravell, 'Paper and Printing in Jonson's *Sejanus* (1605)', *Papers of the Bibliographical Society of America*, 87 (1993), 13–64. The paper for the Jonson quarto may have been bought when Spilman received his knighthood: A. H. Shorter, *Paper Making in the British Isles: An Historical and Geographical Study* (Plymouth, 1971), 16. Spilman may also have been responsible for some unwatermarked paper in English books: e.g. A. Dent, *The Ruin of Rome* (STC 6640; 1603).

1600, was approximately 4 million; by 1700, it was perhaps 5 million. Over the same period, the consumption of paper tripled. In the 1580s, paper imports were running at approximately 40,000 reams annually; by 1620, this had doubled to c.80,000 reams (suggesting a median of c.60,000 reams for 1600). By the mid-1630s imports were running at c.95,000 reams annually; by the 1660s, this had increased further to nearly 120,000 reams (with a peak of 154,000 reams in 1668 when paper stocks were replaced after the Great Fire, which suggests that the trade kept about three months' supply in hand). The annual imports for the last years of the seventeenth-century (when Dutch mills had replaced the French as the main source for paper) are more variable, oscillating around 180,000 reams.[18] This increase reveals more than the sustained growth of the book-trade; it must represent a significant increase in manuscript use: not only were people using more paper, a greater proportion of the population as a whole used more paper. Thus, as a measure of the impact of widening literacy amongst all social classes, paper imports provide an inherently crude, but revealing picture of the scale of the changes taking place.

The diversity of supply, the differing requirements of personal and commercial use (including the way in which paper could convey social and economic status), ensured that not all paper was the same size, or the same quality. In their origins, the sizes of paper reflected the differences between various kinds of animal skins,[19] as well as the physical constraints of the process by which paper was made. The grades were assessed for taxation at different rates. Of the sizes other than pot, crown was c.350 × 460 mm, and royal c.440 × 600 mm.[20] Royal was rarely employed before the eighteenth-century, although in 1600 a shipment was cut into half-sheets, and this appears in a number of books at different printing-houses.[21] Between those mentioned, other sizes were available: Italian flag paper measured c.313 × 432 mm, a size that was generally associated with foolscap, and paper with a grapes watermark. Demy (c.380 × 500 mm), medium (c.420 × 520 mm), and imperial (c.700 × 500 mm) were all larger sizes of paper—the last, the largest practical size of tray that a vat-man could physically work with.

[18] D. C. Coleman, *The British Paper Industry 1495–1860: A Study in Industrial Growth* (Oxford, 1958), 13 and 21.

[19] G. Pollard, 'Notes on the Size of the Sheet', 105–37 esp. 110–15; also, E. J. Labarre, 'The Sizes of Paper, Their Names, Origin and History', in H. Kunze (ed.), *Buch und Papier: buchkundliche und papiergeschichtliche Arbeiten* (Leipzig, 1949), 35–54.

[20] Gaskell, *New Introduction*, 73.

[21] Thus, the first edition of *Every Man out of His Humor* (STC 14766; 1600) should correctly be described as a royal octavo in fours.

Before 1690, imported paper was taxed at 5 per cent of the assessed value per ream (the actual price could, of course, be higher). The differences between the rates for various sizes of paper are quite revealing as to how paper reflected issues of use and status: whilst the assessed value for printing and ordinary paper increased by 80 per cent between 1604 and 1660, the rates for other papers, including foolscap, broadly tripled.

GRADE (per ream)	1604	1660
Brown	1*s*	3*s*
Blue	4*s*	10*s*
Pot (Printing and Copy)	2*s* 6*d*	4*s* 6*d*
Foolscap	2*s* 6*d*	7*s* 6*d*
Rochelle	3*s*	9*s*
Demy	4*s*	12*s*
Royal	6*s* 8*d*	20*s*

Source: D. C. Coleman, *The British Paper Industry* (Oxford, 1958), 123.

For high-quality paper, the actual cost of a ream could be far higher than the assessed value. A bill from Robert Barker, to Sir Thomas Smith for the House of Lords, dated 10 February 1603 (i.e. 1604), priced three reams of fine paper (i.e. Italian flag) at £1 10*s*, or 10*s* a ream, compared to the 2*s* 6*d* that was usual for foolscap.[22] Whilst for most paper the assessed and real costs are likely to have been more closely aligned, this does suggest that the use of assessed rates is likely to understate the true cost of paper as a component of book or manuscript production.

Towards the end of the seventeenth-century, the trade underwent a period of transformation.[23] The war with France from the mid-1660s led to interruptions in supply and finally to a tariff regime against imports. Between 1690 and 1700, the tax was increased to 10 per cent; and, after 1700, to 15 per cent in order to protect the new domestic industry.[24] Local sources of production (at first sporadically, and at the cheaper end of the market) started to proliferate, resulting in different, local watermarks in English books and manuscripts.[25] At the same time, the replacement of presses after the Great Fire, and the impact of Stamp Duty in the early eighteenth-century led to the use of larger sheets, sometimes cut in half, and (owing to the iron press) larger platens.[26] The rapid expansion of

---

[22] Beinecke Library, Yale University, MS Osborn fb 159, f.41ʳ.
[23] For a detailed account: J. Bidwell, 'French Paper in English Books', 583–601.
[24] Coleman, *The British Paper Industry*, 66 and 122.
[25] P. Gaskell, 'Notes on Eighteenth Century British Paper', *The Library*, v: 12 (1957), 34–42;
[26] Pollard, 'Notes on the Size of the Sheet', 130–5.

the book-trade during the eighteenth-century, bolstered by exports to North America, underpinned this new manufacturing capacity and eventually forced the introduction of the first industrial methods. What remained consistent was the growth in paper use driven by the activities of a group of people who filled their leisure with novels, newspapers, histories, diaries, and correspondence, and a book-trade that (freed from licensing) catered for the conspicuous consumption of print and the formation of libraries as an index of civility and taste.

The Manufacture of Paper

Paper was made from the fibrous remains of linen and cotton rags. Wood pulp was not used until the mid-nineteenth-century. The way in which paper was made, on a wire tray, limited the size of the sheet to that of a tray that could be handled within a single person's arm-span, bent at about 120 degrees (i.e. c.700 mm: any wider and it would be both too heavy and too deep to manipulate and shake). These techniques continue to be preserved as several mills have been turned into working museums.[27]

The rags for paper were rotted for four or five days, cut up, blanched with running water, and pulverized until the fibres had broken down; the process was then repeated two or three times depending on the quality of the paper.[28] From a modern perspective, the process seems laborious but it took less than half the time required to prepare parchment; hence, the early success and spread of paper mills. The pulp, once it had been washed clean, was poured into a vat with more water added until it was like porridge. The vat was c.1,600 × 800 mm and contained 1,500 litres (330 gallons): it was warmed by a fire to its side and occasionally stirred. During the eighteenth-century cutting with rotating knives replaced stamping (this speeded the process and created paper with shorter fibres that made it better for some applications than others), otherwise the technology remained the same. Paper production thus required a good supply of rags and plenty of running water.

Papermaking required three people to work as a group: a vat-man, a coucher, and a layer. Their tools were a pair of trays, a pile of felts, and a press. The tray was made up of fine wires running horizontally and thicker vertical wires (known as chains) spaced 18–30 mm apart. Onto

---

[27] Several museums have websites: www.museodellacarta.com, www.museodellacarta.it, and www.papiermuseum.ch are three of the best; also, www.paperhistory.org/museums.
[28] This is an abbreviated account of the process as described by Gaskell, *New Introduction*, 47–50.

the wires was stitched the mark that represented the size of the sheet, place, or quality, and usually the maker's initials. The outer edge of the tray had a thin frame that covered the edge or deckle. The vat-man would dip the tray in the vat, spread the pulp evenly, and give a shake in one direction and then the other in order that as much water would drop through as possible. He then passed the tray to the coucher, who removed the rim and turned the paper upside down onto the felt. Thus all paper has a felt side, and a wire side, the latter being slightly less smooth than the former. While the coucher flipped the sheet onto the felt, the vat-man would take a second tray and repeat the process. The two trays would alternate between the coucher and the vat-man.

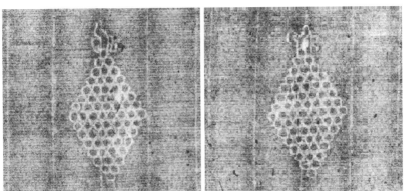

Figure 2.2   Grape watermarks, c.1633–4. Bodleian Library, Oxford, Rawlinson Poetry MS 31, ff.8 and 11 (beta-radiograph, reduced).

As a consequence of two trays alternating, all watermarks have a twin from the other tray that is very similar to, but not exactly the same as the first because the trays are hand-made.[29] In the example above, the 'GR' initials are placed differently against the stalks, and in the left image the bunch touches the chainline, whereas the other does not (figure 2.2). There are further subtle differences such as distances between the chainlines.

Once a pile of sheets has been accumulated, the layer took the pile to a press, where the workmen squeezed it firmly. After the paper had been pressed, the felts were separated from the paper which was pressed again, then hung out to dry. The sequence of the trays would therefore be shuffled. In this state the paper, known as waterleaf, was like blotting paper. Thus, it had to be dipped in size (i.e. gelatine), to fix it for writing or printing on (hence the existence of rag-and-bone men,

[29] See, A. H. Stevenson, 'Watermarks are Twins', *Studies in Bibliography*, 4 (1951), 57–91.

who collected the rags for the paper and the bones and leather for the gelatine from butchers and tanners). The paper was pressed once more, hung out to dry, and then pressed again. By this stage, the texture was dense and the sequencing of the marks irregular. Very occasionally, two sheets remained stuck together from the pressing: hence those copies of books where the recto of a leaf is on one sheet and the verso on another with two blank pages in between.[30] If the paper was primarily to be used for writing it might be hammered or rubbed smooth to give a finer surface finish. Both printing and writing paper were produced from exactly the same trays. It is how they were finished and used that distinguishes them, not the trays on which the pulp was laid. For a very common watermark such as pot, where the same trays might give rise to paper for both manuscript and print, the coincidence of origin and, therefore, supply and date is a useful fact to bear in mind.

A ream of paper was made up of 20 quires, each quire having 24 (in Britain and Holland) or 25 sheets (as in France and Italy), and weighed about 14 lbs for pot and twice as much for royal.[31] The quires were usually folded in half for packing, storage, and shipment, and some outside leaves could be damaged in transport, so that the usable quantity of paper was generally slightly less than the 480 or 500 sheets implied. It is at this stage that the watermark served its original purpose to identify the mill that had made the paper, together with its size and grade, in order that what had been sent to the merchant could be identified.

Paper as Evidence

Paper provides information about the origins and creation of books and manuscripts for two reasons: first, because the trays engaged to make paper had to be repaired or replaced regularly and so can be distinguished from one another; and, second, because the signs of manufacture (the chainlines, wires, and watermarks that left their images in the sheet) are independent of the contexts and circumstances in which the paper was used. It is the coincidence of text, or image, with paper that is informative and significant. When paper is used, in manuscript, print, or art, it possesses both the evidence of its use, and the image of the tray that made the sheet to which that text or image is fused. Thus, the processes and traces of textual replication (the details and idiosyncrasies of script, type,

[30] Thus, R. Greene, *Pandosto* (STC 12288.5; 1609): Folger Shakespeare Library, Washington DC, STC 12288.2, sheet E.
[31] D. J. McKitterick, *A History of Cambridge University Press: Volume 1, Printing and the Book Trade in Cambridge, 1534–1698* (Cambridge, 1992), 15.

or image) are quite separate from the details of the paper being used. This means that paper is informative as to where and when a document came to be, in that it can be matched to other documents with paper from the same tray that were used in other contexts. What we typically want to know is when and why paper and text or image became connected.

There are five pieces of information that a bibliographer needs to establish when studying paper in order to identify the date, or origins of a document: first, where the paper was made and, second, its quality (the two are generally related), in order to understand whether its use is conventional, out of the ordinary, or else in some way socially or pragmatically indicative of its history; third, an accurate tray image (watermark and chainlines) is required, in order to establish a precise point of reference; fourth, a list of similar datable examples should be made so that the relationship of the document being analyzed with other books and manuscripts that share the same batch, or batches, of paper in their making can be assessed; fifth, whether there are any other relevant examples of the paper, especially those that can be associated with the circumstances under which the document of interest was produced. In piecing together this puzzle, it is necessary to account for what is inconsistent or unusual as well as for the evidence that corroborates a date, or identifies responsibility, for any material.

The reliability of paper evidence is sometimes doubted owing to the chance that a 'rogue sheet', or stock of paper might get used long after the rest of a batch. While this is possible, the argument assumes that this would suffice to undermine the analysis of all association by date, or origin, in a way that invalidates both the reasons for, and the results of, any comparison. This is to set a possible witness against all the material that accurately reflects its history. What the critique also fails to do is address the ways in which paper acts as a control against other assumptions that have been made. What has yet to be quantified is the incidence, and recurrence, of stray sheets amongst datable material (e.g. letters), and the distance of the stray from the implied normal result (i.e. the core group of identical watermarks that share a closely related date).[32] In this respect, a study of flag watermarks over a 40-year period has indicated that whilst material can be misdated, rogue sheets are rare enough that one has yet to be found. The exception taken to paper evidence is, at best, an important caveat against carelessness.

---

[32] For instance, it ought to be possible to analyze the watermarks of the correspondence in the State Papers, Cotton, Lansdowne, and Tanner manuscripts and calculate the number of strays against the number of items as a whole. Further, one could then calculate the average variance of a stray to the main group of dates for any given watermark.

A stray is a sheet of paper that was used more than five years after paper from the same tray first circulated. By that time, most paper from a given tray ought to have been either used or bound for occasional use as table books, miscellanies, commonplace books, and so on. Standard statistical probability indicates that 95 per cent of data ought to fall within two standard deviations of a mean, and 99.7 per cent of data within three standard deviations of that time.[33] The period from when a given watermark first appears (i.e. when the paper was imported) to when it ceased to be sold was usually no more than 8–12 months. That means that most examples of a watermark will fall within a two–three year period. After three years, no more than three reams out of 1,000 would not have been used at all, and most of those sheets would not be unbound quires, but a few sheets or singles; after five years, the number of unused sheets would have been very small, and the possibility of one or two unbound quires being available en bloc a very rare occurrence. Unless it is demonstrable from a date, or the history of a document, the notion that a block of loose paper might have survived 15 or 20 years before being used goes against all statistical probability. Rather, related historical and textual evidence is more likely to enable a document to be dated with greater precision within the two–three-year period of its known associative use.

The incidence of stray paper is less likely from sources where there was regular use (be it a printing-house, scrivener's workshop, political or private secretariat, and so on). In rural and private contexts outside the court and universities, greater inconsistency is inevitable as the extent of domestic activity varied. With a printing-house, where the turnover of paper stocks was rapid, it is theoretically possible that a ream or two could have sat in the warehouse, but unlikely. In that instance, a book might contain sheets that were printed some years before the rest of the volume. When paper evidence is inconsistent in this way, what needs to be distinguished is a late use of paper in a book where everything was printed over a limited time-span, from a book that contained material that was printed earlier than the rest of the volume.[34]

If we assume, for a moment, that sheet E of a book is on older paper than the other sheets, then whether the difference proves significant, or not, would depend entirely on what it told us. If the book was entered in 1612, or has an imprint of 1612; perhaps manuscript annotations that it

---

[33] Any number of statistical studies could be cited in support of this, but for convenience, see: D. Freedman, R. Pisani, and R. Purves, *Statistics*, 3rd edn. (New York, 1998), 57–96. Of course, the distribution will be slightly skewed, as the paper could not be used before it was imported, but this detail is not so significant as to vitiate the principle set forth.

[34] Thus *Titles of Honor* (STC 22178; 1631) was started in 1621 and resumed a decade later.

was bought in that year; then there would be no reason to doubt that an older ream had been located and used, and that sheet E was produced at the same time as the rest of the book. The 'stray' paper would be an unused ream. However, if the book was a reprint, first published in 1606, then one would check whether the sheet was reset, or whether an extra run of copies had been printed some years before. In that case, the non-contemporary watermark would verify that the sheet was printed in 1606, rather than reset or reimposed on fresh paper six years later.

Not all books are created at once and paper can be a witness to this fact. A manuscript might start out as a booklet, and then have another block or two of paper added; it may even eventually have some of that paper removed. The evolution can be traced through a combination of the pagination, the variations in script and ink, and their association with different paper stocks. The chronological variation does not, in this case, indicate stray sheets but rather the history of the manuscript in its various stages of preparation.

A dash of scepticism, and a drop of incredulity, applied judiciously, will always serve as useful correctives to analytical narratives that seek to clarify the material and temporal contexts within which a document was prepared. Physical details, like archival records, need to be understood as corroborative forms of information that gain meaning from contexts that are more complex than we like to assume. With manuscripts, the ability to indicate a date range, such as 1610–12 compared to, say, the 1620s, generally suffices. The problem is not the material evidence itself, but the assumptions that are made about watermarks, often owing to carelessness. The issues that need to be faced are the need for exact detail; and a frank recognition of what the analysis is trying to achieve.

There are four main ways in which paper evidence can be used. First, it may alter assumptions about the relationship among documents that have been associated with one another. Used in this way, the study of paper is a tool for scepticism about the production history of texts. Thus, if it is claimed that several books in a sequence were all printed seriatim, but the items were printed in different fonts with the paper evidence suggesting that the books were connected with one another in specific ways, then we might wish to re-evaluate the analysis of printing-house activity with a view to remodelling the production sequence in line with the prevailing practice of concurrent activity.[35] Second, paper may independently corroborate links between documents in a group: if we know A, B, and C, to be written by the same person on the

[35] See pp. 141–8 below for a discussion of this in relation to the 1608 quarto of *King Lear*.

same supply of paper, and we suspect the anonymous document D to be written by that person owing to common scribal practices and idiosyncrasies, then if they all derive from the same stock of paper, that ought to increase our certainty that the attribution is correct because the paper is independent of the script. Third, we might want to know about the social history of paper as a commodity and whether its use can be associated with a specific group: for instance, c.98 per cent of paper employed in England in the early seventeenth-century was French, and Italian paper appears to have been most favoured by people associated with the court.[36] This kind of information is helpful when determining the history of an undated document, as it specifies a context and, therefore, a potentially fruitful direction for further investigative efforts. Fourth, we might want to fix a series of documents at points in time, often because we need to know the sequence they were written in, but sometimes for reasons of textual analysis as well: for instance, if the paper of a manuscript shows it to be earlier than a group of copies that it is generally associated with, then this may be an indication that that first manuscript is related to an earlier stage of the transmission process. This would appear to be true of British Library Harley MS 4064.

Commonsense will usually deal with the apparent exceptions should a watermark fall outside the period in which it might be expected. Most paper was used by, and by far the greatest volume of surviving evidence derives from, (semi-)professional writers who were highly educated: the nobility, court officials, secretaries, authors, academics, students, clergy, lawyers, scriveners. The other main consumer of paper was the printed book-trade. In England, in 1600, the trade accounted for about 20 per cent of paper used; by 1700, overall consumption had tripled, and print made up perhaps 30 per cent of this.[37] Of course, some paper was wasted, and some served as scrap paper, but there is an immediate and apparent difference between a formally prepared manuscript, or letter, and some jottings on an old piece of paper. Similarly, if one is dealing with an irregular user that fact needs to be taken into account.

It may seem counter-intuitive, but most paper with a date other than that indicated by other examples of the same watermark often reveals that previous assumptions about a document were wrong, and that it was written later (not earlier) than had been assumed. For instance, a

[36] M. B. Bland, 'Italian Paper in Early Seventeenth Century England', *Paper as a Medium of Cultural Heritage: Archaeology and Conservation*, ed. R. Graziaplena (Rome, 2004), 243–55; import figures can be found in Coleman, *The British Paper Industry*, 18–21.

[37] See, M. B. Bland, 'The London Book-Trade in 1600', *A Companion to Shakespeare*, ed. D. S. Kastan (Oxford, 1999), 450–63.

letter from the Earl of Pembroke to Sir Michael Hicks, dated '8 May', requesting a six-month extension to a loan, was dated by a later hand as having been written on 8 May 1601 and so bound in the sequence of his correspondence. Hicks, however, was not knighted until the coronation in 1604, and the watermark indicates a date of 1607. There is another letter by Pembroke dated 14 November 1607, again deferring the loan. Textually, and historically, we might well infer that the letter is out of position, but the watermark is absolute evidence that this is so and that the two letters are related. Similarly, a formal copy of the secret negotiations between England and Spain from the early 1630s, dated 12 January 1631, is in fact a copy made c.1642—the flag paper has a rho-lambda countermark that otherwise did not occur prior to mid-1639.[38]

Methods of Analysis and Description

The analysis of paper depends on the ability to acquire accurate images of the watermarks and chainlines. To begin with, it is necessary to look through the paper. Sometimes holding paper towards a window or a lamp is quite sufficient for the purpose; however, most libraries and archives have specific tools such as light-boxes on which loose sheets of paper can be laid, as well as flat light sheets that are inserted between the leaves of a manuscript or book. When these resources are available, they should be used, both in the interests of conservation, and because they free up the hands to hold a ruler for measurement.

The first obvious thing about paper is its colour and, at touch, its texture: whether it is coarse or smooth, and its weight. Some paper may be subject to discolouration from water-staining or chemical washing (which turns it a pale brown), but most 'white' paper will vary from a milky opalescence through cream, to shades of yellow and brown if displaying signs of ageing. Inevitably, the better qualities of paper are less prone to visible ageing than the cheaper ones and, if they are bound in the same volume as other material they will either appear as dense but not coarse (as with Swiss paper), or lighter and brighter (as the Italian and Spanish papers are), than the surrounding documents.

When paper is backlit, the watermark and wires of the tray should be clearly visible. On a loose sheet, the watermark will be found to one side, so that when it is folded once, as with a printed folio or bound correspondence, it will be in the centre of one of the conjugate leaves; if the paper has been folded twice as a quarto, the watermark will be in the

---

[38] Respectively, British Library, Lansdowne MS 88, f.23; Lansdowne MS 90, f.67; and Bodleian Library, Clarendon MS 5, ff.50–1 and 54–5: see, Bland, 'Italian Paper', 243–55.

gutter of the binding; if the book is in octavo, the watermark will be on the inner top edge and have probably been cropped; and if it is a duo-decimo, it will be on the outer edge. For obvious reasons, it is more difficult to measure accurately watermarks in quarto, octavo, and the smaller formats, unless the sheet is disbound—as the earlier example from the first edition of Sidney's *Arcadia* illustrated. The countermark, if present, is a separate mark on the other side of the sheet, normally towards the bottom, that identified the mill if the main mark was of a more generic type.

The Society of International Paper Historians has set out a standard protocol for the description of watermarks, with an exhaustive list of criteria.[39] Many of the categories are concerned with modern machine-made papers. What follows is a synopsis of this standard as it relates to the hand-made period. First, the document needs to be given an identification number or tag, and the repository, the shelfmark (or call number), and the leaf number (e.g. f.37, or C2–3), of the watermark need to be recorded. If the paper can be dated through its text (e.g. if it is a letter, or book with an imprint), this is noted, as should any details, where known, about the author, scribe, recipient, printer, and/or publisher. Second, the size of the sheet (height then width) should be measured in millimetres, and whether it is uncropped, trimmed, or a fragment noted. If the sheet is folded and bound, its dimensions should be multiplied out by the format. If the paper is marbled or coloured it should be so identified. Third, the wire side of the sheet (i.e. the side impressed against the wires and watermark) should be identified and then the felt side, where possible, should be used for measurement.[40]

The second stage in the description of paper focuses on the mark and chainlines, establishing the position of the watermark relative to the tray where this is possible. First, the main mark should be distinguished from the countermark if there is one, and their details should be recorded separately. If the paper is without a watermark, then all that can be recorded is the size of the sheet and the distance between chainlines. Preferably, it should be recorded whether the mark is on the left or right-hand side of the sheet, and where it is positioned, in the middle, or towards the top or bottom. This latter information is usually more helpful for countermarks. Next the image of the watermark is described (pot, pillar, French horn, arms of Burgundy, grapes, double pennant flag, and so on).

---

[39] See, www.paperhistory.org/standard.htm.
[40] The wire side of the sheet is discussed by A. H. Stevenson, 'Chain Indentations in Paper as Evidence', *Studies in Bibliography*, 6 (1954), 181–95.

The watermark is measured first by height, then by width, with the distance from the edge of the mark to the nearest chainline on the left. Measurements can also be taken of the distance between the right outer edge of the mark and the chainline to the right; and, where the sheet is untrimmed, the distance between the lower edge of the paper and the bottom of the mark, as well as the top of the mark and the upper edge of the paper. Next, the distance between chainlines is measured. Ideally, all chainlines ought to be recorded from left to right, although this is not always feasible. As an absolute minimum, if the mark is between two chainlines, then the distance of the compartments on either side of the central compartment with the mark should be measured (i.e. three compartments); if the mark is located on a chainline and across two compartments, then the distance of the compartments on either side of the two in which the mark is located ought to be measured as well (i.e. four compartments). Additional outer chainline measurements are always helpful.[41] The ruler should then be placed against the chainline to the left of the mark, and the number of wires over 20 mm counted. Finally, it should be added that if the mark is a complex image, it may help to measure the component parts; and that initials, names, or the identity of the papermaker (if known) should be recorded as well.

Finally, it is desirable to have as accurate an image of the water-mark and chainlines as possible. There are several methods. Drawing or tracing may suffice for private purposes, but for direct comparison it is necessary to resort to photography, digital imaging, dylux, or various forms of radiography, of which beta-radiography is the most common.[42] With folios, it is usually preferable that the beta-radiograph have a horizontal (landscape) orientation in order to record the maximum number of chainlines as well as the mark. In part, the option chosen will depend on the resources of the library, and whether the image is easily accessible or hidden behind type or script. For obscured marks, beta-radiography presents the clearest image as it only preserves an image of the paper and not the text, but a number of libraries no longer offer this facility. If the watermark is obscured, and radiography is not available, then one option is to seek another source of the image, and then compare the two to confirm the match.

It is important to realize how subtle the changes between one mark and another can be; and that measurements alone will not enable the

[41] R. L. Hill, 'The Importance of Laid and Chainline Spacing', in M. Zedoun Bat-Yehouda, ed., *Le Papier au Moyen Âge* (Tournhout, 1999), 149–63.

[42] For a recent discussion, see: A. de la Chapelle, 'La Bêtaradiographie et l'étude des papiers: beaucoup plus qu'une belle image', *Gazette du livre médiéval*, 34 (1999), 13–24.

identification of different marks: what they will do, if all the images are not available, is provide a list of examples to confer with. In particular, it is important to distinguish between marks that derive from different states of the same tray, and those that derive from different trays. This is where the measurement of chainlines proves to be crucial, for marks that derive from different states of the same tray will always have exactly the same distance between their chainlines, even though there has been a shift in part of the image, whereas marks that derive from different trays will have different distances between the chainlines.

In the example below (figure 2.3), the watermarks are twins with grapes that appear to have been affected in the same way by the pressure of the pulp, with the one on the left illustrating the pressure of the pulp on the pillar as the tray is shaken by a right-handed workman. Despite

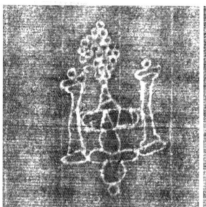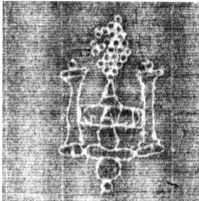

Figure 2.3   Pillar watermarks with grapes, initials GALD, c.1629–30. Bodleian Library, Oxford, Rawlinson Poetry MS 160, ff.53 and 168 (beta-radiograph, reduced).

their similarities, however, they are not variants of the same mark because the distance between chainlines differs from one to the other.

Both these watermarks measure 61 × 38 mm. The distance between the chainlines for the one on the left is 20, 20.5, 19 and 20.5 mm; the distance between the chainlines for that on the right, 20, 18.5, 20.5 and 20.5 mm.[43] In contrast, the two images opposite do represent different states of the same mark (figure 2.4). In this instance, it would appear that the tail of three circles has either come loose from, or been fixed to, the chainline (the right pillar in the left-hand image does show greater signs

[43] All the beta-radiographs for Rawlinson Poetry MS 160 are kept as REF XXII.97, together with an analysis of the manuscript by Bruce Barker-Benfield, prepared in 1987.

of wear, which suggests that it may be the later state). The distance between the chainlines for both images is 18.5, 20, 20.5, and 19 mm.

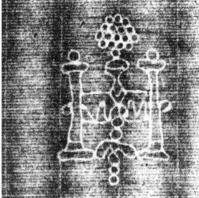

Figure 2.4 Pillar watermarks with grapes, initials MM, c.1629–30. Bodleian Library, Oxford, Rawlinson Poetry MS 160, ff.149 and 208 (bata-radiograph, reduced).

Fine Paper

Italian paper with a flag watermark is the most common fine paper in early seventeenth-century England. Other fine papers have a crossbow, the hat of a monsignor and, earlier, a lotus flower.[44] Papers with a cross enclosed by a pendant, or three vertical circles, are Spanish: they are rare after the first decade of the seventeenth-century because domestic shortages limited the Spanish export trade.[45] Spanish and Italian papers have wide chainlines, superior whiteness, and a light texture: Bacon and Northampton, as well as Jonson, had a taste for paper of this kind and used it almost all the time. Only rarely, as with Pope who chose 'Genoa' for fine-paper copies of his earliest books, was it used for printing.[46] The contexts of use indicates how more expensive paper was an index of social and economic status, as only those with access to it, with money and taste, would use or have texts prepared on paper of this kind.

---

[44] The lotus flower watermark is found, for instance, in Trinity College, Dublin MS 638: a collection of poems by boys at Westminster School for Queen Elizabeth, prepared c.1586. See also, G. Castagnari, *L'opera dei fratelli Zonghi: l'era del segno nella storia della carta* (Fabriano, 2003).
[45] See, M. B. Bland, 'Italian Paper', 243–55. Both kinds of Spanish paper are to be found in letters sent by John Digby, Earl of Bristol, from Madrid during the Spanish marriage negotiations: thus, Bodleian Library, Oxford, MS Clarendon 4, f.35 (pendant; 18 June, 1623); and f.44 (circles; 24 September, 1623).
[46] Foxon, *Pope and the Early Eighteenth-Century Book Trade*, 19–21.

Every few years, the flag watermarks would evolve in ways that help to identify an approximate period for their use. The earliest flags are draped around the pole rather than flying from it, the next stage was to have a bulbous base to the pole. At various later stages, this was shaped like a nail, then more angled like a screw and, sometimes, in the 1620s, it was flared like a trumpet or rifle-butt. From the late 1620s, the '3' was repeated twice, and in the late 1630s, a rho-lambda countermark was added. Both the examples, here, are from the 1620s (figure 2.5). The mark on the left is from a contemporary copy of a letter by Sir Thomas Roe to Secretary Calvert, dated 18 October 1624. Overall, the watermark is 52 × 44 mm; the G is 16.5 mm high, the 3 16 mm high, the distance from the left chain to the G measures 11 mm, and the inner distance between the G and the pole is 3 mm. The compartments are 27 mm and 26.5 mm wide. The mark on the right is found in a letter by John Davenant, Bishop of Salisbury, to Seth Ward dated 4 November 1628. Overall, this mark is 51 × 43 mm; both the G and the 3 are 14 mm high, the distance from the left chain to the G is 12 mm, and the inner distance between the G and the pole is 5 mm. The compartments are both 26 mm wide.

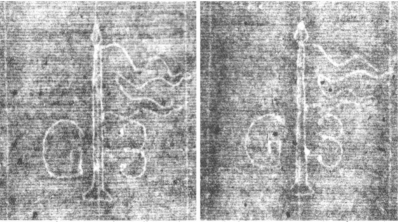

Figure 2.5   Flag watermarks. Bodleian Library, Oxford, MS Tanner 73/2, f.482 (18 October 1624); and MS Tanner 72, f.298 (4 November 1628: beta-radiographs).

A number of important literary documents were written on Italian paper, and this can be an indication of the context in which they were prepared and circulated.[47] In the following example

---

[47] For instance, John Fletcher to the Countess of Huntington (Huntington Library, San Marino, MS HA 13333); Folger Shakespeare Library, Washington DC, MS V.a.125.

(figure 2.6), which has been turned upside down, the flag is visible between the 'hon' of 'honest' to the 'w' of sweare.

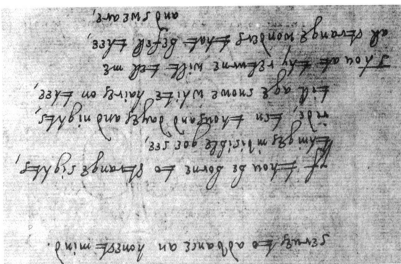

Figure 2.6 John Donne, 'A Songe' (Goe and catch a fallinge starre), scribe not identified: Houghton Library, Harvard University, MS Eng 966.4, f.203ʳ (photograph).

This manuscript of Donne's poems, together with three sermons and the paradoxes and problems, was probably written c.1624–6.[48] It is one of a number of Donne manuscripts on fine paper—an aspect of the manuscript tradition that has been little commented upon. It suggests not only that these texts by Donne were valued, but that the source of the texts (a few poems, mainly by Sir John Roe, are included) was thought to be reliable, although the underlying copy must have descended via an intermediary. Similarly, two Group One manuscripts have unusual, high-quality paper stocks, and are written in highly practised hands. The Leconsfield manuscript (Cambridge University Additional MS 5778) is on paper with a circular peacock watermark that is particularly rare in English manuscripts; whilst the Dowden manuscript (Bodleian Library,

---

[48] The sermons are on Psalm 38.9 (spring/summer 1618), Ecclesiastes 12.1 (21 February 1619), and Matthew 21.44 (18 April 1619), the last dedicated to the Countess of Montgomery before Donne's departure to Germany. The presence of 'To Christ' ('A Hymn to God the Father') indicates a date after 1623. The paper indicates a date c.1624–6. See also, M. Potter, 'A Seventeenth Century Literary Critic of John Donne: The Dobell Manuscript Re-examined', *Harvard Library Bulletin*, 23 (1975), 63–89; E. M. Simpson and G. R. Potter (eds.), *The Sermons of John Donne*, 10 vols. (Berkeley and Los Angeles, 1953–62), x, 428–30

Oxford, MS English Poetry e.99) is on paper manufactured by the firm of Nicholas Heusler in Basle that has a house and dragon watermark.[49] A small stock of that paper is also to be found in Huntington Library MS HM198 part 2, mixed in with the main arms of Burgundy paper.[50] The Huntington manuscript includes poems by Donne, but is more broadly a miscellany connected with the Inner Temple.[51] Both manuscripts were prepared c.1615–18, which is earlier than has been assumed, and both were clearly prepared for a person of some importance. The date is of some significance as it means that the manuscripts were prepared very close to the time that Donne took holy orders.

What these examples indicate is that unusual paper is a sign that a manuscript was prepared with greater care and expense than most: it may suggest that the manuscript could have been the work of an author, a scrivener working to specific requirements, an aristocratic household, or that it may have been especially prepared for a particular patron whose identity may not always be apparent; at which point, both the character of the hand, and its consistency, is of singular relevance. Further, whilst the origins of these manuscripts are yet to be established, the determination of a likely period in which they were prepared, and an understanding of their context, is the first step towards resolving the identity of those responsible for preparing them.

As well as the rarer papers from Italy, Spain, and Switzerland, better and larger papers were available from France. The two most common watermarks are the fleur-de-lys and the arms of Burgundy (the crest having three-quarters with horses rampant, and the maker's initials in the fourth) surmounted with a crown. These are the usual forms of large paper found in most printed books and manuscripts. For example, Trinity College, Dublin, MS 877 was prepared on paper of this kind c.1620 (figure 2.7). This manuscript was half-completed with poems by Donne before being used in the early 1630s as a miscellany. These later additions indicate that the manuscript had associations with the south-west of England. It is possible that the empty half had been intended for prose works by Donne, in much the same way as is found in the Dobell manuscript, as the paper belongs to a single stock. As can be seen, the differences between the twin watermarks of this manuscript are more clearly pronounced than, for instance, Bodleian Rawlinson Poetry 31 (figure 2.2, above) as they are set at different angles from each other; what is

---

[49] W. F. Tschudin, *The Ancient Paper-Mills of Basle and Their Makers* (Hilversum, 1958), 177 (mark 294).
[50] The paper is at ff.31–6 and ff.41–56 of the manuscript.
[51] For a description see pp. 125–6 and figure (127) below.

equally apparent from the images are the ways in which the continual pressure of shifting pulp against the wires gradually distorts the shape of the mark during the life of a tray.

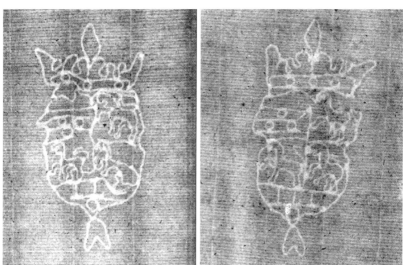

Figure 2.7   Crown watermarks (arms of Burgundy), c.1618–20. Trinity College, Dublin, MS 877, ff.9 and 105 (backlit photographs, reduced).

Large paper copies of printed books came to replace parchment as the premium medium for presentation copies. There are, nevertheless, a few early examples of books printed on parchment, notably the Vatican copy of Henry VIII's *A Vindication of the Seven Sacraments against Martin Luther* that the king later repudiated.[52] The exceptional nature of this book, its polemical as well as its political purpose, underlines its unique status in the context of commercial book production. In more typical circumstances, a dozen or so special copies were printed on a grade of paper one size larger than the main run. In general, this practice appears to have become more common after 1600. When books were printed on pot, large copies would be printed on crown, as with Jonson's *Workes*.[53] There are exceptions: the ordinary copies of Samuel Daniel's folio *Works* (1602) and Michael Drayton's folio *Poems* (1619) are on a smaller than

[52] Henry VIII, *Assertio septem sacramentorum adversos Martinum Lutherum* (STC 13078; 1521). For an illustration, see A. Grafton (ed.), *Rome Reborn: The Vatican Library and Renaissance Culture* (New Haven CT and Washington DC, 1993), 69–71 (plate 62).
[53] B. Jonson, *Workes* (STC 14751–2; 1616). Large paper copies (by STC sigla) include: L.O39.CAL.F(2).HN.PML.PN.TX(2). At least five large paper copies remain in private hands.

usual paper with a unicorn watermark;[54] it is the large paper copies that were printed on pot. More uncommonly, it would appear that all copies of Isaac Casaubon's *A Response to the Letter of the Illustrious Cardinal Perron* are not only set in great primer but printed with wide margins on crown paper,[55] the latter being another case of a monarch paying for a special commission. Sometimes, however, there were books that had to be printed on crown, such as Shakespeare's *Comedies, Histories, and Tragedies*. The sheer volume of text to be set required the shift up from pot to crown paper, and the trade seems to have been reluctant to print large paper copies on demy. There are, however, some continental examples of both folios and quartos in demy for important classical texts.

As with many things about the early book-trade, paper use drew upon a series of commonly accepted conventions. Understanding the principles that informed those conventions is relatively simple, in that special items required special paper, and that paper could also reflect social and economic patterns of use. The problem in studying paper is how we might sift the evidence in ways that are productive rather than exhaustive, and exhausting. There are, in fact, at least two methods that can be employed most fruitfully to address this problem: first, by focusing on and mapping the use of fine and large papers in order that the various differences in paper use can be understood, particularly with regard to what might be thought of as either not conventional, or deliberate in some way; second, with paper such as pot and pillar, by focusing on localized and resolvable problems in order that specific reference points can be established and so expanded upon. By sharpening the focus in this way, the diversity and complexity of the information can be made more manageable. In the end, it is this ability to control the information that will lead to greater descriptive and analytical clarity in the study of early modern paper and its uses.

[54] S. Daniel, *Works* (STC 6236–7; 1601–2); M. Drayton, *Poems* (STC 7222–3; 1619). Also. B. Juel-Jensen, 'Fine and Large-Paper Copies of *S.T.C.* Books and particularly Drayton's *Poems* (1619) and *The Battaile of Agincourt* (1627)', *The Library*, v: 19 (1964), 226–30; and, 'Fine and Large-Paper Copies of *S.T.C.* Books: A Further Note', *The Library*, v: 23, 1968, 239–40. Daniel's presentation copy of his *Works* to Queen Elizabeth is now Pierpont Morgan Library PML 15592. At least 12 other presentation copies survive.
[55] *Isaaci Casauboni ad epistolam illustr. cardinalis Perronij, responsio* (STC 4740; 1612).

3   The Structure of Documents

FREDSON Bowers's most enduring book is the *Principles of Bibliographical Description*,[1] in which he consolidated his ideas and reputation for analytical and descriptive bibliography. Following Greg, who argued that editorial practices had to be technically precise in their methods,[2] Bowers made the exact description of documents a prerequisite for the analysis of all textual materials, and he was particularly acute at mapping patterns and discontinuities in printed books that were of significance. His methods received their most extended development in Hinman's monumental *The Printing and Proofreading of the First Folio of Shakespeare*.[3] Yet the intensity of this gaze on individual texts obscured those more complex associations of concurrent work that McKenzie illuminated in 'Printers of the Mind'.[4] That response is sometimes misunderstood as a refutation of analytical and descriptive bibliography. It is not. McKenzie insisted that the complexity of books was a function of the trade and the methods of manufacture were far more flexible than then prevalent theories allowed. His caveat against analytical bibliography was that, whilst it could establish certain facts about the production of a book, those facts could not be stretched to make generalizations about the organization of output, edition runs, or the work of individuals; and further, he insisted that physical evidence needed to be understood alongside related archival information, and be inclusive of all materials.

Analytical bibliography maps the recurrences and differences in the making of books and manuscripts to localize specific events in the production process. Descriptive bibliography records the structure, format, and physical characteristics (including the script or type) of books and manuscripts in order that each specific state of a document can be identified, and related items distinguished from, or connected to one another: thus, descriptive bibliography informs both cataloguing practices, and textual scholarship. In principle, the format, structure,

---

[1] F. T. Bowers, *Principles of Bibliographical Description* (Princeton, NJ, 1949). In the same year Bowers founded *Studies in Bibliography*. For two very different assessments of Bowers, see: G. T. Tanselle, 'The Life of Fredson Thayer Bowers', *Studies in Bibliography*, 46 (1993), 1–154; and, H. Amory, 'Review: *The Life and Work of Fredson Bowers*', *TEXT*, 9 (1996), 466–74. Tanselle discusses the *Principles* on pp.40–8.

[2] Greg, 'Bibliography—An Apologia', 239–66.

[3] C. Hinman, *The Printing and Proofreading of the First Folio of Shakespeare*, 2 vols. (Oxford, 1963).

[4] McKenzie's article, based on his exhaustive study of the early Cambridge University Press accounts, was originally published by Bowers: McKenzie, 'Printers of the Mind'.

and binding of manuscripts and printed books (that is, the way in which sheets of paper were folded, collected, modified with insertions or removals, and bound together) is common to both. The study of these physical characteristics enables an understanding of how these items were produced, as well as a comparative analysis of materials, so that the extent to which any book or manuscript varies from established conventions of textual representation can be analyzed.

In recent times, the shift in bibliographical scholarship towards a study of the uses of the book and the history of reading practices has moved the focus away from the primary skills of material analysis and description. As a consequence, narratives about the history of the book sometimes fail to notice the way in which the structure of a document communicates meaning. Books and manuscripts reveal through the aesthetics of their page design, form, and function, preconceptions about their use, including the extent to which they were conceived of as being privately kept, or socially exchanged and circulated texts (hence a manuscript that was prepared for a patron or employer might differ from the smaller, less formal volumes kept as diaries, commonplace books, miscellanies, and as journals for recipes). Practical decisions about format, size, and binding are primary considerations that define the shape and physical appearance of the book. For this reason, matters of presentation should not be regarded as 'incidental' to a document, but as fundamental to the history of the book: form affects meaning.[5]

This chapter is concerned with the format and structure of books and manuscripts (that is with the decisions that were made about their material characteristics before they became text-bearing artefacts). In many instances, those decisions will have been made with an awareness of what was to be reproduced and the length of the text that needed to be accommodated, together with the type to be used, or script employed. These issues have to be resolved first as they determine how much paper is required, how it is to be folded, and so bound. If a manuscript is an original where the details of length and format were not yet known, then it was common for it to be written in folio (i.e. the paper was folded once) so that extra sheets or quires of paper could be added at the end. This practice was also usual for correspondence.

By studying the structure of a document, it is possible to understand the primary technical and economic considerations that went into its making, the language of its presentation, the reasons why decisions were made, and the relationship of the item with other documents. It is important to put this structural and contextual analysis before the study

---

[5] McKenzie, 'Typography and Meaning', 198–236; *Bibliography and the Sociology of Texts*, 4.

of the precedence, alteration, and correction of a work since textual analysis tends to separate one document from another owing to its concern with error and difference. Further, a concern with the text tends to obscure other signs that may be of cultural and historical value in understanding what a particular copy represents. Thus, some contemporary bindings give expression to political or social obligation and intent. In other instances, the extent to which printed books were manuscripts (the content of which did not always relate to the 'text'), owing to their marginalia and other annotations, is still inconsistently treated by scholars and repositories, who since the early seventeenth-century have privileged print over the written word.[6]

If the structure of a document is part of its bibliographical language, then the art is to read the complexity of books and manuscripts in their modes of production and use. To do so requires a grasp of descriptive techniques. At first sight, the *Principles of Bibliographical Description* fulfils this need. It details the concepts, formulae, and processes involved in describing books, including how to determine and record variant states, issues, editions, and reimpositions of type, together with the size and format of the sheet, and the order of the signatures. It is, in its way, a work of acute technical virtuosity that is focused on printed books, particularly literary texts. As with McKerrow, Bowers did not discuss how to apply these methods to manuscripts or inscriptions, and he only lightly touched on maps and plates, ignoring volvelles (rotating paper wheels pinned with a rivet through the page in books of mathematics, navigation, and astronomy) and similar attachments. The method fused the formula for collating texts according to their signatures with the more general practices found in the catalogues of the better booksellers. The result was both more limiting, as well as less comprehensive, than Bowers envisaged, whilst being over-elaborate as a practical technique for distinguishing most printed texts from one another.

The reason it is instructive to understand the format of documents is because structure shapes reading practices.[7] An octavo or duo-decimo is a pocketbook: it can be carried and read casually. A folio weighing 2 kg or more is less likely to be portable, and was generally read at a desk, lectern, or some similar space. The ease of use with the octavo and smaller sizes, as well as the fact that such books were rarely more than 30 sheets in length (with most under a dozen sheets), meant that runs for pocketbooks were, as a sweeping generalization, likely to be

---

[6] McKitterick, *Print, Manuscript and the Search for Order*, 12–17. See also, R. C. Alston, *Books with Manuscript: A short Title Catalogue of Books with Manuscript Notes in the British Library* (London, 1994).

[7] McKenzie, 'Typography and Meaning', 223–8.

higher than for folios, where the extra costs of composition and paper meant that the returns on a first edition were carefully calculated and the potential for loss minimized. The same sense of scale and proportion in relation to reading practices is true of manuscripts. Yet the issues are not only those of cost, portability, and (if published) copy-runs, but the intimacy of the reading space. Smaller volumes are often found in conjunction with smaller scripts and type sizes. At the most extreme reduction of format, texts of this kind are inherently unreadable in any sustained manner: the tiny psalm-books (32mo and smaller) set in brevier and pearl served more as *aide-memoires* than reading texts, reflecting the oral and memorial habits of repetition and ritual, as well as tokens of cultural and religious identification.

Bowers did not discuss why books have the format, structure, or binding they do, and what this might communicate about their purpose and use. These matters, he felt, were critical issues. Rather he claimed that descriptive bibliography 'may be described as "pure" scholarship'. Against this, one might place the practical insight of Hugh Williamson:

> Aesthetic factors in book production are difficult to pin down for examination and description. Efficiency in the presentation of its contents, economy in manufacture, and durability in use and store are the prime physical virtues of a book, but to attract and please is as important for the book as for an orator. Taste as well as reason must attend the choice of format.[8]

In retrospect, it is possible to see that Bowers (owing to his desire to trace agency and responsibility for every textual act) isolated one class of material within a methodology that ought to have encompassed the full variety of evidence, just as his analytical work isolated individual literary documents from the concurrent complexities of their making. With that caveat made, the guidelines that were first outlined by Greg,[9] and developed by Bowers, retain their usefulness as the most concise means of describing any particular artefact, including (with a little adaptation) manuscript, and its relationship to other materials.

Precision in the description of books and manuscripts is a necessary skill as it is the means by which the bibliographer records and controls information, including copy-specific details where multiple examples survive. This is as true for works of law, history, geography, science, mathematics, music, and theology, as for commonplace books, charts,

---

[8] Bowers, *Principles*, 3; H. Williamson, *Methods of Book Design: The Practice of an Industrial Craft*, 2nd edn. (Oxford, 1966), 24.
[9] Greg, 'A Formulary of Collation', *Collected Papers*, 298–313.

broadsides, pamphlets, and ephemera, as well as literature. The starting point is the way in which a sheet of paper has been folded because the sheet is the primary unit of documentary organization. What needs to be remembered about format and structure is that the decisions that gave rise to any particular document were normally made in relation to other texts, and their format and structure, as well as the item in hand.

Format

If the principles of structural description are simple, the permutations can be quite complex. In what follows, it should be assumed that we are dealing with sheets of paper: the size and details do not particularly matter—those issues were addressed in the previous chapter and, for practical purposes, a sheet of A3 will substitute for a trimmed sheet of pot; nor is it significant whether the sheets are blank, a manuscript, or a printed text. The primary concern is the relationship between the parts that make up a document, together with the removal and addition of leaves, and how one goes about describing these characteristics.

Take a sheet of A3 paper. If this were not folded, and printed on one side only, it would be known as a broadside. This format was chosen for texts that could be pasted up on a post or a wall: proclamations, ballads, playbills, and their ilk.[10] Next, fold the sheet of paper once. The paper now has two leaves with inner and outer pages, four in all. This format is known as folio. In order to get eight pages we could do one of three things. We could fold another sheet and place it in sequence, we could fold another sheet and place, or quire, it within the first (a folio in fours), or we could fold the sheet of paper again as a quarto, giving half the page area but twice the number of leaves. With a quarto, pages 2–3 and 6–7 will be on the one side of the paper, and pages 1, 4–5, and 8 on the other. In a printed book, these are the inner and outer formes.

If we now wanted to create a document with 16 pages, the number of options more than doubles: we could have four separate folio sheets, or four sheets quired as a single gathering. There could be two quires with two folio sheets in each; a quire of three folio sheets (a folio in six) with a singleton before or after; two quarto sheets in sequence; two quarto sheets one inside the other (a quarto in eights); or the paper could be folded for a third time as an octavo. With an octavo, pages 2–3, 6–7, 10–11, and 14–15 are on one side of the sheet, pages 1, 4–5,

---

[10] See, for instance: T. Stern, '"On Each Wall and Corner Post": Playbills, Title-pages and Advertising in Early Modern London', *English Literary Renaissance*, 36 (2006), 57–89; T. Watt, *Cheap Print and Popular Piety, 1550–1640* (Cambridge, 1991).

8–9, 12–13 and 16 are on the other. Folio, quarto, and octavo are the most common formats found in early printed books and manuscripts.

It is possible to keep folding the paper and smaller formats do exist. These are most often associated with psalm-books and pocketbooks of devotional piety. If an octavo is folded again it becomes a decimo-sexto. The problem with decimo-sexto and the smaller formats (32mo, 64mo, 128mo) is that they could not be easily stitched through the middle. In order to achieve the small page area, but not have a problem in the binding, the paper was cut in half or quartered to produce a decimo-sexto or 32mo in eights. With folio and octavo books, the chainlines are vertical on the page and the wirelines horizontal. With quarto and decimo-sexto, the chainlines are horizontal, and the wirelines vertical.

The other important format is the duo-decimo of 12 leaves. This may be either a single sheet folded uncut, or one cut and then folded in two sections: for this reason, mistakes in the gathering and binding of this format are not unknown. The most usual method of folding a duo-decimo was to cut the right third from the rest of the sheet, set with pages 12, 13, 16, and 9 on one side, and 10, 15, 14, and 11 on the other; then the left two-thirds that contains pages 1–8 and 17–24 was folded as a typical octavo, and the right third was folded twice and placed inside.[11] The resulting page is tall and narrow and thus ideal for rapid reading (like a newspaper column). A further consequence is that whereas quarto and octavo books have the occasional half-sheet, duo-decimos tend to have eights and fours.[12] It is possible to fold the sheet uncut like a 'z', or to turn the left side inwards, and fold the right side over the top. It is also possible to have very narrow long pages. These are unusual methods for a book in this format. With the common format of duo-decimo, the chainlines are horizontal and the wirelines vertical. If the format is a long duo-decimo then the chainlines would be vertical and the wirelines horizontal, with the mark on the top edge.

Generally, a sheet of pot will yield a trimmed folio of c.290 × 190 mm, a quarto of c.190 × 140 mm, an octavo of c.140 × 95 mm, and a duo-decimo of c.145 × 65 mm. Yet sometimes with manuscripts, music, or illustrated books, variations upon the standard practices occur. The most common difference is for the paper to be bound as an oblong: thus, there are a number of music part-books arranged as oblong quartos, whilst oblong octavos were sometimes used for verse miscellanies (figure 3.1).[13]

---

[11] Or, it is placed following (i.e. B⁸ C⁴): e.g. R. Thorius, *Hymnus Tabaci* (STC 24033; 1626).
[12] A full series of format diagrams can be found in Gaskell, *New Introduction*, 87–107.
[13] For instance, Bodleian Library, Oxford, MS Tenbury 1018; and Beinecke Library, Yale University, Osborn MS b114.

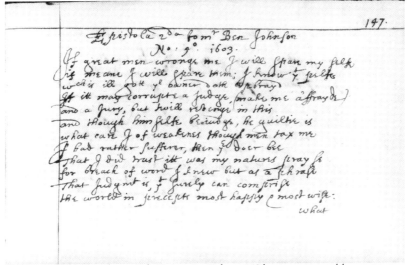

Figure 3.1   Beinecke Library, Yale University, Osborn MS b114, p.147, an oblong octavo.

Another unusual example of a non-standard format is the diary of Archbishop Laud, which consists of three sheets of royal folded as a long decimo-sexto, making it very long and thin.[14] It is a volume in which Laud kept intensely private records, from irrational fears and court gossip to his dreams of failed communions.[15] One of the immediately striking things about this format is the way in which it departs from convention. Whether private or public, choices about format depended on the text being prepared and its length; the purposes to which the volume would be put and so its size; and the social profile of those involved in its creation and use.

Understanding format is necessary because the sheet is the unit with which all scribes, compositors, and pressmen worked. In relation to this, they had to calculate the size of the page, how many sheets might be involved in preparing the copy of a text, and how many copies might be required. From that they could calculate how much paper would be necessary for the job to be completed, and from that they could begin to estimate cost. Measuring the page, counting the number of leaves in each gathering, and multiplying the sums out to establish the size of the sheet may often lead to a predictable result, but it reinforces the sense of the book as a physical object and on occasion it yields answers that are

---

[14] St John's College, Oxford, MS 258. The diary thus measures 20 × 8 cm, not 16 × 10 cm.
[15] M. B. Bland, '"Invisible Dangers": Censorship and the Subversion of Authority in Early Modern England', *Papers of the Bibliographical Society of America*, 90 (1996), 190–3.

not expected. The Herbert manuscript of *Biathanatos*, for instance, was prepared as a folio with extra wide margins to be cut down, not as the quarto it would seem to be at first glance from its size and shape.[16]

Pagination and Signatures, Rectos and Versos

With printed books, the organization of the sheets to be gathered was usually alphabetical, although asterisks, hands, paragraph marks (¶), daggers (†), and other signs might be employed for preliminaries. Once the alphabet was exhausted it was repeated again in duplicate (Aa), then triplicate (Aaa), and so on.[17] In principle, the sequence of signatures in printed texts makes it easier to refer to a leaf by its place in a gathering rather than by the page number. There are a number of reasons for this, not least because the pagination of early printed books is not always strictly logical whereas the signature sequence typically is, and can always be precisely recorded. Some texts might also be numbered by the column, or foliated by the leaf. With manuscripts, formal signatures are rare and the foliation or pagination has been checked by the curatorial staff, so references to a folio or page are generally more convenient.

The pagination of printed books was subject to error because the skeleton forme with the running title and pagination was set separately from the text page which included the signature. The skeleton was used again and again to avoid resetting minimally changing text, and because it served as a reference point to ensure that the pages of the next forme were arranged in the same place relative to the sheet as the previous forme or gathering. As a consequence, it is not uncommon to find that a compositor might not replace the pagination, or invert the numbers when setting, pick up a numeral from the wrong box, or mis-distribute a numeral when the type was being returned to the tray. These kinds of detail can help establish the relationship of one forme to another, and sometimes an overlap or gap may indicate concurrent setting, or occur because parts of the book were set in different printing-houses. Hence, pagination can be very instructive as to how a book was printed, but it does mean that it is a less accurate form of record than the signature, and some books were set without any pagination at all. The formal structure and the relationship of the leaves within a gathering, however, can always be described.

---

[16] Bodleian Library, Oxford, MS e. Musaeo 131; British Library, MS Royal 18.A.xlv; see, M. B. Bland, 'Jonson, *Biathanatos*, and the Interpretation of Manuscript Evidence', *Studies in Bibliography*, 51 (1998), 154–82; see also, p. 69 below.

[17] What follows summarizes Bowers, *Principles*, 191–254; Gaskell, *New Introduction*, 321–35.

A Caueat, and a Comfort for Beleeuers. 627

uing vpon it, that nothing fhould be able to defeate him of that happineffe hee
wayted for: So in the beginning of that difcourfe, hee propounds a generall
Doctrine, which concernes all which are in Chrift Iefus: Touching whom this
he delinereth, that *to them there is no condemnation*; now hee prooues this by his
owne example at large, &c¹? Whereupon I inferre, that whatfoeuer *Paules* re-   ¹ Verf. 1.&c.
ported there of himfelfe is not fingular, that is, fuch as wherein ordinary beleeuers are not interreffed with him; for then to what end is his experience and
example brought in as a proofe for a Doctrine which concernes all? Certenly,
it is the condition and ftate of all true Beleeuers, *That neither height nor depth,*
nor any other Creatures can feparate them from the loue of God, which is in Chrift Iefus
our Lord ª. But I ftay my felf in this; It were no hard thing to be plentifull in the   ª Verf. 39.
enlargement of this proofe.

There be fome things which are vfually obiected by fome againft this Do-   Obiections a-
ctrine: which it fhall not be amiffe to make anfwere to,   gainft the
                                                                                Doctrine an-
   1. It is faid, that there are diuers fpeeches in Scripture, where falling, and for-   fwered.
faking, and things of the like nature are threatned to the faithfull, and they are   1. *Obiection.*
called vpon to feare and care, fuch as feeme to argue a poffibility of finall lo-
fing all grace which they haue once receiued. For examples fake, *Let him that*
thinke he ftandes, take heede left hee fall ª. Bee not high minded, but feare, &c ª   ª Cor. 10. 12
Quench not the Spirit ª. Worke out your Saluation with feare and trembling ª. Now to   ª Rom. 11. 20.
what end are thefe fpeeches, if the faithfull cannot fall, fo as to lofe that faith,   ª 1 Thef. 5. 19
with which they haue beene once endued? I anfwere thus: That whatfoeuer   ª Phil. 2. 12.
God workes in, and for the faithfull, hee worketh it by meanes. As hee will   *Anfw.*
continue them in faith, and keepe them in the ftate of grace: fo he will doe it
by a courfe: and one fpeciall meanes, by which hee preferues the faith of his
children, is fuch exhortations as this, by which (he bleffing them vnto them,) he
preuents fecurity, and ftirres vp care of vfing all good meanes confecrated by
him, by which they may bee vpheld in grace, and builded vp in faith. So that
thefe, aduertifements doe not prefuppofe the falling away of Gods Elect: but
are purpofedly vfed in the wifdome of God to preuent the fame.

   They prooue that we in our felues may fall, and had therefore need to refolue
with *Dauid, That it is good for vs to draw neere to God ª,* but they doe not argue the   ª Pfal. 73: 2.
purpofe of God to fuffer to fall, but rather the contrary: for well may wee fay,
that if God would forfake, hee would neuer fo often call vpon his children to
ftand faft.

   2. Many true beleeuers haue fallen and failed greatly: as *Dauid* in the mat-   2. *Obiect.*
ter of *Vrieh, Peter* in the bufineffe of denying his Mafter: fhall it be thought that
thefe loft not their faith, when they committed fuch foule offences? How could
faith and fuch groffe euils, be at once together in the fame men? I anfwere di-   *Anfw.*
rectly, that neither *Peter* nor *Dauid* loft their faith quite in thofe their falls. We
muft learne to diftinguifh betwixt the being of faith, and the working of faith:
Faith may bee, where it doth not worke. There may bee life in the roote of a
tree, though in the winter feafon the fame be without both leafe and fruit. In a
mans body their may bee life, although for the prefent being in a fwound, he
doth neither moue nor breathe: like to that, which *Paul* faid of *Eutichus, falling*
from the third loft, and taken vp dead: His lefe is in him ª. In a drie fommer there   ª Act. 20. 10.
maybe a fecret fpring of a Well in the earth, though not fo much as a drop of
water doe flow from it: So there may be a certen feed of faith in a Chriftian, e-
uen then when by fome great temptation he is ouercome and fallen into a grie-
uous fin. So then it is true, faith did not worke in *Dauid* when hee committed a-
dultery. It was not powerfull in *Peter*, when he denied his Mafter: but yet the re-
couery of both, argueth that there remained, as *Theophilact* faith out of *Chryfoftome* Luke 2.
touching *Peter, the hidden feedes of faith and grace in them both.* No fooner was *Da-*
uid throughly dealt with by *Nathan*, but he cryed out, *I haue finned ª.* No fooner   ª 2 Sam. 12. 13
                                                                                 did
M ɯ 3 L l l 2

The signature was important to compositors, pressmen, binders, and warehouse managers and the sequence is usually accurate because more depended upon it. First, type was arranged according to the side of the sheet on which it was to be printed and thus the signature enabled the outer forme to be distinguished from the inner; second, it helped the pressmen get the orientation between one side of the sheet and the other right when printing so that the text was aligned on both sides of the sheet;[18] third, it avoided confusion in the gathering and sorting of materials by the warehouseman; and fourth, it provided guidance for a binder to fold and gather the sheets together.

Mistakes did occur in signature sequences, including both omission and mis-signing. Hence, sheet 3L2 of the *Sermons* of Samuel Hieron (STC 13379; 1620) was first signed 3M3, prompting a manual correction to be overstamped on that leaf (figure 3.2). More often, two leaves within the same gathering might be signed the same, e.g. C2. Provided cancels and inserts have been recorded, and the formalities of recto and verso observed, what page is meant by C2^v is always understood. Put simply, C2 refers to the leaf, C2^r to the first page of the leaf, C2^v to the second page of the leaf: thus 'C2, blank' means both sides of a leaf are blank; 'C2^v, blank' means only the second page of a leaf is blank. Sometimes, in error, references to a leaf or sheet are given where the '^{r}' is dropped and only '^{v}' is specified: when cited in this way, the document concerned ought to be re-examined, however much one might comprehend the reasons for the lack of precision or carelessness involved: to describe a reference as C2–C2^v involves a non-sequitur as the first descriptor (C2) already implies the second. If there are two or three repeated alphabet sequences in a book, then the subsequent C2s are preceded by a superscript number, as in ^{2}C2 or ^{3}C2, in order that the group of repeated sequences to which the specific leaf belongs can be identified.

Quires, Cancels, and Inserts

Paper was sold in quires of 24 or 25 sheets at a time, with 20 quires to a ream. Some manuscripts are prepared as a single quire of this kind, but it is more usual to quire two or three sheets in folio texts, or to quire two sheets per gathering in longer quarto books, and for the same reason— to do so made sewing easier and the spine more compact; the limit being, as with the smaller formats, the number of conjugate leaves that have to be stitched at a time: four being the preferred upper limit. If a

---

[18] For details about imposing formes: Moxon, *Mechanick Exercises*, 223–33; Gaskell, *New Introduction*, 78–117.

folio is in sixes (three sheets per gathering), the first page will be on the same outside of the sheet as page 12, page 2 will be opposite page 11, and so on: this arrangement of material, particularly for printed books requires some care in the production.

As well as paper being folded together, leaves and sheets could be added or removed. There are many reasons why a scribe or printer might do this,[19] including adding illustrative material (engravings, maps, diagrams, mathematical tables), or resetting because a better text became available, or because of a significant omission or other blunder by a compositor. The use of cancels owing to censorship is rarer as books were licensed before they were printed. Cancels and inserts reflect the malleability of the codex form, and the ease with which it could be altered, albeit one copy at a time. Early modern books and manuscripts were hand-made, with several artisan crafts working in conjunction with one another: scriveners, printers, engravers, and binders tailored their products towards individual needs and wishes; whilst private compilations of papers, commonplace books, and miscellanies reflect their unique and idiosyncratic characteristics. Hence all texts were to some extent adapted as circumstances required, and the making of cancels and inserts was inevitable.

Whilst manuscripts could have initials and other spaces decorated if room was left by the scribe, illustrative materials frequently required separate treatment from the text in printed books. Printers' ornaments began to appear from the late fifteenth-century, whilst woodcuts and metal casts could be included with a little forethought; however, copperplate engravings were prepared by specialists and printed on a different press to that used for text production. As a consequence, engravings could be added to a book in one of two ways. Either the engraving was printed off on a separate sheet and inserted when copies of the book were made up, or (as with engraved title-pages) the printer would set the text and print this off for the conjugate leaf, and then the engraved page would be printed separately. The latter would not involve an extra inserted leaf into a gathering, but the former would. This was done by pasting the plate to the back of the adjacent leaf. Similarly, if a page was to be cancelled it was sliced through the middle of the text and then cropped leaving a short stub (occasionally one finds a sliced page that has not been removed as it ought).[20] The difference between an insert and a cancelled leaf is that an inserted leaf is added with its stub pasted to the recto

---

[19] See, Bland, 'Invisible Dangers', 156–8 and 163–5, where the examples of Camden and Purchas are discussed.
[20] See, R. E. Stoddard, *Marks in Books, Illustrated and Explained* (Cambridge MA, 1985), 13.

(front, or 'r') of the related leaf; whereas a cancelled leaf is first removed, and its replacement is pasted on the verso (back, or 'v') to the stub of the once conjugate second leaf.[21]

Simple alterations to the primary structure of a gathering are quite common, as is the replacement of a single cancelled leaf by a bifolium (i.e. two leaves with the stub pasted to the back of the second), so that there are five leaves. More complex cases can be perplexing, particularly as it can be difficult to dig down into the gutter of a binding to establish what happened (librarians tend to be twitchy about such manipulations of a volume). One particularly unusual example, which will illustrate what can happen when changes are made to a duo-decimo, is John Benson's pirated edition of Ben Jonson's *Q. Horatius Flaccus his art of poetry* (STC 13798; 1640), which includes the 'Execration upon Vulcan', 'The Masque of Gypsies' and 20 of Jonson's poems.

In November 1639, Benson acquired a manuscript, or manuscripts of the 'Execration upon Vulcan' and 'Epigrams' that he corrected against some stolen sheets of the as yet unpublished 1640 *Workes*, and published as *Ben Ionson's Execration upon Vulcan* (STC 13770; 1640).[22] The licence was first dated 1640, but taking advantage of the legal calendar which ended in March, he changed this to read 1639 to imply that he had owned the copy for more than a year.[23] Shortly thereafter, he acquired a manuscript of the *Masque of Gypsies* and another of the first version of Jonson's translation of *Horace his Art of Poetry*. He reissued all the texts in duo-decimo, but while the volume was at the press, he acquired a further, better manuscript of *The Masque of Gypsies*. As it was first printed, the volume was a standard duo-decimo, except for sheet E, which had eight leaves with E5–8 removed in the normal way. This was because the miscellaneous poems began with sheet F, and they may have been set up concurrently, or even prior to *The Masque of Gypsies* that precedes them.

With the new source for *The Masque of Gypsies*, Benson had to make cancellations to both D and E, to which he then added sheets d and e. With sheet D, he cancelled leaves D5–10, leaving four at the beginning and two at the end.[24] D3 and D4 were thus singletons, but they were contained within the enclosure of D1/12 and D2/11. After D4, Benson inserted the new sheet d. The stubs of D3 and D4 were pasted to d12ᵛ, creating an unusual 18-leaf gathering.

[21] For a full-scale study of cancels: R. W. Chapman, *Cancels* (London, 1932).
[22] The matter is fully dealt with in M. B. Bland (ed.), *The Poems of Ben Jonson*, Oxford, forthcoming.
[23] Huntington Library RB62053 and Beinecke Library, Yale University, Ih J738 640e copy 1 have the date 1640, the other 20 copies seen all read 1639. There are 29 known copies.
[24] The only copy with the original issue of D is Cambridge University Library, Syn 8.64.13.

Sheet E is slightly more surprising. It has generally been assumed that it was cut in half, leaving the four singletons E1, 2, 3, 4 followed by e¹² — both e12 and the original E12 being blank. In fact what happened (as demonstrated by two copies where the final blank is present with the stub in between the end of the text and the blank) is that e12 was cancelled and E12 retained. This is because E12 is conjugate with E1 and thus, once again, the singletons and additions could be contained by the outer conjugate leaves.

This example illustrates how early modern book production was not guided by a strict mathematical logic (as we tend to infer), but rather by a visceral and a practical sense of how one might preserve the integrity of the artefact. Mathematical logic would have placed the four leaves E1–4 between D and e and left any or all of them at risk of being lost. That was much less likely to happen if the four singletons were E2–4 and e1, leaving E1 conjugate with E12, with the loose leaves sandwiched alongside the new sheet between them.

Methods of Notation

The use of signatures for recording the structure of the book has more to do with the history of binding than with production because, in practice, there is no necessary reason why sheet B ought to be printed before sheet D, particularly if the book is a page-for-page reprint.[25] What the formula records, therefore, is the order of the material as it ought to be bound, with J, U, and W not used. Some books, such as the third volume of Jonson's 1640 *Workes*, were able to be bound in several different yet equally inclusive ways.[26] Hence, the collation needs to be accompanied by a description that combines brevity with accuracy. As some books exist in both standard and large paper copies, or maybe on crown rather than pot, it is also useful to measure the page and multiply this out to the implied size of the trimmed sheet. Thus, a two-sheet pot quarto pamphlet, with the title-leaf and first page of the text unnumbered but with the number of A2^r implied by the sequence that follows, would be recorded as:

c.280 × 380 mm, 4°: A–B⁴; $3.
pp.16: (2) *1* 2–14.
A1^r, Title; A1^v, Blank; A2^r–B4^v, Text; B4^v, 'FINIS.'.

---

[25] See, McKenzie, 'Printers of the Mind', *Making Meaning*, 46–7.
[26] See, M. B. Bland, 'The James A. Riddell Collection of Jonson's 1616 and 1640 *Workes*', *Huntington Library Quarterly*, 67 (2004), 489–503.

There are a great many early modern pamphlets, two to four sheets in length, that can be described this simply. They cost 1–2*d* stab-stitched (½*d* per sheet of pica unbound).[27] A publisher might expect to make £1–3 after production costs if he sold all the copies himself. If quantities were sold on to other stationers, it would be at a discount, but with the knowledge that those copies would not be sent to Bucklersbury to wrap tobacco and spices.[28] They were ephemeral and usually survive in only a single or a few copies, if at all,[29] but to the trade they provided valuable cash-flow and incidental work while larger projects were at the press.

The longer a book is, the more likely it is that the volume might have some complexity to its structure. Of course, a great many books collate A–M⁴ or A–V⁴ with sheet A reserved for the preliminaries; whilst even pamphlets could have cancels or inserts. What follows are some examples of the more complex structures that might be found. For instance, the collation and description for a six-sheet quarto with the first blank leaf missing, the title on the second leaf, a dedication by 'A. B.' on leaf A3, the preface on A4, with C3 lacking a signature, leaf D3 signed D2, page 32 numbered '24', and an errata list with 20 corrections on the penultimate page, would read:

> c.280 × 380 mm, 4°: A⁴(−A1) B–F⁴; $3 (−C3; 'D2' for 'D3').
> pp.46: (6) *1* 2–39 (1); '24' for '32'.
> A1, Wanting, presumed blank; A2ʳ, Title; A2ᵛ, Blank; A3ʳ⁻ᵛ, Dedication to Sir John Smith; A3ᵛ, Signed 'A. B.'; A4ʳ⁻ᵛ, Preface; B1ʳ–F3ᵛ, Text; F3ᵛ, 'FINIS.'; F4ʳ, Errata (20); F4ᵛ, Blank.

If we then located a second copy with A1 blank, the formula would read A–F⁴; the pagination sequence, '(8) *1* 2–39 (1)'; the description 'A1, blank'; and the copy-specific information for the first exemplum (citing library and shelfmark) would be 'lacks A1'. Or, else, A1ʳ might be signed 'A' and the description would read 'A1ʳ, Signed; A1ᵛ, Blank' (the fact that the title-page is not signed need not be recorded as the lack of a signature on that page was habitual). Sometimes, of course, this kind of clarity is not possible because only a single copy of a book survives and blanks were often removed in binding—especially in later bindings.

---

[27] F. R. Johnson, 'Notes on English Retail Book-Prices, 1550–1640', *The Library*, V:5 (1950), 83–112; D. J. McKitterick, '"Ovid with a Littleton": The Cost of English Books in the Early Seventeenth Century', *Transactions of the Cambridge Bibliographical Society*, 9.2 (1997), 184–234. The rate of ½*d* per sheet was adjusted accordingly for larger or smaller type.

[28] See, B. Jonson, 'Epig. II: "To my Bookseller"', *Workes* (STC 14751–2; 1616), 3T1ʳ.

[29] See, figure 4.9 (p.113) for an illustration of a pamphlet where only the title-page survives as a reverse offset on the final verso of another pamphlet produced at that time.

Whilst the removal of blank leaves is sufficiently common as to be unexceptional, and generally limited to the first and/or last leaf of a book, the cancellation and replacement of the internal pages is a rather more significant matter and not always obvious at first glance. For instance, almost all the surviving copies of Jonson's *The Alchemist* (STC 14755; 1612) have E2 cancelled and replaced: a fact overlooked by Greg, as well as the Oxford and subsequent editions.[30] There is no particular reason to think that the cancel was required by authority; rather, the variants (e.g. E2^v, line 32: *Ebrew,/Hebrew,*) suggest that the cancel was caused by an unhappiness with the work of a compositor who did not adhere to the standards that Jonson desired. What is unusual is that the changes were corrected through a cancel rather than recorded in an errata list.

Although printers could use all the alphabet (upper and lower case) and ancillary signs, some initial preliminary material may lack a signature. Unsigned preliminary materials are represented by π, with χ denoting an inserted illustration on a separate leaf. Thus, the description of a quarto book of 16 sheets with unsigned preliminaries that have a dated dedication, a preface, and an errata list with 12 corrections, E3 cancelled and replaced with a new leaf, I3 not signed, an engraved diagram inserted between K3 and K4, and the final page blank, would read:

c.280 × 380 mm, 4°: π^4 A–D^4 E^4($\pm$E3) F–I^4 K^4(K3+χ1) L–P^4; \$3 (–I3). π1^r, Title; π1^v, Blank; π2^r–3^r, Dedication to Sir John Smith; π3^r, Signed 'A. B.', dated 17 March 1604; π3^v–4^r, Preface; π4^v, Errata (12); A1^r–P4^r, Text; K3+χ1, Engraved diagram of an orchard, 175 × 125 mm; P4^r, 'FINIS.'; P4^v, Blank.

If the leaf with the engraved diagram had, instead, been an inserted leaf of text, it would be recorded as K^4(+K3.1). If it was a double-page illustration, the insert would be recorded as K^4(K3+χ1.2). Similarly, if the cancelled leaf had been replaced by a bifolium, the collation would read E4(–E3, +E3.1–2). Each version of this equation records precisely what has been added and removed.

The description of all materials from a printing-house or publisher involves having to record books with quite specialized features. Music, with both staves and text, tends to be complex to describe in terms of

---

[30] W. W. Greg, *A Bibliography of the English Printed Drama to the Restoration*, 4 vols. (London, 1939–59), I: 440–1; C. Herford, P. Simpson, and E. Simpson (eds.), *Ben Jonson*, 11 vols. (1925–52), V: 275–81. The two copies at the University of Texas, Austin (Wh J738 612a, and Pforzheimer 539), have the original state.

layout, but was structurally quite simple, usually being single folios gathered in a sequence.[31] Mathematical books, with volvelles attached to some of their leaves are more awkward, and there is no standard convention for describing them. One option is to use χ. The problem with χ is that it potentially confuses an inserted full-page illustration with a piece of paper that has been cut out and attached to a specific part of the page, and so the letter rho (ρ) has been chosen. The example that follows is a quarto in eights in two parts, with an unsigned preliminary half-sheet including an engraved title-page; this is followed by the signed dedication and preface, a half sheet of preliminary verses signed 'a', the text in eights, a cancel and insert at F7, an extra inserted leaf after Q5, a single-page diagram after L6, a double-page engraved insert after 2B3, and volvelles on P4, V2, and 2A8. The volume before the cancels and inserts is 60 sheets, with part 2 beginning at sheet T, and with S and 2H being single-sheet gatherings. The first four leaves per gathering are signed, except for A, S, and 2H where the first three leaves are signed; the half-sheet of verses is signed on both leaves.

c.280 × 380 mm, 4° in 8s: π^2 A^4 a^2 B–E^8 $F^8(\pm F7)$ G–K^8 $L^8(L6+\chi 1)$ M–O^8 $P^8(P4^r+\rho 1)$ $Q^8(+Q5.1)$ R^8 S^4 T^8 $V^8(V2^v+\rho 2)$ X–Z^8 $2A^8(2A8^r+\rho 3)$ $2B^8(2B3+2\chi 1.2)$ 2C–$2G^8$ $2H^4$; $4 (- A4, S4, 2H4)$. $\pi 1$, Blank; $\pi 2^r$, Engraved Title; $\pi 2^v$, Blank; $A1^r$–2^v, Ded. to Sir John Smith; $A2^v$, Signed 'A. B.'; $A3^{r-v}$, Preface; $A4^{r-v}$, Contents; $a1^{r-v}$, Poem, signed 'C. D.', $a2^r$, Poem, signed 'E. F.'; $a2^v$, Poem, signed 'G. H.'; $B1^r$–$S4^r$, Text, Book One; $L6^r+\chi 1$, 190 × 140 mm; $P4^r$, Volvelle, 90 mm; $S4^v$, Blank; $T1^r$–$2H3^v$, Text, Book Two; $V2^v$, Volvelle, 100 mm; $2A8^r$, Volvelle, 85 mm; $2B3+\chi 1.2$, 190 × 280 mm; $2H3^v$, 'FINIS.' $2H4^r$, Errata (32); $2H4^v$, Blank.

To be fair, most books are not this complex; but the point is that they can be and, if they are, that the methods exist to describe their structure in a precise, concise way. Any attempt to understand the work of a printer or publisher involves understanding all their relationships to the extent that these can be reconstructed, including the work of engravers and image-cutters. The work of these people is easily overlooked and treated as part of the stock of available resources. Yet these extras always had to be paid for in the first instance. Behind every material trace that a book contains is a human and a financial relationship.

---

[31] See, McKitterick, *Print, Manuscript and the Search for Order*, 40–3, who also emphasizes the need for bibliography to account for the full range of historical evidence (6–7); D. W. Krummel, *English Music Printing, 1553–1700* (London, 1975).

Complex books, with extra illustrative materials could be frequently reprinted, as was Blundevile's *Exercises* (STC 3146–51a.5; 1594–1638), a 102-sheet mathematical text set as a quarto in eights. The book, though large, is scarce and the fifth edition does not survive at all. We know that William Stansby must have printed this c.1617–18, and any attempt to reconstruct his workflows at that time has to account for the missing output. Most of the copies of the other editions that do survive want, in part, their volvelles.

With other books, such as Ralegh's *The history of the world*, the collation may help distinguish between the first and second editions. Not all copies of those editions retain the final leaf with the printer's dated colophon. Where this is wanting, the easiest way to distinguish between the suppressed 1614 edition (STC 20637), and the surreptitious 1617 edition (STC 20638), which is a page-for-page reprint (including pagination errors), is through collation. With the 1614 edition, 2V1 is cancelled and replaced; in 1617 it is not.[32] The collation for 1614 is:

c.330 × 440 mm, 2° in 6s: π^2 A–E^4 a–c^6 d^2 ^{2}B–F^6 G^6(G2+χ1.2) H–P^6 Q^6(Q5+2χ1.2) R–Y^6 Z^6(Z4+3χ1.2) 2A–M^6 2N^6(2N3+4χ1.2) 2O–T^6 2V^6($\pm$2V1) 2X–3I^6 3K^4 4A–5C^6 5D^6(5D4+5χ1.2) 5E–O^6 5P^6(5P4 +6χ1.2, 5P5+7χ1.2) 5R–6T^6 6V–Y^6 7A–C^6; $3.

Similarly, the two states of *Q. Horatius Flaccus his art of poetry*, together with a description of the contents, should read:

First issue. c.330 × 440 mm, 12°: A–D^{12} E^{12}(–E5–8) F–G^{12}; $5 (–C3, F1).

Second issue. c.330 × 440 mm, 12°: A–C^{12} D^{12}(D5+d^{12}, –D6–10) E^{12}(E4+e^{12}(–e12), –E5–11) F–G^{12}; $5 (–C3, F1). A1, Blank; A2^r, Signature within ornamental border; A2^v, Blank; A3^r, Blank; A3^v, Engraved Portrait; A4^r, Title; A4^v, Blank; A5^r–6^v, Dedication to Thomas, Lord Windsor; A6^v, signed 'I. B.'; A7^r, Poem, Sir Edward Herbert; A7^v–9^v, Poem, Barten Holyday; A10^r, Poem, Zouch Townley; A10^v–12^v, Poem, signed 'I. C.'; B1^r–C2^r, Horace his art of poetry; C2^v, Blank; C3^r, Sub-Title, Execration upon Vulcan; C3^v, Blank; C4^r–C8^v, Execration; C9, Blank; C10^r, Subtitle, Masque of Gypsies; C10^v, Blank; C11^r–E/e11^v, Masque of Gypsies; E12, Blank; F1^r, Subtitle, Epigrams; F1^v, Blank; F2^r–G11^v, Epigrams; G12, Blank.

---

[32] See, Bland, 'Invisible Dangers', 184–90.

In order to prepare descriptive notes of this kind, it helps to consult multiple copies of the same edition, for the imperfect evidence of one copy may be rectified by reference to another. This is not to imply that there is such a thing as a perfect copy of an early printed book, rather there is a putative state of physical completeness from which all copies may depart through the absence of a leaf or leaves.[33] Thus, any particular copy of *Q. Horatius Flaccus his art of poetry* may lack the blanks A1, C9, E12, and G12, without rendering that copy textually incomplete, but each of these leaves exists in some of the copies of that book.

Title-pages

As well as the structure of a book, it is also usual to record the exact details of the title-page. Historically, the title-page developed from the incipit, and by the late fifteenth-century had become a standard feature of printed texts.[34] The two most important details it contained were the title and the publisher; the printer and author being of less significance and not always recorded, or sometimes recorded only by their initials. A great many title-pages are explanatory, indicating the nature of their contents; or, with sermons and plays, the circumstances of preaching or performance: for a prospective purchaser, these details gave a very brief synopsis of the nature of the material, and a few extra copies of the title-leaf could serve as an advertisement.

The forme with the title-page was generally the very last part of a book to be printed, and could be subject to several stop-press states. If the book was shared between two or more publishers, it might well have variant imprints, and sometimes the layout might be adjusted to improve the visual balance of the page. A replacement title-page might also be printed for a reissue, to freshen the impression.[35] The title could be printed in both black and red, with the type for each colour set separately, and the page printed off twice. The full range of roman, italic, and black-letter fonts might be used as well, including the very large titling fonts that are not present in the body of the text. For all these reasons, title-page transcriptions record an exact line-for-line state of the copy being described, in order that variants in other copies may be identified and the reason for them determined.

---

[33] The idea of physical integrity derives from a pragmatic understanding of the component parts of a document, and is different from (although Bowers conflated it with) the concept of ideal copy put forward by Greg (*Collected Papers*, 374–91).
[34] See, M. M. Smith, *The Title-Page: Its Early Development 1460–1510* (London, 2000).
[35] For example, S. Daniel, *Dramatick Poems* (STC 6243.8; 1635), from the 1623 *Works*.

The method of title-page transcription as developed by Greg and Bowers employed a number of scribal conventions to record typographical features that digital technologies have rendered obsolete: italics were underlined, small capitals double-underlined, and adjacent full capitals underlined three times; black-letter was recorded with subscript dash marks, and red with dots.[36] Ornaments and devices were measured and identified, but the differing sizes of fonts were not distinguished because they could not be represented in typescript. Those methods can now be simplified. For practical purposes, the best option is a digital image of the title-page supported, if need be, by a transcription engaging a full range of fonts to make the distinctions that were once achieved by secondary means. Where digitization of the title-page is not practical, then the standard procedures can be applied using fonts and extended character sets, with dotting for red retained. The other forms of underlining are unnecessary. These examples illustrate the method:

1.] THE | NORTHERN | LASSE, | A | COMOEDIE. | [Rule, 108 mm] | As it hath beene often Acted with good | Applaufe, at the *Globe*, and *Black-Fryers*. By his | Maiefties Servants. | [Rule, 107 mm] | Written by RICHARD BROME. | [Rule 107 mm] | *Hic totus volo rideat Libellus*. Mart. | [Rule, 107 mm] | [Ornament with head, 18 × 59 mm] | [Rule, 101 mm] | LONDON: | Printed by AVG. MATHEVVES, and are to | be fold by NICHOLAS VAVASOR, dwelling | at the little South dore of S'. *Pauls* Church. | 1632.

2.] [Within double rules, 313 × 198 mm; in black and red:] S. THOMÆ | AQVINATIS SVMMA | THEOLOGICA: | IN QVA | ECCLESIÆ CATHOLICÆ DOCTRINA VNIVERSA, | ET QVICQVID IN VETERVM PATRVM MONVMENTIS | eft dignum obferuatu; quicquid etiam vel olim vocatum eft, vel hodie vocatur | ab hæreticis in controuerfiam; id omne vt eruditè, folidè & delucidè, | ita piè atque fideliter explicatur; | IN TRES PARTES AB AVCTORE SVO DISTRIBVTA. | *OLIM QVIDEM EX MANVSCRIPTIS* | *exemplaribus, quorundum Louaniensum Theologorum, deinde aliorum* | *doctissimorum virorum, ac nouissimè nonnullorum Duacensium Theolo-* | *gorum operâ, ab infinitis mendis repurgata; ita vt fuum primæuum nito-* | *rem vel nunc habeat, vel ad eum proximè accedat.* | QVID POST RELIQVAS OMNES IN HAC EDITIONE | præftitum, exponetur Epiftola ad Lectorem. | [Engraved device of the phoenix and the fire, with the motto 'DO FLAMMÆ ESSE SVVM, FLAMMA DAT ESSE MEVM.'; 116 × 140 mm] | DVACI, | Sumptibus MARCI WYON, Typographi Iurati, | fub figno Phœnicis. | [Rule, 81 mm] | ANNO M. DC. XIV. | [Between bottom rules:] *CVM GRATIA ET PRIVILEGIO.*

[36] For some examples, see Gaskell, *New Introduction*, 368–80.

Describing Manuscripts

Unlike printed books, for which title-pages became standard in the late fifteenth-century, most manuscripts were produced without one. When they do occur, as a separate leaf on a political pamphlet prepared by a professional scrivener, for instance, or on a manuscript intended for the press, the formal nature of their presence indicates either a specific context such as the circulation of a text through the commercial trade, or a deliberate imitation of the presentational language of print. For many other manuscript texts, a brief summary title was written at the top of the first page indicating the nature of the text.

When catalogued, multiple manuscripts in a single volume may be listed as separate items; or, else, are foliated (pagination is rarer). As a consequence, a specific leaf can be cited without reference to the gathering of paper to which it belongs. The problem of prior pagination sequences (where these exist) is superseded by archival cataloguing practice and what is meant by f.198 ought to be unambiguous. A codicological analysis focused on the structure of a document is thus purely concerned with understanding how a manuscript was prepared, as well as how and why it came to have its present form. In some cases, as with correspondence, the manuscript volume may be nothing more than a collection of separates gathered as single folios in a sequence. Other manuscripts might be sammelbände of several items, or a single document that has been prepared in several stages, starting out as a booklet and being built up over time.[37] The evidence for these patterns is established through the relationship of paper, script, and structure.

Most early modern manuscripts were not prepared with a signature sequence; however, the folding of the folio, quarto, or other formats was no different to print. A collection of single folio sheets represents one extreme of what a manuscript volume might be. At the other end of the spectrum are the table-books and notebooks that the trade sold ready bound with the regular structure of a book that has no added or removed material. Frequently, these volumes were never completely written through, but the integrity of the volume was established at the outset. In between these casual and formal states, were manuscripts tailored to individual needs, prepared in sheets and quires and then later bound once the text was complete, or abandoned.

Owing to the lack of signatures in manuscripts, there are two options for description: to imply a sequence as if it were a printed book; or, to

[37] See, R. Hanna, *Pursuing History: Middle English Manuscripts and Their Texts* (Stanford, CA, 1996), 21–59.

number the gatherings sequentially. For various reasons, not least the avoidance of confusion, the latter is preferable; but it does mean that descriptive conventions do need to be strictly observed. With a printed book, F^{12} means sheet F has 12 leaves, F12 means the 12th leaf of the sheet. The same gathering in a manuscript would be 6^{12}, and the leaf 6.12: both the superscript and the point are absolutely necessary.[38]

A few examples of seventeenth-century manuscripts will convey the variety of possible structures. For instance, National Library of Scotland MS 2067 is a verse miscellany with poems by Donne, written by William Drummond of Hawthornden. It is a ten-sheet quarto in eights that was not originally bound, but left as a booklet that could later be compiled with other items. It never was, and collates as it was first prepared:

c.310 × 410 mm, 4° in 8s: 1–5^{8}.

Similarly, Derbyshire Record Office MS D258/10/15 is an unbound two-sheet quarto in eights with the sixth leaf removed, and collates:

c.310 × 410 mm, 4° in 8s: 1^{8} (–1.6).

The relationship between the page area of a manuscript and the size of the sheet is subject to greater variation than with print and so the placement of the watermark and the direction of the chainlines need to be confirmed as well. One example of this is the autograph of Jonson's *The Masque of Queenes* (British Library MS Royal 18. A.xlv) written on Italian paper that had been cropped down to look like a royal quarto. It is however a folio gathered in single sheets:

c.210 × 340 mm (from c.313 × 432 mm), 2°: 1–10^{2} 11^{2}(–11.2).

Another folio manuscript, this time in the hand of a professional scribe who has been nicknamed 'Feathery' after the style of his hand, is Bodleian Library MS Rawlinson Poetry 31, bound in contemporary limp vellum.[39] This volume is gathered as a folio:

c.285 × 390 mm, 2°: 1–3^{8} 4–5^{6} 6–7^{8}.

A more complex example is the Wedderburn miscellany (National Library of Scotland MS 6504). This volume, which is related textually to

---

[38] See, Gaskell, *New Introduction*, 330, who gives a single example.
[39] P. Beal, *In Praise of Scribes*, 58–108 and 211–68.

Drummond's MS 2067, was originally a manuscript of 144 leaves on crown paper bound in limp vellum, to which two leaves were added in the 1660s and nine removed. Two of these original leaves have been used as pastedowns. The manuscript collates:

$$c.330 \times 390 \text{ mm}, 4^\circ \text{ in 8s: } 1-7^8 \ 8^8 \ (-8.3) \ 9^8 \ (-9.2, .3) \ 10^8 \ (-10.3) \ 11^8$$
$$12^8 \ (-12.1) \ 13-14^8 \ 15^8 \ (15.3+.3.1-2) \ 16^8 \ (-16.6, .7, .8) \ 17^8 \ (-17.1) \ 18^8.$$

Similarly, St. John's College, Cambridge, MS S.23 is a quarto in 16s, with four leaves removed:

$$c.280 \times 380 \text{ mm}, 4^\circ \text{ in 16s: } 1^{16}(-1.3) \ 2-5^{16} \ 6^{16} \ (-6.9, .13, .15).$$

As these examples indicate, the structure of early modern manuscripts may be more varied than printed books. Trinity College, Dublin, MS 877 is, for instance, a volume originally consisting of 288 leaves, of which 277 are present with two of the other leaves copied. Another sheet at the front has a nineteenth-century index. Nine leaves (ff.1, 12, 47.1, 47.2, 266.1–.4, 279.1) are lost, with ff.1 and 12 recopied on Irish paper of the nineteenth-century. Two leaves are cancelled: f.159.1 with a knife or scissors, f.247.1 having been torn out; f.167 has been cancelled and replaced. It collates:

$$310 \times 400 \text{ mm}, 2^\circ: 1^6 \ (\pm 1.1) \ 2^6 \ (\pm 2.6) \ 3-4^{12} \ 5^{12} \ (-5.12, 5.1 \text{ bd. after}$$
$$5.11) \ 6^{12} \ (-6.1) \ 7-9^{12} \ 10^{16} \ 11-13^{12} \ 14^8 \ 15^{10} \ (-15.6) \ 16^{10} \ (\pm 16.4) \ 17^8$$
$$18-21^{12} \ 22^{10} \ 23^{12} \ (-23.9) \ 24^{12} \ 25^{12} \ (-25.5/.8, 25.6/.7) \ 26^{10} \ (-26.10).$$

Studying the relationship of the structure, paper, and scribes, makes it possible to understand what happened to this Donne manuscript. It looks as if the volume was initially prepared by scribe A (who was possibly a professional scrivener), c.1618–20.[40] The scribe prepared a volume of 150 sheets (300 leaves), and completed ff.13–161, with 162–3 blank, being quires 3–15. Apart from the two lost leaves between ff.47 and 48, there are three other changes to these quires. First, two sheets were taken from quire 14 and moved to quire 10 for copying, the reason for which is not evident. Next, folio 147 (14.1) was torn out and pasted back in (it is not a cancel as such), its verso blank except for the words 'The Marchant, &c.', which begins the following leaf; on leaf 148 the scribe adds in the margin a sentence of omitted text. This suggests that a mistake occurred when, turning over the leaf, the scribe started at the

---

[40] See also, pp.46–7 above. Trinity College, Dublin, MS 877 will be discussed in Bland, *Jonson and Donne: Manuscript Traditions, Connections, and Revisions*, forthcoming.

next recto and not the verso. Later at 15.6 a leaf is removed, probably owing to a serious transcription error, with the text starting again on the next leaf. Further, another sheet was removed from the gathering: this suggests that the scribe was copying in unbound quires.

Quires 3–15 originally constituted 78 sheets of which the scribe had removed one from the final quire, leaving a further 72 sheets (144 leaves) blank. As the first part of the text ends with Donne's *Paradoxes and Problems*, it is possible that the remaining sheets were intended for some of Donne's Sermons (as with the Dobell Manuscript: Houghton Library MS Eng 966.5). Then, sometime c.1625, two scribes added material to f.104 (the Hamilton obsequy), and then another scribe added poems to f.162. The next step appears to have been taken by scribe E (c.1630) who added in a selection of poems on ff.164–74. The manuscript was then passed to scribe F who used it as a miscellany, moving one quire of paper (six sheets) to serve as an index, which was placed at the front. This index must have been a quire (hence the original being a 150-sheet folio), as two sheets from quires 15 and 16 had already been removed (hence these are 10-, not 12-leaf quires). Further indeterminate sheets were removed from quires 17, 22, and 26. Soon after scribe F completed the volume, the manuscript must have been bound. It was later rebound in the nineteenth-century.

Complex examples of preparation and reorganization are not unusual in larger manuscripts. Thus, National Library of Wales, MS 5390D was prepared by members of the Salusbury family of Lleweni, who were also responsible for the equally complex Christ Church, Oxford, MS 184.[41] MS 5390D has had 18 leaves removed:

c.285 × 390 mm, 2°: 1^4 2–10^6 11^8 12^6 13^6 (-13.2) 14–15^6 16^6 (-16.1) 17^{14} $(-17.2, .3, .13)$ 18^{14} (-18.14) 19^{10} 20–25^6 26^6 (-26.2) 27–29^6 30^6 (-30.2) 31^{12} $(-31.4, .6, .12)$ 32^6 (-32.2) 33^8 $(-33.1, .3)$ 34^8 35^8 (-35.8) 36^8 37^6 (-37.5) 38–39^6 40^6 (-40.1) 41^2 42–43^4 44^6 (-44.5) 45^2.

The reason collations like this are important is that, often, scholarly arguments are made about the existence of a text within a manuscript without an understanding of how that manuscript was put together. Not only may manuscripts be prepared by different scribes at different times, but a manuscript may be a composite document in which one part is only related to another through the later binding practices of an owner. It is to that subject that the discussion now turns.

---

[41] See, M. B. Bland, '"As far from all revolt": Sir John Salusbury, Christ Church MS. 184 and Jonson's First Ode', *English Manuscript Studies*, 8 (2000), 45–8, 72–3 and 75.

Booklets and Sammelbände

During the later medieval period, the booklet had been the standard format for commercial manuscript production. This enabled work to be divided up between professional scribes who were expected to be able to write near-identical hands. As a consequence, a copy of a text could be prepared more rapidly with two or more scribes than by a single scribe alone. The use of booklets, however, went much further than the commercial trade: for lawyers, they were composite documents for case histories; for scholars, they were a means of circulating knowledge; for the clergy, they were a way of grouping sermons and homilies. It is a practice that lingered in the early modern period as booklets could be easily circulated and copied into personal collections and then passed on or returned. A small group of poems by Robert Herrick and Thomas Carew, for instance, survives as a two-sheet booklet amongst the papers of Robert Boyle.[42] Printed pamphlets were, in effect, booklets by another name that could be later bound together in a single volume.

From the mid-fifteenth-century onwards, sammelbände need not be exclusively manuscript or printed, but both could be mixed together. Similarly, gathered collections of loose papers might include a few printed sheets, most often pamphlets and broadsides. Regrettably, later librarians, collectors, and booksellers, either separated manuscript and print for ease of classification, or found greater profit in each item than the whole, and have broken many of these composite volumes apart.[43] In the process, much of our sense of the continuity between manuscript and print, and between one text and another, has been lost.

What the sammelbände offers through its unexpected associations is a sense of how texts might have been read together, in much the same way as the verse miscellany brings to the fore associations between texts that are now regarded as significant literature, and others that are all but unknown except to specialist scholars who work with manuscript verse. In some cases, collections were composed of closely related material: a volume of 22 items concerned with contemporary accounts of the new world, once in the Holford collection, was acquired and broken up by the Philadelphia book-dealer Dr George Rosenbach in 1925. It had been arranged as an account of the first English plantations, with the Virginia material first, in chronological order, then the Bermuda pamphlets, and finally three other items that formed a contextual appendix: it is now

---

[42] Royal Society, RB MS 42, ff.111–17, collates 1^4 $2^4(-2.4)$, with a pot 'R | DP' watermark.
[43] McKitterick, *Print, Manuscript and the Search for Order*, 50–2; A. Gillespie, 'Poets, Printers, and Early English *Sammelbände*', *Huntington Library Quarterly*, 67 (2004), 189–214.

dispersed amongst seven libraries. One item has extensive marginalia; another was completed in contemporary manuscript.[44] Later groupings, however, may simply be volumes of convenience, with diverse papers grouped together in a single binding: when looking at sammelbände, it is necessary to consider how and when their coincidence came to be, and the purpose the volume might have served.

With manuscripts, in particular, care needs to be taken in describing material as the use of microfilms is common, and so misunderstandings about the internal structure of documents can arise when they are not physically examined, or the differences between the component parts are not understood. British Library, Harley MS 4064 is a volume of this kind, and the verse miscellany that has most interested literary scholars is only one of its four parts; nor are the parts coherent, and there is no evidence that they were brought together before the early eighteenth-century. It would, therefore, be mistaken to infer anything from these other items in the volume about the miscellany, or to read the miscellany as deriving from the same source as them.[45]

One example may illustrate both the nature of a sammelbände, and the relationship between its parts. British Library, Lansdowne MS 740 is made up from several booklets and leaves; items 3a, b, and c (ff.56–141) of which derive from the endpapers and quires of an earlier verse miscellany. The binding is from the late seventeenth-century, with the gilt stamped arms of the first Marquess of Lansdowne. The parts are:

1. ff.1–39: An incomplete collection (39 leaves of 42), in a single hand, of extracts in Greek, c.1618–20? Many leaves are damaged, some with a loss of text. The leaf prior to f.1 has a fragment of the missing first leaf. The paper is Spanish, of a cross within a pendant.

2. ff.40–55: A booklet of two quires, in verse, in three different hands (40–4, 45, 46–55: the last italic). The paper is northern French pot, with the initials DM. Late 1580s–early 1590s?

3a. f.56: A single leaf, related to ff.138–41 (in the same hand), containing a list of books and prices. No watermark, or pagination; perhaps an endpaper; written c.1640.

3b. ff.57–137: A verse miscellany in a single hand, except for ff.70–2, which is in the same hand as the book lists on ff.56 and 138–41. The miscellany is built up from three different stocks of French paper (none being pot), the earliest of which is found on ff.74–81, 87–91,

[44] L. A. Morris, *Rosenbach Abroad: In Pursuit of Books in Private Collections* (Philadelphia, 1988), 12–33.
[45] See, A. F. Marotti, *Manuscript, Print, and the English Renaissance Lyric* (Ithaca NY, 1995), 21 and 149. The manuscript is also described as Egerton MS 4064 (21) and so indexed (374).

94–7 (c.1602–3). By c.1620, the volume had been expanded to become a 304-page quarto (with the now missing pages recorded in angle brackets): [2] 1–32 <33–8> 39–54 <55–6> 57–76 <77–80> 81–4 <85–6> 87–8 <89–96> 97–164 <165–6> 167–8 <169–206> 207–10 <211–20> 221–32 233–4 <235–90> 291–6 <297–8> 299–300 <2>. Thus, the miscellany lacks 93 leaves, the first of which is amongst the final list of book prices. Many of these leaves were probably blank, especially ff.235–90, a unit of 14 sheets. Written c.1603 to c.1620.

3c. ff.138–41: Four leaves numbered on the bottom outer verso 299, 295, 293, and 291, indicating their relationship with the previous material. The list of books and prices was evidently written upside down and in from the back. As with f.56, this material is very much later than the original copying of the manuscript, c.1640.

4. ff.142–67 (+155.1): A separate booklet in two hands, containing part of a long poem by Anne Southwell, together with the paratext. The manuscript is in three hands: hand A is found on ff.142ʳ and 167ᵛ; hand B, on f.142ᵛ, has a distinct mixed script; hand C, the scribe, is responsible for ff.143ʳ–67ʳ, and is corrected by hand A. The paper is northern French pot with the initials H and BR. This material has no relationship to item 3.[46]

5. ff.168 and 168.1: A single folio leaf cut down, with no watermark, containing a Latin poem and translation; ff.168ᵛ and 168.1 are blank.

6. ff.169–70: A half-sheet with no watermark, containing mathematical calculations, a translation from Lucian's second dialogue, and ten lines of verse from Dryden's *Marriage à la Mode*.

7. ff.171–3: Three leaves of verse in a single hand, perhaps fragments with partial watermarks present on ff.171 (a sword within a wreath?) and 173 (the bottom part of a small crest?); f.173ᵛ has accounts, with the signature Jo: Davies, and a note 'Poems by | Dr Evans | JW'.

The material in Lansdowne 740 was gathered together in the 1680s from a variety of sources. It is not only that the constituent parts are quite independent of one another, it is important to realize that the miscellany at its heart was built up in three separate stages.[47] The ability to recognize the physical differences both between the parts, and within the miscellany, derives from the analysis of the paper and the scribal hands. Whilst the latter is more immediately obvious, the history of the paper is perhaps an even more significant source of primary information.

---

[46] J. Klene, *The Southwell-Sibthorpe Commonplace Book: Folger MS V.b.198* (Tempe AZ, 1997) has speculated that part 3 and part 4 of the manuscript are linked; they are not.
[47] See also, pp.124–5 below.

Bindings

During the last 20 years, the bibliographical study of bindings has undergone a significant transformation with a greater emphasis on the role of the trade in the making of books. Earlier scholarship had focused on structure and ornament, particularly if the bindings were elaborate, or else could be localized to a particular workshop, or collector. Thus, when Greg discussed the scope of bibliography, he thought the study of bindings as, at best, a branch of art history because he did not connect the binding with meaning, or the networks of patronage that it might represent as being linked to the concerns of textual scholarship.[48] The traditional concern with tooled and luxury bindings also meant that the impact of increasing literacy on the trade, and the materials that were used, received less attention than it ought.

The technical aspects of sewing and attaching the cover have been described many times and are summarized, with a few historical notes, by Gaskell.[49] Since then, and in far greater detail, the structure of early bindings has been discussed by Szirmai,[50] whilst McKitterick, Foot, and Pickwoad have shifted attention towards the practical, commercial, and cultural aspects of the trade, and Pearson has given a detailed account of English binding styles, materials, and techniques as they evolved between 1450 and 1800, as well as a localized account of the trade in Oxford.[51] These studies of the trade have provided a new context within which to understand the work of earlier scholars in the field.[52]

---

[48] Greg, *Collected Papers*, 240 called it 'a bookish art'; see also, M. M. Foot, *Bookbinders at Work*, 3–12, who summarizes the debate.

[49] Gaskell, *New Introduction*, 146–53.

[50] J. A. Szirmai, *The Archaeology of Medieval Bookbinding* (Aldershot, 1999).

[51] D. J. McKitterick, 'Customer, Reader and Bookbinder: Buying a Bible in 1630', *Book Collector*, 40 (1991), 382–406; M. M. Foot, *Studies in the History of Bookbinding* (Aldershot, 1993); —, *Bookbinding as a Mirror of Society* (see fn. 1: 19); —, *Bookbinders at Work* (see, fn. 1: 50); N. Pickwoad, 'Onward and Downward: How Binders Coped with the Printing-Press before 1800', in R. Myers and M. Harris (eds.), *A Millennium of the Book* (Winchester, 1994), 61–106; D. Pearson, *Oxford Bookbinding 1500–1640: Including a Supplement to Neil Ker's Fragments of Medieval Manuscripts Used as Pastedowns in Oxford Bindings* (Oxford, 2000); —, *English Bookbinding Styles, 1450–1800* (London, 2005). See also, D. Pearson (ed.), *'For the Love of the Binding': Studies in bookbinding history presented to Mirjam Foot* (London, 2000); and M. M. Foot (ed.), *Eloquent Witnesses* (London, 2004).

[52] As well as the work of A. R. A. Hobson, G. D. Hobson, and H. M. Nixon, see, G. Pollard, 'Changes in the Style of Bookbinding, 1550–1830', *Library*, V: 11 (1956), 71–94, later expanded as part of 'Commentaries on the Physical Form of Books', typescript, Bodleian MS Pollard 284, 68–127; H. M. Nixon and M. M. Foot, *The History of Decorated Bookbinding in England* (Oxford, 1992); and, J. B. Oldham, *English Blind-stamped Bindings* (Cambridge, 1952); —, *Blind Panels of English Binders* (Cambridge, 1958).

It is the realization that binding was more than a decorative craft that has begun to alter approaches to its significance. We are proverbially taught that the value of a book cannot be assumed from its covers; yet this view of the function, or aesthetics, of the structure and binding of a book is textual in its assumptions rather than historical: in other words, if we assume that it is the *text* that matters, then the binding of any given copy of a work may only be of incidental interest; however, if we assume that it is the *book* that is of interest (and, thus, the complex social relationships and spaces within which patronage as well as ownership and reading take place), then the structure and binding of a volume is an integral part of the history of any given copy and may reveal aspects to the meaning of an artefact that a strictly textual approach would not notice. If paper is the material that gives a book its voice, the binding is the architecture in which that voice finds resonance.

Scholars interested in literary editing had tended to regard binding as incidental to their concerns, in part because the drama was so dominant as a field in early modern studies and because a great many dramatic texts are preserved in nineteenth-century morocco dress. It is not uncommon to find plays and pamphlets in bindings of ruby, emerald, or sapphire morocco, as well as brown or black, often with the discreet gilt-stamped name of Bedford, Rivière, or Zaehnsdorf on the edge of the inside board.[53] Many of these ephemeral texts had once been preserved in sammelbände. Even in the eighteenth-century, incunabula and other important books had received similar treatment as collectors represented rarity and age by replacing damaged or unpretentious bindings with coverings of more conspicuous value. In these instances, unless other kinds of historical record survive, it is not possible to assess the role a binding played in the early transmission of a book. Yet the impact of the later binding trade on a group of highly valued texts is only part of the story. Fortunately, not all books have been rebound and a perspective that takes in a broad conspectus of all the evidence reveals just how important the original bindings could be.

Binders were an important part of the early modern book-trade, and it would not be unreasonable to estimate that by 1600 there may have been as many as c.100 binders in London, with that figure increasing significantly during the following century.[54] The binder was responsible

---

[53] The firm of Rivière merged with Bayntum of Bath in 1939; part of the establishment is a museum on the history of binding.

[54] This broad estimate is based on the data prepared for Bland, 'The London Book-Trade in 1600', 450–63, allowing for manuscripts and imports and the rate of work given by Foot, *Bookbinders at Work*, 117.

for the integrity of a book or manuscript, including the collation of the gatherings, the addition of plates or attachments, and the cancellation and insertion of appropriate leaves. The process of collation, as a bibliographer practises it, is to understand exactly how, when, and what a binder stitched together in making a book, and to account for anything else that has been added or removed subsequent to that fact, as books have always had to be repaired and rebound depending on the conditions of their storage and use. The second step is to be able to describe and assess the materials used both from the perspective of the extent to which it differs from standard practices, and the extent to which those standard practices slowly evolved.

The complete book was not finished by a scribe or a printer: in fact, a scribe or printer might only be responsible for a section of the work, it having been shared amongst two or more of them. Equally, a publisher could sell a book bound; or one gathered, beaten, and stab-stitched ready for binding (figure 3.3): it is not surprising, therefore, to find the well-known publisher William Ponsonby described by Fulke Greville and John Ramsay as a 'book-bynder': an important part of a publisher's business was his standard trade and customized bespoke binding services.[55] The reason for this was quite simple: the binding was the most variable expense available to a customer when they purchased a book. Owing to that expense, they often chose to have two or three items bound together. Thus, with trade bindings, only a few copies need be finished at any one time, and these could be blind-stamped or gilded if extra finishing was required.

The materials available to a binder commonly included calf, sheep, vellum, goat (black turkey and blue morocco being common), pig (used quite often in German bindings), velvet, embroidered silk, gold and silver thread, gold leaf, red dye, brass clasps and cornerpieces, silk ties, and a variety of ornaments, including arabesques and rules, that could be heated and applied either blind, or finished with gold leaf. The fore-edges of the paper might be stippled, or gauffered, with a pattern after gilding, and in the later seventeenth-century marbled end papers first appear, as do red calf and morocco bindings. Other colours, such as citron, were also possible. The possible permutations therefore range from the simplest limp vellum wrapper to highly elaborate velvet bindings embroidered with silver and gold thread. The more elaborate the binding, the greater the cost, and the more time and skill that was required of the binder.

[55] M. G. Brennan, 'William Ponsonby: Elizabethan Stationer', *Analytical & Enumerative Bibliography*, 7 (1983), 91–110 (see, pp. 93 and 102); see also, Foot, *Bookbinders at Work*, 35–40.

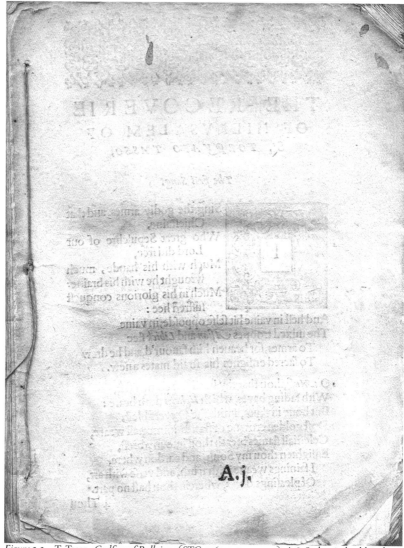

Figure 3.3   T. Tasso, *Godfrey of Bulloigne* (STC 23697–97a; 1594), A1ʳ: Stab-stitched binding. The copy lacks either of the variant title-pages (personal collection).

The evidence as to how much various bindings cost is fragmentary but fairly consistent and survives from several different sources.[56] The

---

[56] Foot, 'Some Bookbinders' Price Lists of the Seventeenth and Eighteenth Centuries', *Studies*, 15–67; —, *Bookbinders at Work*, 106–26 gives some German examples.

trade usually priced bindings according to well-known books of various sizes and bulk, such as a Camden, or a Ralegh. The price was adjusted for the degree of decorative work involved. Sixteenth-century calf bindings have a bitter chocolate colour; those of the seventeenth-century vary from mid-brown lightening to dark tan towards the end.[57] Increasingly, as well, sheep came to replace calf as a cheaper alternative, as more skins were required to meet demand. That expansion ultimately led to half- and quarter-bound boards, and cloth in the nineteenth-century. Goatskin was the most common of the expensive materials.

A broadside from 1619, being *A generall note of the prises of binding of all sorts of bookes* (STC 16768.6), gives a fair guide to prices and styles. A folio roman Bible gilt over once cost 11*s*; with gilt fillets only, it cost 3*s* 4*d*; the two volumes of Foxe's *Book of Martyrs* with fillets cost 12*s*, in hard boards 7*s*; Ralegh's *History* with fillets cost 3*s* 6*d*, the folio *Workes* of Gervase Babington (STC 1077–8; 1615), 2*s* 6*d*. For books 'in ouills' Camden's *Britannia* 'with maps' (i.e. STC 4508–9; 1607–10) cost 4*s* 6*d*, Ralegh's *History* 2*s* 6*d*, Plutarch's *Liues* 2*s* 4*d* and Comines' *Historie* 1*s* 6*d*. A duo-decimo like the *Practice of Piety* was 1*s* 4*d* gilt all over, and 1*s* with edges gilt and fillets. Smith's *Sermons* with ovals in quarto cost 10*d*; the psalms or a book of common prayer in quarto with gilt fillets cost 1*s* 2*d*. The *Statutes* in folio cost 2*s* 6*d*; whilst Michael Dalton's *Countrey iustice . . . of the Peace* in octavo cost 6*d*. Schoolbooks were normally bound in sheep rather than calf, with Cicero's *Orations* in decimo-sexto costing 3*d*, and an octavo grammar 2*d*. For Latin books costs were similar: small quartos cost 10*d*; a *Dictionarium poeticum* 1*s*.

Accounts are a further source of information: thus, in 1608, Robert, earl of Salisbury, paid Thomas Herbert 12*s* 8*d* for seven days' work and a further 30*s* for six dozen vellum skins.[58] Sometimes (with care) binding prices may also be inferred. Thus, an unbound copy of Jonson's 1616 *Workes* cost 9*s*, one bound copy 12*s*: the former price accords exactly with a rate of ½*d* a pica sheet adjusted by a ratio of seven-eighths as the *Workes* is set in english roman.[59] What we do not know (as the original binding for the 12*s* copy does not survive) is the extent to which the 3*s* binding was worked or gilded, but in view of the price for binding a Ralegh at 2*s* 6*d*, it seems likely that it was embellished in some way.

How an owner chose to have a text bound, or the bindings that they acquired, is revealing about the social and cultural values that shaped a collection, and (in cases of patronage) the role of the author in the

---

[57] For a comprehensive account, see Pearson, *English Bookbinding Styles*, 41–163.
[58] For instance, H. M. C., *Hatfield House, Part XXIV: Addenda 1605–68* (London, 1976), 149.
[59] The *Workes* has 257 sheets (with 15 blank pages): $257 \times 0.5 \times 0.875 = 112\frac{1}{2}d$; $9s = 108d$.

presentation of a copy. For instance, Jonson's large paper presentation copy of his 1616 *Workes* to John Wilson, headmaster of Westminster School, is bound in dark calf, stamped and tooled with a central diamond panel, and inscribed by Jonson. However, a copy at Princeton is bound in black turkey with gilt rules and stamped dentelles, all edges red, then gilded. It was probably given to an aristocratic patron: hence the lack of an inscription. Another black turkey binding, again without an inscription but with a large 'Pyramis and Thisbe' ornament stamped on the front and back boards, is now in the collection of Robert Pirie: it was also probably a gift to a member of the nobility.[60] Jonson's inscribed copy to Edward Heywood, on the other hand, was rebound for Robert Hoe in the late nineteenth-century by Lortic Fils in red morocco lavishly gilt with brown morocco inner doublures, and cased. It may have been originally bound in gilt calf.[61] Similarly, the evidence of bindings from Jonson's library indicates that whilst his folios were bound in calf, smaller sizes were typically in plain vellum: the only velvet binding amongst his books being a gift copy of Lucan's *Pharsalia* from his friend, the translator Tom May.[62]

Authors could distinguish between presentation copies in a strict hierarchy of bindings.[63] Francis Bacon, for instance, gave copies of his *De Dignatate et Augmentis Scientiarum* (STC 1108; 1623) to the Bodleian, Cambridge University Library, and Trinity College, Cambridge: the first two are bound in turquoise velvet with gold thread (figure 3.4), the Trinity copy is bound in burgundy velvet, without the thread, but stamped with gold rules.[64] Similarly, a copy of Vesalius' *De Corporis* (1543) with hand-painted illustrations, that may have been a presentation copy to Charles V, was bound in purple velvet.[65] More typically, John Golburne had the vellum binding of his translation of Cipriano de Valera's *Two Treatises* elaborately gilded for the dedicatee, Sir Thomas Egerton.[66]

[60] PML 16254; Princeton University, Robert Taylor Collection, STC 14751; H. M. Nixon, *Five Centuries of English Bookbinding* (London, 1979), 62–3 (plate 25). Pirie also owns Sir Kenelm Digby's large paper presentation copy of Jonson's 1640 *Workes* to Elizabeth of Bohemia, bound in blue morocco.

[61] Huntington Library, RB62101.

[62] Library of Congress, Batchelder PA 6479 .E5M3 1627 (STC 16887; 1627).

[63] For instance, Bp. John Davenant to Dr Samuel Ward regarding STC 6293, 12 September 1640, Bodleian Library, Oxford, MS Tanner 65, f.118; also, Davenant to Ward concerning STC 6294, 8 December 1634, MS Tanner 70, f.41.

[64] F. Bacon, *De Dignitate et Augmentis Scientiarum* (STC 1108; 1623): Bodleian Library, shelfmark Arch A.c.6; Cambridge University Library, shelfmark Sel. 2.84; Trinity College, Cambridge, shelfmark R.4.60.

[65] Norman collection, Christies. The copy sold for $1.6525 million in 1998 to a private bidder.

[66] Huntington Library, shelfmark RB69718.

Figure 3.4   F. Bacon, *Opera . . . tomus primus: qui continet De dignatate et augmentis scientiarum libros IX* (STC 1108; 1623): Bodleian Library, Oxford, Arch A.c.6.

As well as gift bindings, there are others that always indicate a certain kind of personal association with the text. For instance, embroidered bindings with flowers, plants, birds, and so on, were usually made for women. Most of the texts with these bindings are Bibles, psalm-books, liturgies, and occasional volumes of godly devotion.[67] A Bible, book of common prayer, and psalm-book from 1625, in the Pierpont Morgan Library, has a list of five names, all of them women, all different.[68] Like similar volumes, it was almost certainly the book carried by the bride at her marriage, and was passed down from generation to generation: an inference that could be confirmed, or disproved, by checking the parish records. The devotional book that is handed down from mother to daughter has an iconic status quite separate from its text; as do the images of books (often indicative of godly piety) that appear in early modern paintings and sculpture, sometimes with a finger inserted in the otherwise closed volume to suggest the act of remembering the place in the act of reading. As with clothes, jewels, and animals, books in paintings reveal something about their owners, and generally what is depicted is not the open text (itself a very suggestive image, like that of a blank page), but the binding.

Coda: Monumental Inscriptions

A small group of early modern texts are preserved as inscriptions, particularly on funeral monuments. These can be quite difficult to record and describe. The best option available is to photograph the monument and the cartouche(s) that contain the text. It may be possible to measure both the monument and the lettering and therefore to give a sense of scale and composition. Perhaps the most important relationship, however, is the context within which an inscription is found, and particular thought needs to be given to how it is best represented and recorded. These decisions have to be made on the basis of both practicality and circumstance. What ought to be recorded, in particular, are the materials and the style of script used.

---

[67] See, G. Barber, *Textile and Embroidered Bindings* (Oxford, 1971); Foot, *History of Bookbinding*, 61–5. Folger STC 2535.2 (1610).
[68] Pierpont Morgan Library, shelfmark 16033. It is one of 25 English seventeenth-century embroidered bindings in the Morgan collection.

4　Producing Texts

THE application of ink to paper, whether by quill or movable type, was the most common method of recording and preserving a text during the early modern period. Having determined the kind of paper to be employed and the structure of the document, it was through ink that the printed or manuscript text became a dual witness to the histories of material process and intellectual content. The marriage of form and meaning, whether performed with a casual nonchalance that accepts all the stale pieties of convention, or entered into with an acute sense of the expressive limits and possibilities involved, occurred at the moment a text began its alliance with the page. As a consequence, this chapter is concerned with the methods of textual replication in manuscript and print, from the basic skills of literacy to the ways in which the making of a text left traces that indicate how it was produced.

Not all manuscripts became printed books: most did not. Private and financial documents, personal correspondence and jottings, estate records, legal opinions, administrative and political papers, personal miscellanies, commonplace books, compilations of recipes, and similar items required the primary skills of literacy but not the resources of the press. These documents are as expressive of their origins, and forms of production, as are the more publicly available materials we associate with the commercial manuscript and printed book-trades. The public materials were produced with an eye to profit or, at least, economic survival; some other manuscripts might be written in the course of employment, or to please a patron in the hope of some reward, but the difference is this: their distribution through a network depended on connection, not coin. Manuscripts reserved for private use were the dominant mode of textual production in the sixteenth and seventeenth centuries and, despite the fact that we have obviously lost vast swathes of what once existed, they remain the single largest and most diverse body of textual evidence that survives.[1]

In production and use, manuscript and print were intimately related. Some manuscripts consciously imitated the layout and conventions of printed texts; whilst every printed book was first a manuscript; and even when a book had been printed, it might well be marked up and

---

[1] Bland, 'The London Book-Trade in 1600', 457–60 attempts to estimate the approximate levels of paper used by the printed book-trade (20 per cent) compared to known import data. That estimate is generous, and allows for lost texts and ephemera: it is unlikely to have so understated the levels of print production that the broad conclusion is invalidated. What was not employed by the printed book-trade was used for manuscript activity.

corrected for a later edition by hand. Readers might annotate or emend, making a book into a composite document and leave their traces, like the inky thumbprint of a pressman, in the margin. On the title-page, or elsewhere, a name, a motto, the price, a date of purchase, or a record that the volume was a gift might be noted. Details like these can be revealing about the production history of a book, as with the Anglo-Saxon gospels edited by Archbishop Parker, who presented a copy to John Savile, the brother of Sir Henry, 'ix Augusti 1571': a date within days of publication.[2] For many, the difference between print as a mechanized form of mass manuscript production, and print as a technology with other aesthetic, technical and socio-economic concerns, was not at first self-evident: that awareness evolved as access to books became more common throughout the sixteenth and seventeenth centuries. It was the spread of literacy that changed the market for books.

Literacy and Script

There is an intimate relationship between the ability to write and the ability to read; the word in the mouth, and the word in the hand. The coordination of those skills is the prerequisite for literacy whether they were taught by a parent, a tutor, or at school. We first learn literacy by connecting the sounds that have been received as language to their abstract representation, and then we learn how to make those abstract signs for ourselves. From first familiarity with letterforms, through the recognition of semantic units of meaning, to the ability to read in silence together with the gradual mastery of writing, as well as the control and preparation of a quill, the learning of literacy then, as now, developed alongside other forms of moral and intellectual instruction.

Education was not available as a matter of right in the sixteenth and seventeenth centuries, but that does not mean that those who were illiterate had no access to, or were not influenced by, the written culture of the time. In the early fifteenth-century, literacy had been uncommon outside the educated elites; by 1700, it had permeated through much of society. True, small communities, who lived by the agricultural year, had little use for printed or written texts where, for most purposes, custom and gossip prevailed; nor did the servants who cleaned, cooked, sewed,

---

[2] J. Foxe (ed.), *The gospels of the fower euangelistes tr. in the olde Saxons tyme out of Latin into the vulgare toung of the Saxons* (STC 2961; 1571): Alexander Turnbull Library, Wellington, shelf-mark Howard 25. See also, P. J. Lucas, 'Parker, Lambarde and the Provision of Special Sorts for Printing Anglo-Saxon in the Sixteenth Century', *Journal of the Printing Historical Society*, 28 (1999), 41–69.

or worked in a garden need to learn to read or write. Forms of common wisdom and entertainment, like anecdotes, jokes, riddles, and ballads, required memory but not the written word; proverbs might preserve skills ('a stitch in time saves nine') that required no other instruction.[3] Yet in a world where many did not need to read, almost every village had its parish church (or at least a shared living) with a cleric who was literate in both English and Latin (increasingly often having attended university), and many landed households employed a tutor, secretary, or steward—or perhaps several staff with scribal abilities.

Amongst the gentry, and those who aspired to that rank, as well as those who engaged in commerce and trade, or who owned property, literacy became a means to enhance economic and social mobility. From the late fifteenth-century on, it became more common for men to be given formal education, sometimes at the universities and Inns of Court, whilst more often women might learn how to read and write an italic hand. The spread of literacy amongst women outside the more wealthy households was particularly significant as their children, in turn, might be taught by them. For women, as for men, the crucial issue was the need to manage property, as Billingsley argued when he advocated the acquisition of basic skills:

> Lastly, the practise of this Art is so necessary for women, . . . that no woman suruiuing her husband, and who hath an estate left her, ought to be without the vse thereof, at least in some reasonable manner: For thereby she comes to a certainty of her estate . . . whereas otherwise for want of it, she is subiect to the manifold deceits now vsed in the world.[4]

The growing presence of both manuscript and print, and the spread of grammar schools through the smaller market towns meant that, by the middle of the sixteenth-century, basic skills were being acquired across a broad spectrum of society, especially in urban centres. The spoken and written words were cheek by jowl: the pulpit and the stage could serve as conduits for the communication of complex ideas; whilst the ability of one person to read within a group meant that others might be exposed to a text: communal reading, at home or in a tavern, was a common form of social entertainment.

---

[3] See, in particular, Fox, *Oral and Literate Culture in England 1500–1700*; also, D. Cressy, *Literacy and the Social Order: Reading and Writing in Tudor and Stuart England* (Cambridge, 1980); F. Schurink, *Education and Reading in Elizabethan and Jacobean England* (Oxford University MS D.Phil c.1941/5, 2004).
[4] M. Billingsley, *The pens excellencie* (STC 3062.2; 1618), B4^v–C1^r.

The ability to read some things did not mean that all who did read could read everything; a different level of competency was required for a complex book than a broadside ballad or the catechism, nor did an ability to read imply an ability to write.[5] Writing, and especially writing with clarity and precision, required time and patience: those who wrote the manuscripts that now interest scholars the most, such as verse texts and prose tracts, were either paid for their services (as secretaries or scriveners) or belonged to a relatively small, socially elite group. The copying of letters, advice tracts, and verse from separates and booklets, was not something done in a few minutes. Amongst the elite, the need to control information, and organize access to it as a resource, was not only a political problem, but one that is reflected on a personal level in the practice of keeping a diverse variety of personal compilations.

The practical evidence for early instruction in the arts of literacy is scarce. Professional writing manuals, such as those by De Beau Chesne and Billingsley, are deceptive in that they present a professional ideal rather than real practice, and the scripts that they exhibit have a clarity and legibility few achieved; nevertheless they were reprinted—perhaps more often than we can now establish.[6] Hornbooks and elementary schoolbooks, as well, are among the rarest of early printed materials because they were used until worn out.[7] The earliest example of an ABC with the Lord's Prayer (STC 21.4), that was first entered to John Wolfe on 6 November 1587, dates from c.1620; whilst the earliest ABC, with the Pater Noster, Ave Maria, and so on, dates from c.1535 (STC 17.4), some 60 years after the introduction of printing in England. In both instances, the evidence is relatively late; what the examples reveal, however, is that the initial steps in reading were oral and memorial: first a person (not always a child) associated a sound with each letter, and then recited a text that they knew by heart to coordinate those sounds with the combinations of letters they saw on the page. In so doing, they professed their faith.

Billingsley had some sharp remarks to make about the teaching of writing skills by his contemporaries.[8] Of course, he had his own agenda

---

[5] See, I. M. Green, *The Christian's ABC: Catechisms and Catechizing in England c.1530–1740* (Oxford, 1996); —, *Print and Protestantism in Early Modern England* (Oxford, 2000); M. Spufford, *Small Books and Pleasant Histories: Popular Fiction and Its Readership in Seventeenth-century England* (London, 1981); T. Watt, *Cheap Print and Popular Piety, 1550–1640* (Cambridge, 1991).

[6] For Billingsley (publ. 1618–41), STC 3061–2.8 and Wing B2909A; De Beau Chesne and Baildon (publ. 1571–1615), STC 6445.5–50; also, STC 3361.3–.7 and 3363.7.

[7] See, A. W. Tuer, *History of the Horn-book*, 2 vols. (London, 1986); STC 17.7–22.5.

[8] See also, Woudhuysen, *Sir Philip Sidney and the Circulation of Manuscripts*, 29–45.

when he wrote of 'lame Pen Men' who 'onely haue a certaine confused kind of writing, voide eyther of *Life*, *Dexterity*, or *Art* it selfe' (the choice of epithets is instructive) and who pasted bills to posts promising 'to teach anyone (not standing vpon the capacity of the pupill) to write a sufficient hand in a moneth, and some of them doe say in a fortnight'.[9] His qualification about the capacity of the pupil, and the speed at which 'a sufficient hand' was achieved, are a reminder that, for many, literacy was only ever an elementary and partially acquired skill; and that in underemployed urban areas, teaching it was a means of survival. In London, wrote Billingsley, 'a man can goe in no corner of this City, but hee shall see and heare of a world of squirting Teachers, not one of them almost worthy to carry a Pen-mans Incke-horne after him'.[10] For those without secure employment, private teaching allowed little more than a temporary respite from hardship that could be supplemented by love-letters and other personal notes that the poor were too unskilful to compose for themselves. These people were not professional scriveners.

The teaching of writing is intimately linked to the ability to spell, and poor spelling practices (then, as now) only made access to literacy more difficult. Francis Clement, for instance, thought it appropriate for children to have learnt their ABC by the age of four, and to have the basic writing and spelling skills in place by seven or eight. He is frank, however, that these standards were rarely achieved:

> Children . . . almost euerie where are first taught either in priuate by men or women altogeather rude and vtterly ignoraunt of the due composing and iust spelling of words: or else in common schooles most commonly by boyes, verie seldome or neuer by anie of sufficient skill.[11]

Quite what was a 'sufficient skill' is not so clear, even where teachers were available, but the implication is that the children struggled at the moment when they should have learned with the greatest facility:

> For how fewe be there vnder the age of seauen or eight yeares, that are towardly abled, and praysablie furnished for reading? And as manie there be aboue those yeares that can neither readily spell nor rightly write euen the common wordes of our Englishe.[12]

---

[9] Billingsley, *The pens excellencie*, B1ᵛ–2ʳ.

[10] Billingsley, *The pens excellencie*, B3ʳ.

[11] F. Clement, *The petie schoole* (STC 5400; 1587), A2ᵛ. The preface is dated 21 July 1576.

[12] Clement, *The petie schoole*, A2ᵛ.

For all the vividness of this account, many a 'pen-man' and teacher taught with more art and dexterity than Billingsley and Clement allow. With time, imperfect skills could be improved and the most common errors rectified. Even if some of those who learnt Latin at school later forgot much of what they had been taught, the essential skills that were acquired of reading and writing remained.

Literacy was primarily a written skill and was driven by a mastery of manuscript techniques—something that discussions seeking to connect the spread of literacy to the 'impact of print' usually overlook. Children were taught how to cut and hold a quill. Clement describes the third or fourth quill of the wing of a goose or raven as best, followed by the pinion feather (found at the joint with the terminal section of the wing). These quills were valued for their strength and roundness. They were prepared with a penknife (their original purpose) 'slantwise on the backe-part downeward about the quarter of an inch from the end' and then on the other side cutting from a point slightly higher.[13] The description that Clement offers of the technique is fairly complex: a rift was cut into the mid-back of the quill and, on the other side, a slash was made that was then cut back to form the nib. The quill was then cut in again from both sides. The fineness of the nib would depend on the quality of the quill, the experience of the person cutting it, the firmness of the hand, the sharpness of the blade, and the keenness of their eyesight. As well as quills, students were taught how to make ink. Clement's recipe for this involved leaving a quart of water to stand with a mixture of Arabic gum (two ounces), oak galls (five ounces), and copperas, otherwise known as green vitriol (three ounces).[14]

Children were first taught to write dry (without ink) to conserve paper, or to write in wax so that the blank surface could be recovered through heat: practised repetition was the key to developing ease with a quill and a fluid hand.[15] Clement recommended that in writing 'let not your paper lye to hard' (in other words, that it ought not be in direct contact with a wooden surface) in order to protect the nib and prevent the paper being torn and punctured. Consistency, then as now, was valued as an aid to legibility. Word separation, Clement advised, should be 'the space of the small a'.[16] Pen trials of young children are also

---

[13] For a full description, see Clement, *The petie-schoole*, D3^{r-v}.

[14] Clement, *The petie-schoole*, D2^r.

[15] For an extended treatment of erasable texts, and their use more generally for notetaking, see P. Stallybrass, R. Chartier, J. F. Mowery, and H. Wolfe, 'Hamlet's Tables and the Technologies of Writing in Renaissance England', *Shakespeare Quarterly*, 55 (2004), 379–419.

[16] Clement, *The petie-schoole*, D5^v.

sometimes found in printed books on blank pages or around the margins: there are several copies of Jonson's 1616 *Workes* so marked.[17]

The first alphabet taught at school was secretary hand because, as Billingsley noted, 'it is the onely vsuall hand of England, for dispatching of all manner of businesses'.[18] Those who had no need for a business hand (including some aristocrats and many women) wrote, and were presumably first taught, italic; similarly, from the mid-sixteenth-century, italic was practised at university. Otherwise, secretary hand is found throughout a vast range of documents, from parish registers and wills to private papers and accounts. For many people it was the common hand for correspondence and private notes. Hence, Shakespeare preferred secretary hand. Bacon, in contrast, was fully digraphic (he could switch from secretary to italic with ease: figure 4.1), whilst Donne wrote an italic hand, and Jonson mixed some secretary features into his italic script.[19] During the seventeenth-century, the shift towards italic became pronounced, and after the Restoration secretary hand is rare.

There are various formal characteristics that distinguish secretary hand from italic. It is, in all respects, a more elaborate script, although it can be written with cursive efficiency. Most importantly, while many of the letters are recognizably similar to their italic equivalent, several have different forms: most notably miniscule *c*, *e*, *h*, *k*, *p* and, to some extent, *r*. Of these, *c* is written like the left and top side of a square and can be confused with *t*; *e* is written in reverse and can be confused with *o*; *h* has a descending stroke that swings open to the right and is easily confused with *y*; *k* is often an *l* crossed with a raised *z̃*; *p* begins with a 2 that then circles back anticlockwise and down on the diagonal to form the bowl and descender; *r* is double-sided and may have a stroke at its base. Of the other letters, the open *a* can be confused with *u*. Clement gives quite detailed instructions about the formal aspects of writing various letters, whilst McKerrow provides several examples of each of the letterforms and a discussion of the technical issues.[20] Both sources should be consulted.

[17] For instance, University of London, shelfmark B. S. 1272; National Art Library (V&A), shelfmark Forster SF⁰ 4689; Jesus College, Oxford, shelfmark I.Arch.3.6; Pembroke College, Cambridge, shelfmark LC.I.29; Boston Public Library, shelfmark XfG. 3811.5A; Brown University, shelfmark PR2600 1616; Columbia University, New York, shelfmark 822,34; University of Texas, shelfmark Ah J738 +B616 am.

[18] Billingsley, *The pens excellencie*, C2ʳ.

[19] For Jonson and Donne, see P. J. Croft, *Autograph Poetry in the English Language: Facsimiles of Original Manuscripts from the Fourteenth to the Twentieth Century*, 2 vols. (London, 1973).

[20] McKerrow, *Introduction*, app. 8, 341–50; G. Dawson and L. Kennedy-Skipton, *Elizabethan Handwriting 1500–1650: A Guide to the Reading of Documents and Manuscripts* (London, 1968); www.nationalarchives.gov.uk/palaeography.

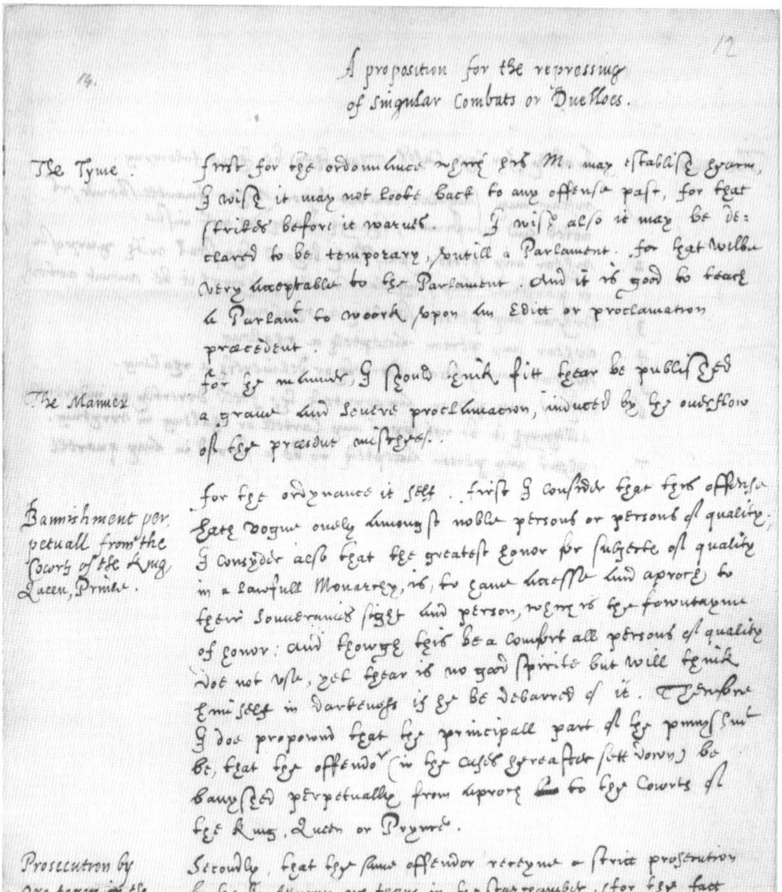
14.

12

A proposition for the repressing
of singular Combats or Duelloes.

The Tyme: first for the ordinance which his M. may establish therein, I wish it may not looke back to any offense past, for that strikes before it warnes. I wish also it may be declared to be temporary, untill a Parlament. for that wilbe very acceptable to the Parlament. And it is good to teache a Parlamt to worke upon an Edict or proclamation precedent.

The Manner: for the manner, I should think fitt that there be published a grave and severe proclamation, induced by the overflow of the present mischeefs.

Banishment perpetuall from the Courts of the King, Queen, Prince.: for the ordynance it self. first I consider that this offense hath vogue only amongst noble persons or persons of quality; I consider also that the greatest honor for subjects of quality in a lawfull Monarchy, is to have access and aproche to their Soueraignes sight and person, which is the fountaine of honor: and though this be a comfort all persons of quality do not use, yet there is no good spirite but will think himself in darknes if he be debarred of it. Therfore I doe propound that the principall part of the punishment be, that the offendor (in the cases hereafter sett down) be banished perpetually from approch to the Courts of the King, Queen or Prynce.

Prosecution by Ore tenus in the Starchamber.: Secondly, that the same offendor receyve a strict prosecution by the Kgs Atturney ore tenus in the Starchamber. for the fact being notorious will allwaies be confessed and so made fitt for an ore tenus; and that this prosecution be without respect of persons, be the offendor never so great, and that the fyne sett be irremissible.

Figure 4.1 Francis Bacon, 'A proposition for the repressing of singular Combats or Duelloes' (secretary hand with italic marginal text), c.1614: National Library of Scotland, MS Adv. 33.1.14, vol. 31, item 14.

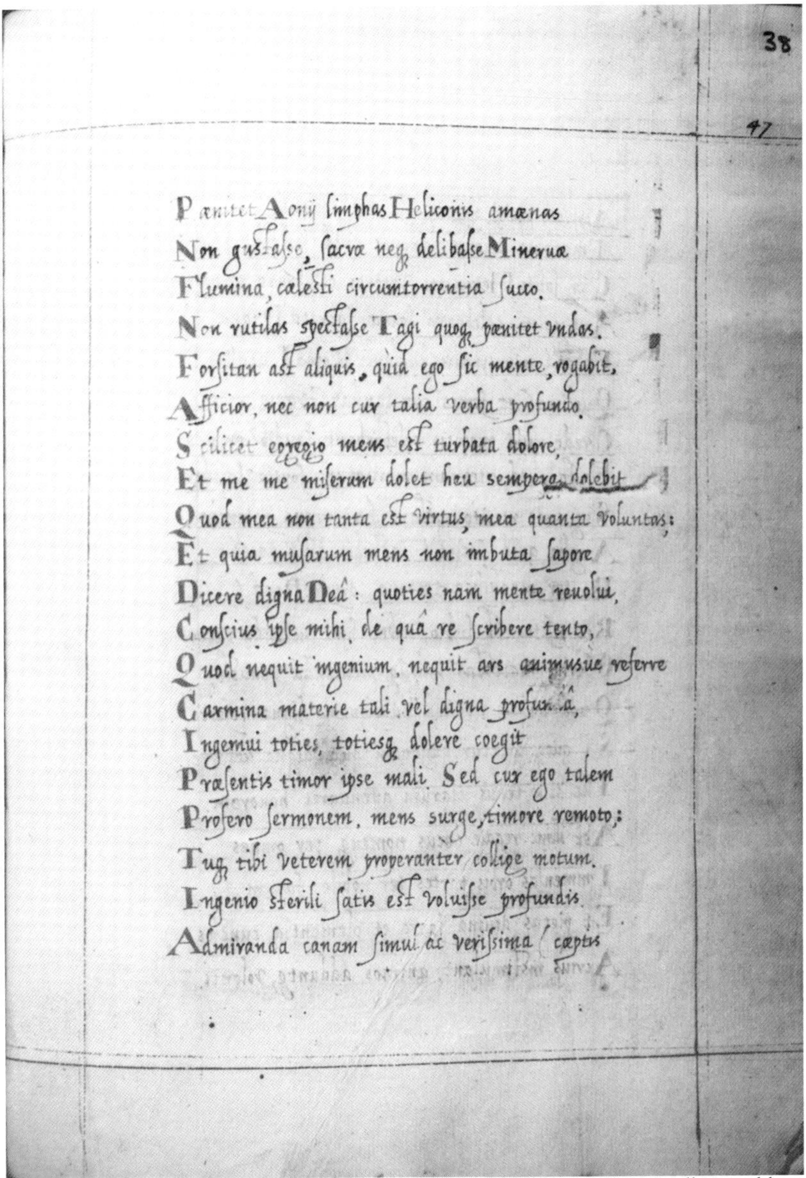

38

47

Pænitet Aonÿ limphas Heliconis amœnas
Non gustasse, sacvæ neq delibasse Minervæ
Flumina, cælesti circumtorrentia succo.
Non rutilas spectasse Tagi quoq pænitet undas.
Forsitan ast aliquis, quià ego sic mente, rogabit,
Afficior, nec non cur talia verba profundo.
Scilicet egregio mens est turbata dolore,
Et me me miserum dolet heu semper dolebit
Quod mea non tanta est virtus, mea quanta voluntas:
Et quia musarum mens non imbuta sapore
Dicere digna Deâ: quoties nam mente revolui,
Conscius ipse mihi, de quà re scribere tento,
Quod nequit ingenium, nequit ars animusue referre
Carmina materie tali vel digna profunda,
Ingemui toties, totiesq dolere coegit
Præsentis timor ipse mali. Sed cur ego talem
Profero sermonem, mens surge, timore remoto;
Tuq tibi veterem properanter collige motum.
Ingenio sterili satis est voluisse profundis.
Admiranda canam simul ac verissima (cœptis

Figure 4.2 Trinity College, Dublin, MS 638, f. 47ʳ: the schoolboy italic of William Gibbins at Westminster School in a presentation manuscript for Queen Elizabeth, 1586.

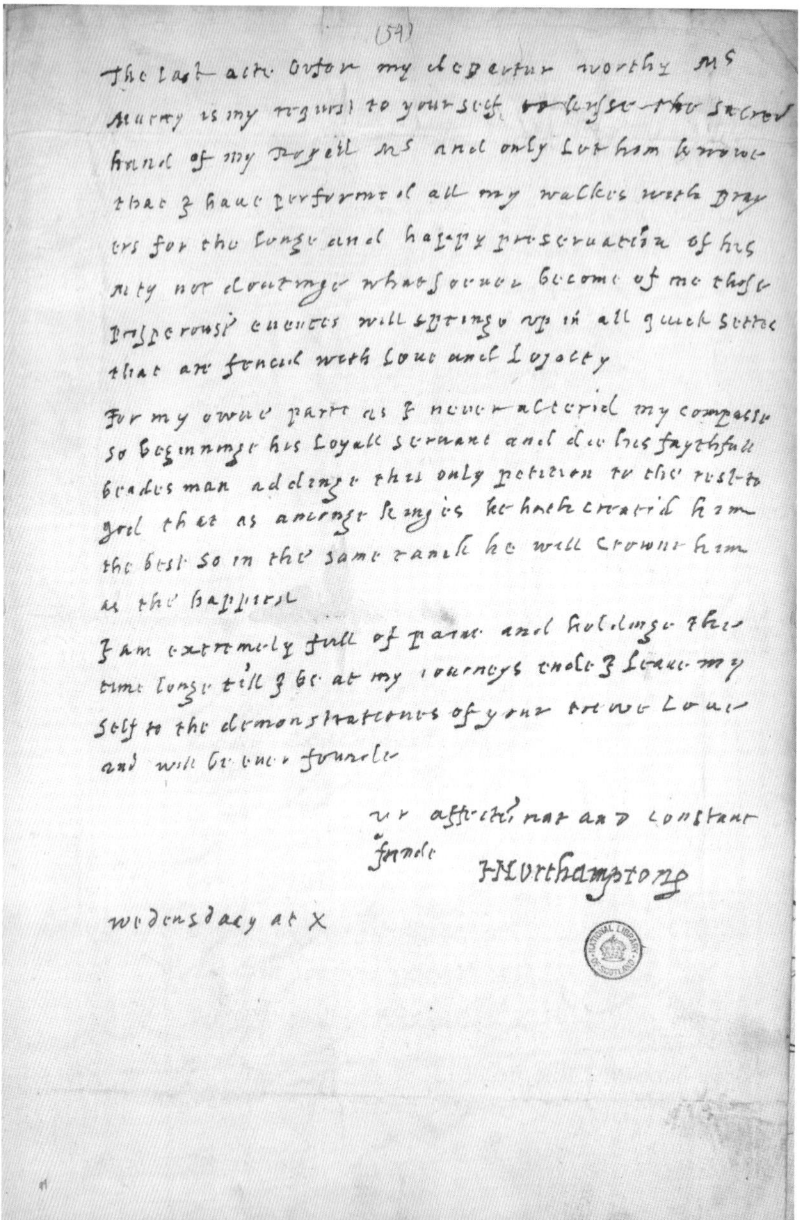
(59)

The last acte before my departur worthy Mr
Murray is my request to your self to kysse the secret
hand of my royall Mr and only let him knowe
that I haue performed all my walkes with pray
ers for the longe and happy preseruation of his
Mty not doutinge whatsoeuer become of me those
prosperouse euentes will springe up in all quick settes
that are fenced with loue and loyalty

For my owne parte as I neuer altered my compasse
so beginninge his loyall seruant and dienge his faythfull
beadesman addinge this only petition to the rest to
god that as amonge kinges he hath created him
the best so in the same ranke he will crowne him
as the happiest
I am extremely full of payne and holdinge the
time longe till I be at my iourneys ende I leaue my
self to the demonstrationes of your trewe loue
and will be euer founde

yr affectionat and constant
frende
H Northampton

wedensdaey at X

Figure 4.3 Henry Howard, earl of Northampton, his last letter the day he died, Wednesday 15 June 1614 (Julian Calendar): National Library of Scotland, MS Adv. 33.1.7, vol. 22, item 59.

The italic hand, and training in the finer calligraphic arts, remained at first the preserve of the well educated.[21] By the time a young man had finished at a school such as Westminster, he was expected to display a mastery of writing skills in keeping with later expectations of position and preferment. As part of the ethos, royal visits to the school were celebrated with collections of Latin and Greek verse, with every boy responsible for his own contribution to the manuscript (figure 4.2).[22] Quite intentionally, the hands were expected to be sufficiently similar so as to ensure visual continuity from one poem, and one boy, to the next. In practice, they were not used for everyday purposes, but they do reveal the level of skill developed through formal training. In more personal ways, the practice left its elegant traces in the hands of those who had been taught to write with this mastery, such as Bacon and Jonson.

Clarity of style involved a fusion of thought with the visual elegance conveyed by the written word. A good hand was an expression of good manners, reflecting a courtesy towards those who might have to read the advice, opinion, or ideas of another. Humanistic italic was, in this sense, not only an expression of a cultured mind and classical education (although italic miniscule was, in fact, Carolingian in its origins),[23] but of a Roman civility that found its most acute expression in the letters of Cicero and the younger Pliny, which the boys were expected to read.

The calligraphic skills of those who attended the great schools and the universities were not universally adopted throughout the political and social elite. Whilst Elizabeth wrote a skilled hand, James wrote with neither care nor precision (see figures 6.1 and 6.2; pp. 156–7). Bacon might have been a master of the calligraphic arts, and Northampton (who in the 1590s had worked as a secretary for Essex) measured and chaste (figure 4.3); others, such as Buckingham, cultivated a large scrawl that reflects his power and influence, even if he did sign his letters to the king and Prince Charles as their 'most humble slaue and doge Steenie' (figure 4.4): the character of the hand is revealing of the character of the man. Similarly, Lady Arbella Stuart and Lady Mary Wroth are justly appreciated for their disciplined and elegant script, but the large and laboured hand of Katherine, Lady Aubigny and duchess of Lennox, is a more telling example of the cursive italic common amongst gentry-born women, revealing more care than practice or use, for all of Jonson's praise of the qualities of her mind (figure 4.5).

---

[21] A. Fairbank and B. Dickens, *The Italic Hand in Tudor Cambridge* (Cambridge, 1962).
[22] C. M. Bajetta, 'The Manuscripts of Verse Presented to Elizabeth I: A Preliminary Investigation', *Ben Jonson Journal*, 8 (2001), 147–206: see esp. pp. 155–6, where Trinity College, Dublin, MS 638 is not listed.
[23] Morison, *Politics and Script*, 266–76 and 290–3.

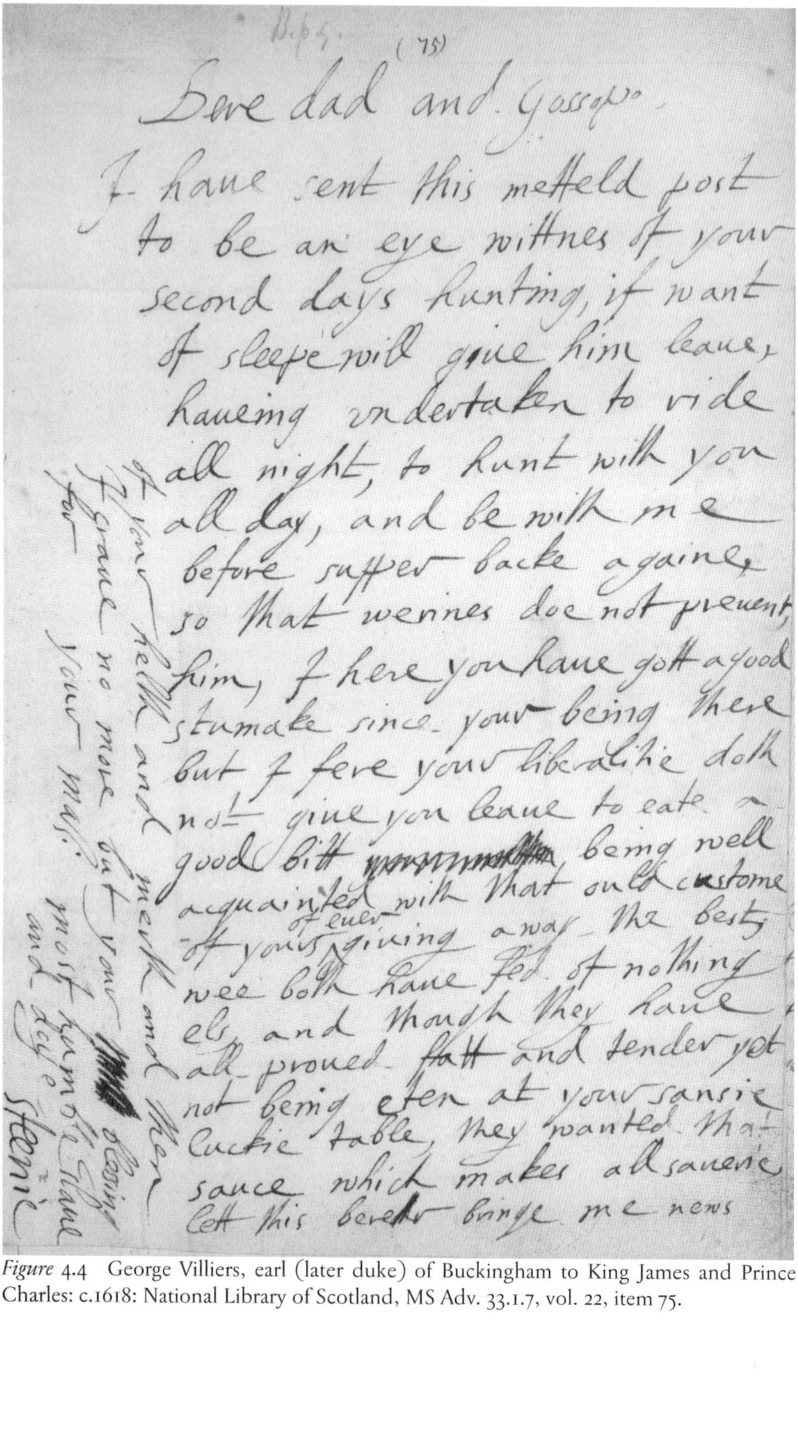
(75)

Deare dad and Gossope.

I haue sent this metteld post to be an eye wittnes of your second days hunting, if want of sleepe will giue him leaue, haueing undertaken to ride all night, to hunt with you all day, and be with me before supper backe againe, so that wearines doe not preuent him, I here you haue gott a good stumake since your being there but I fere your liberalitie doth not giue you leaue to eate a good bitt being well acquainted with that ould custome of euer your giuing away the best, wee both haue fed of nothing els, and though they haue all proued fatt and tender yet not being eten at your sausie luckie table, they wanted that sauce which makes all sauerie lett this bearer bringe me news

of your helth and merth and then I craue no more but your blessing your Ma[jes]t[ie]s most humble slaue and doge Steenie

Figure 4.4 George Villiers, earl (later duke) of Buckingham to King James and Prince Charles: c.1618: National Library of Scotland, MS Adv. 33.1.7, vol. 22, item 75.

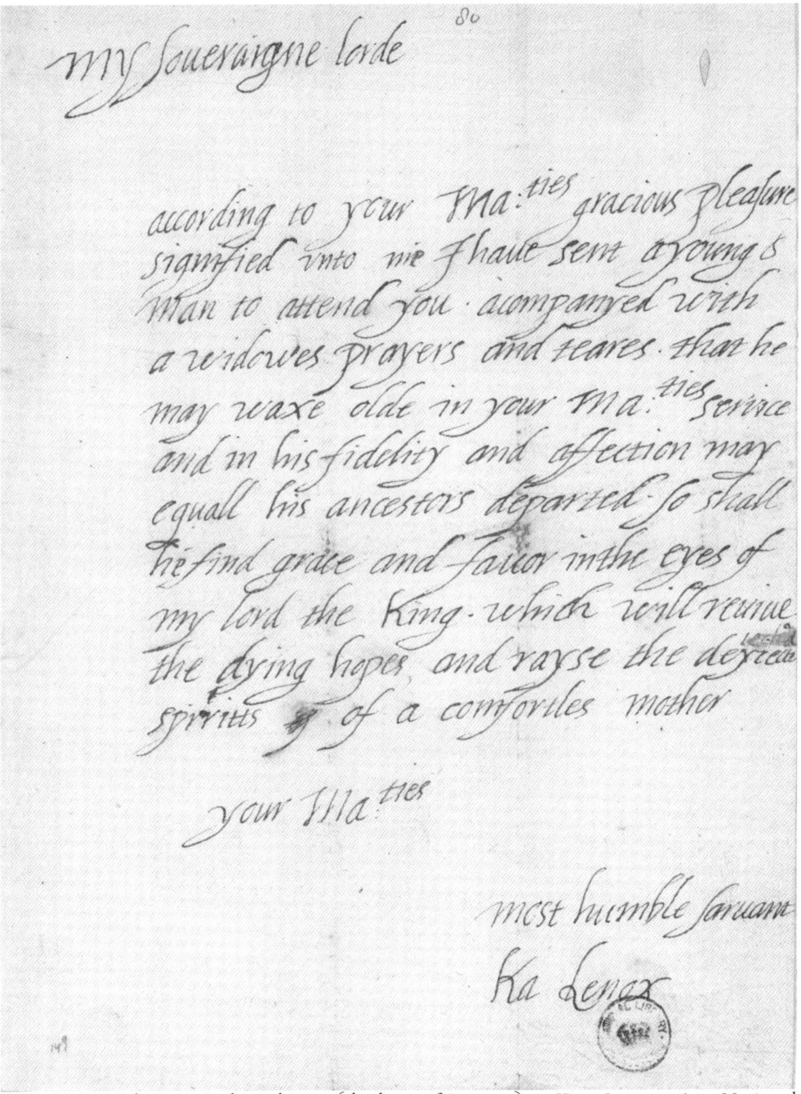

80

my Soueraigne lorde

according to your Ma:ties gracious pleasure
signified unto me I haue sent a young
man to attend you · acompanyed with
a widowes prayers and teares · that he
may waxe olde in your Ma:ties service
and in his fidelity and affection may
equall his ancestors departed · so shall
he find grace and fauor in the eyes of
my lord the King · which will reuiue
the dying hopes and rayse the dejected
spirits of a comfortles mother

your Ma:ties

most humble saruant
Ka Lenox

149

Figure 4.5 Katherine, Lady Aubigny (duchess of Lennox) to King James, 1624: National Library of Scotland, MS Adv. 33.1.7, vol. 22, item 80.

The use of script to validate liability or authority lends to each hand a unique legal status. The idiosyncrasies of a signature guarantee loans, wills, marriage vows, treaties, execution warrants, and so on.[24] Then, as

[24] See, P. Beal, *In Praise of Scribes*, 3–5.

now, we recognize individual combinations of palaeographical habits as self-defining: hence the danger and skill of the forger's art. That same individuality of script left its traces across all texts that were copied, as the nature of the hand influenced the ability of others to read what was before them, whether the final product was in manuscript or print.

For many texts that interest literary scholars a holograph is wanting. Hence, when source documents are irrecoverable, other papers in the hand of an author or scribe may afford an insight into textual issues. At all times, it must be understood that for every fair copy, there were many other forms of less legible document that might impact upon the intelligibility of a text. Indeed, one of Greg's arguments for ascribing the manuscripts of Heywood's *The Captives* and *The Escapes of Jupiter* as autograph was that 'no sane person would have employed a scribe who wrote such an atrocious hand'.[25] More generally, it helps to know whether a source document, from which subsequent copies derived, was written in secretary or italic, by a skilled or less accomplished hand, and whether the script was disciplined or highly cursive. The cultural and pedagogical conditions under which writing was first learnt, as well as the purposes for which a manuscript was prepared, will have shaped the characteristics of the hand in which it was written.

Manuscripts and Their Uses

The vast range of manuscript material poses descriptive problems both of classification concerning its purpose and use, and of determining its circumstances of production.[26] The idea that a manuscript is simply the result of pen put to paper does not get one very far: documents were created for a wide variety of reasons, and that context determined potential access to the material as well as influencing the script that was used. The distinction is not one of subject classification as such: literary papers, for instance, might include private notes or presentation copies; what helped to shape the format and script of a document, in the first place, were the circumstances under which it was created and to what end. At the risk of being a little glib, it might help to distinguish seven broad groups that, in certain respects, will inevitably overlap.

First, there are private documents that were never intended for any eyes other than the person responsible for compiling them or, at most,

---

[25] Greg, 'The Escapes of Jupiter', *Collected Papers*, 156–83, esp. 158; similarly, Beal in the *Index of English Literary Manuscripts*, I: ii, 219–21.
[26] See also, H. Love, 'Oral and Scribal Texts in Early Modern England', *The Book in Britain . . . 1557–1695*, 93–121.

members of the family, whether spouses or siblings. These papers might include ideas jotted down on a loose sheet, entries in a private diary, records of events and dreams, jokes and anecdotes, collections of mottos, calculations, nativities and horoscopes, notes, drafts of letters or other compositions, as well as annotations in the margins of books and manuscripts. The character of these materials does not require that they be legible to others, so care in writing is more a matter of personal habit and preference than good manners. The types of document involved include loose papers as well as table-books and small pocket volumes sold pre-bound; small cursive hands, whilst not universal, are common.

Second, educational materials form a closely related group of semi-private papers. These manuscripts may have been reviewed by a teacher or tutor, but were not usually intended for a life beyond their immediate instructional value. At one extreme, the group might include private copies of texts in Greek, Hebrew, or Arabic, as well as mathematical calculations; and, at the other end of the scale, basic exercises that might be categorized as juvenilia. In its most social form, this material includes the presentation manuscripts of Latin and Greek verse prepared by the schoolboys at Westminster and Eton. Generally, these manuscripts were written with greater care than private papers.

Third, there are documents that were intended to circulate through personal and scribal networks as socially communicated texts, including letters to family and friends, works of scholarship,[27] and separates or booklets of verse and prose from which copies were to be taken. Private correspondence might cover a great many issues, and it is sometimes difficult to draw a line between the political and the personal as both might be touched on in the same letter; likewise, letters by scholars and antiquaries provide a rich source of information about the book-trade as well as intellectual and political matters in Britain and Europe. These exchanges were not always confined to the recipient: for instance, the boys at Westminster knew of Camden's European friends.[28] The writing of letters between women, as well, was a sign of status as writer and recipient could maintain familiarity at a distance owing to their skill.

As with letters, social connections were the link that enabled access to the separates and booklets that formed the underlying documents for the private compilations that were clearly put together from disparate sources. Some of these loose items survive. Usually, manuscripts of this kind are more carefully written in slightly larger script than the private

[27] See, Woudhuysen, *Sir Philip Sidney and the Circulation of Manuscripts*, 116–33.
[28] G. Goodman, *The Court of King James the First, to which are added letters*, 2 vols. (London, 1839), 126.

copies (although there will always be exceptions) because they were intended to be passed from hand to hand. The material was most often written on single folio, and sometimes quarto, sheets.

Fourth, local archives, record offices, and some private owners, hold considerable quantities of estate papers that document the household and business transactions of a family: accounts, rentals, leases, marriage contracts, inventories, and much else besides. Some of this material was written by the family, other items were prepared by stewards and notaries, generally in table-books, or on quired sheets, with property transactions written on parchment. Often in the same collections as these records are other personal papers and correspondence. Family archives have been of greater interest to economic and social historians than literary scholars, but they provide much contextual information: the management of an estate required literacy, numeracy, and a clear hand, as details about property, assets, or finances might be required at any time. Hence, an employee who wrote regularly, such as a steward or tutor, might be asked to help with other transcriptions. Estate papers, therefore, record the activities of a household and its staff, and thus the identity of those who might compile other documents for the family.

Fifth, collections of political, professional, and administrative papers were prepared by secretaries and other trained professionals.[29] This material includes assize, customs, and tax records; the acts, speeches, political papers, and correspondence of government and its officials, some of which was scribally circulated; chancery proceedings; parish records, including the minutes of parish wardens, and ecclesiastical visitations, inquisitions, and interrogations; wills, probates, wards and prerogative court of Canterbury administrations; the documents of city corporations; bills, and business papers; records of the guilds and companies as well as the schools, universities and Inns of Court; legal opinions, advice tracts; and so on. These papers are vitally important for our understanding of early modern society, and some have been edited. The modern printed record, however, emphasizes the information they contain over the people who kept them; the lives of secretaries, lawyers, physicians, clerks, and clergy involved more than their professional duties: Eleazar Hodgson, for instance, was a physician who circulated copies of poems by Donne.[30] Along with the country gentry, students, and scholars, the professional elite were the primary consumers of written and printed material. In order to understand their involvement

---

[29] See Woudhuysen, *Sir Philip Sidney and the Circulation of Manuscripts*, 66–87.
[30] Beal, *In Praise of Scribes*, 92: Beal incorrectly identifies Hodgson as a law student; the list by Francis Davison that identifies him is British Library Harley MS 298, ff.159ʳ–160ʳ.

in manuscript activities, we have to locate them back to their working environments and the documents that they produced.

Sixth, manuscripts were produced, whether as a record of events or as works of imagination, belief, or knowledge, with the intent that they be the principal copy to be preserved, to be presented to another, or else to serve as the source document for later publication in manuscript, print, or through performance as plays, speeches, or sermons. These papers might be authorial, scribal, or secretarial, but in most cases they were not the work of a professional scrivener. With these manuscripts, terms such as fair or foul papers are not particularly helpful in describing documents that vary from those prepared with immaculate care to others that were replete with deletions, insertions, interlineations, and marginal additions. In most cases, the usual format for this material was quired folio sheets, but other formats are not unknown depending on the context for which the manuscript was prepared. For printed books, most manuscript copy does not survive, and we do not usually know in what condition the papers were before text was set, though comments by printers suggest that sometimes the copy was less than satisfactory.[31]

Seventh, and finally, there are the manuscripts that were prepared by professional scriveners for clients and customers. Like members of the Stationers' Company, scriveners belonged to a guild that was originally known as the Writers of the Court Letter in the fifteenth-century, and that was incorporated as the Company of Scriveners from 1617.[32] Members were apprenticed and trained in the calligraphic arts, as well as in the preparation of financial, legal, and other documents. They had a dual function: first, a scrivener was like an early modern copy shop producing manuscripts to order, and sometimes in advance; second, they prepared legal documents and were moneylenders. It was this latter function that led to their eventual mutation into merchant banks. Hence, a scrivener might copy or make public a wide array of material, including much that has been outlined above, such as compilations of verse, correspondence, speeches, presentation copies, advice texts, and legal documents like indentures, bonds, bills, and wills: Milton's father was the scrivener who prepared William Camden's testament in 1623.[33]

---

[31] See, McKitterick, *Print, Manuscript and the Search for Order*, 117–23; J. K. Moore, *Primary Materials Relating to Copy and Print in English Books of the Sixteenth and Seventeenth Centuries* (Oxford, 1992: OBS 24). Sometimes, as well, private documents (such as Laud's *Diary*) served as copy for the press: a use for which they were never intended.

[32] See, F. W. Steer (ed.), *Scriveners' Company Common Paper 1357–1628: With a Continuation to 1678* (London, 1968). For a survey of the London scriveners, see: Woudhuysen, *Sir Philip Sidney and the Circulation of Manuscripts*, 52–66 and 174–203. See also, p. 184 below.

[33] Camden's will is PROB 11/142, ff.351ᵛ–2ʳ.

We know very little about the organization of a scrivener's business, or of their relationship with the printed trade.[34] Beal has reproduced an image of a German shop in the mid-sixteenth-century that shows a master and three assistants, one perhaps an apprentice, at work.[35] There are a variety of documents—an indenture, bound volumes, rolls, and loose sheets hung up to dry; there are different working areas, including a sloping desk, a counter and a desk of the more usual kind. There is an hourglass to keep time, and various writing implements. It is likely that these circumstances are not too different to those found in the late medieval period, or the early seventeenth-century.[36] It is possible, of course, that the scriptorium may have offered other services, such as the retailing of paper and writing materials, including precut quills.

When a customer wanted a manuscript to be copied, several things could happen. A scrivener would want to establish what kind of copy was required, whether it was to be on ordinary or higher-quality paper, or else parchment, whether special pen work was necessary, the number of copies required, and the time available for the work to be done. If it was to be a single copy of a short document then it might be prepared by a single scribe; but if it was lengthy, or if multiple copies were required, then the work might be divided. One way of doing this was for one scribe to copy the first and another the second part of a document, and for them to then exchange parts. Equally, if a single copy of a larger document was wanted quickly, it might be broken into booklets with each scribe responsible for a section. The important point about these arrangements was their flexibility: sometimes a scribe would simply take over from another in the middle of a page, or even in mid-sentence.[37]

Professional documents have a distinctive appearance: the layout of the page is consistent, the handwriting regular, level (not sloping upwards or downwards), and fair; if there are several hands, they will be highly skilled. Typical manuscripts were usually prepared in folio gatherings, and they are frequently found bound as a sammelbände.[38] Common texts available by scribal copy include political letters and papers, relations of events and proceedings, parliamentary speeches, views of contemporary political issues, discourses on marriages and the arraignments of nobles, treason reports and Star Chamber proceedings,

---

[34] For a survey, see Woudhuysen, *Sir Philip Sidney and the Circulation of Manuscripts*, 58–9.
[35] Beal, *In Praise of Scribes*, 12–13.
[36] See, Rouse, *Illiterati et uxorati*.
[37] Beal, *In Praise of Scribes*, 77–90 with illustrations.
[38] See the catalogue of the Feathery scribe: Beal, *In Praise of Scribes*, 211–68.

negotiations of state, historical synopses, observations on privileges and ancestry, and similar matters of antiquarian and political interest. These texts were not generally available through the printed book-trade. The people who acquired these items would employ the services of a scrivener for their will and other personal documents, and they were also those who were most likely to seek a scrivener's services as a moneylender.

The reason for having made distinctions by the types of manuscript and their context in this way is to shift the emphasis from a concern with content towards the appearance of the page. It is only possible to develop a sense of how manuscripts look and differ in their scribal and formal characteristics if a wide range of material is examined. In many cases, the context will make it obvious as to the origins of the document involved: a personal compilation of verse in a small pocketbook in what is else a collection of estate papers would indicate that the manuscript is a private copy of socially circulated texts by a member of the family who is probably identifiable from other items such as correspondence. There are, however, many manuscripts that lack the immediate associative evidence in which to situate them. For these items, the appearance of the page will suggest something about the original context.

The question 'Who was responsible for this manuscript?' is one that is often insolvable, but that does not mean that the manuscript does not leave a trail of clues and an indication of its likely origins. The paper, format, script, and textual history all reveal something about when and by whom a manuscript was prepared. For instance, British Library Harley MS 4064 is a quarto sammelbände that was brought together at the end of the seventeenth-century. In its midst is a verse compilation that was copied c.1610–12 by two scribes: scribe A, was responsible for the miscellany of items by Jonson, Roe, Edward Herbert, and others with which the collection begins; whilst scribe B stepped in to help with the copying of one of Jonson's poems (figure 4.6), before resuming later to copy the poems by Donne. The quarto format and rough-hewn hand of scribe B, suggests that this was not a professional copy, but rather a document prepared by the members of a household.[39] In comparison, National Library of Wales Peniarth MS 444C, includes a genealogy of Venetia Digby and Jonson's poem to her sons. It is a professional manuscript with a single autograph correction in Jonson's hand (figure 4.7): he engaged a professional scrivener because by the 1630s his tremor made calligraphy difficult.

---

[39] The Donne material is part of the Group One tradition: I have discussed the relation of the manuscript to the tradition and the dating in my forthcoming *Jonson and Donne: Manuscript Traditions, Connections, and Revisions.*

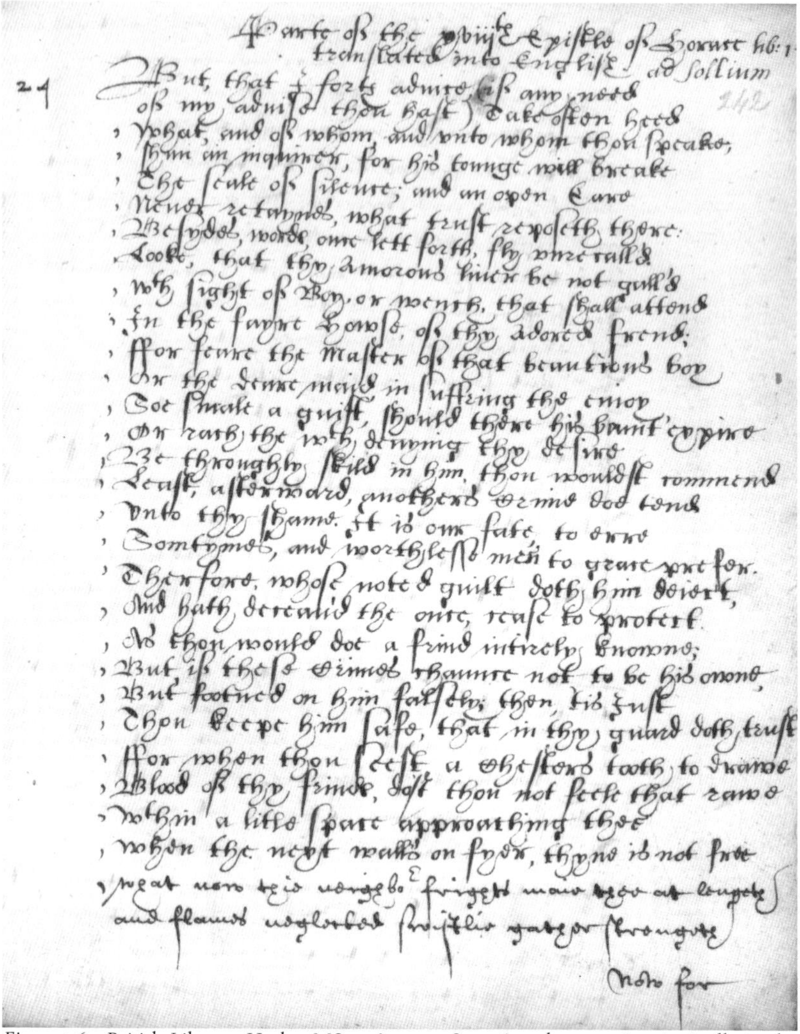

Figure 4.6 British Library, Harley MS 4064, p. 238; c.1612: the page is principally in the hand of scribe B, with the final two lines and pagination by scribe A.

Presentation manuscripts, such as Peniarth 444C or *The Masque of Queenes* typically bear signs of the care with which they were prepared. As well as the script, superior paper and either a gilt vellum or gilt goatskin binding are indications of a special status.[40] Manuscripts like these might either be prepared by the author, or by a professional on the author's behalf.

[40] British Library, Royal MS 18.A.xlv: *The Masque of Queenes* has been rebound.

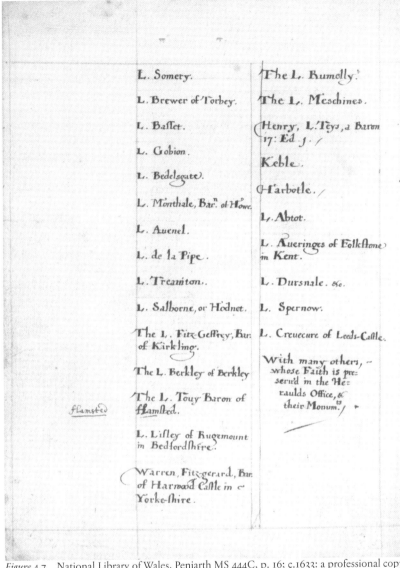

L. Somery.

L. Brewer of Torbey.

L. Baffet.

L. Gobion.

L. Bedelsgate.

L. Monthale, Bar. of Howe.

L. Auenel.

L. de la Pipe.

L. Treanton.

L. Salborne, or Hodnet.

The L. Fitz-Geffrey, Bar. of Kirkling.

The L. Berkley of Berkley

The L. Touy Baron of ffamfted.

L. Lifley of Rugemount in Bedfordſhire.

Warren, Fitzgerard, Bar. of Harmood Caſtle in & Yorke-ſhire.

ffamſted

The L. Rumolly.

The L. Meschines.

Henry, L. Teys, a Baron 17: Ed. j.

Keble.

Harbotle.

L. Abtot.

L. Aueringes of Folkſtone in Kent.

L. Dursnale. &c.

L. Spernow.

L. Creuecure of Leeds-Caſtle.

With many others, whose Faith is preſeru'd in the Heraulds Office, & their Monum. /

Figure 4.7   National Library of Wales, Peniarth MS 444C, p. 16; c.1633: a professional copy by a scribe with a single correction in Jonson's autograph.

One particularly unusual presentation manuscript was clearly never finished: Glasgow University Hunter MS U.8.27 is a six-sheet quarto, bound in gilt vellum that was intended as a presentation copy for Prince

Henry. It is unclear whether this copy of Richard Kellie's *The Tragedie of Lord Boroscho of Poland*, a poem written as a single stanza per page, is authorial or scribal, and no other witness survives. Although the poem itself is complete, each page was then intended to be finished with light decoration, including double rules above and below the text: it is this rubrication that is unfinished. What marks the manuscript out as the intended royal presentation copy, however, is another feature: it is written throughout in gold (figure 4.8).

As with printed books and pamphlets, manuscripts do not exist in isolation. Their production can be as various, and the network of their connections as complex, as any printed text. The script that they are written in can veer from the Petrarchan ideal of chasteness and clarity to a kind of visual chaos. To assume that the source documents for book production, whether manuscript or printed, were prepared to make life as easy as possible for those who followed defies logic, life, and the rich diversity of evidence. Hence, where statements about the nature of the copy for printed books exist, they usually indicate difficulty if only to excuse the faults.[41] It is only through recognizing the vicariousness of manuscript activity, and the specificity of its production, that we can begin to recover the life of the page and the interconnections between the written word and the printed book.

An Early Modern Printing-House: The Plantin-Moretus Museum

Before the practical aspects of printing are discussed, mention should be made of the Plantin-Moretus Museum in Antwerp, as it is the only sixteenth- and seventeenth-century printing-house that survives, and for that reason alone it offers a glimpse of the way in which such a business operated. The museum has very large archives, relating to all aspects of the book-trade, which again make it unique.[42] It is rather larger than most London printing-houses would have been, and has some features (a type foundry, a courtyard garden, paintings and designs by Rubens, and a large library) that a London business is unlikely to have shared; but with a little imagination, it is easy to make allowances and understand what a smaller business would have looked like.[43]

---

[41] McKitterick, *Print, Manuscript and the Search for Order*, 97–138.
[42] See, L. Voet, *The Golden Compasses: A History and Evaluation of the Printing and Publishing Activities of the Officina Plantiniana at Antwerp*, 2 vols. (Amsterdam, 1969–72). The museum has a useful website: http://museum.antwerpen.be/plantin_Moretus/index_eng.html. The St Bride's Library also has early printing material and a website: http://stbride.org.
[43] See also, D. F. McKenzie, *The Cambridge University Press 1696–1712: A Bibliographical Study*, 2 vols. (Cambridge, 1966), which includes much primary detail in the second volume.

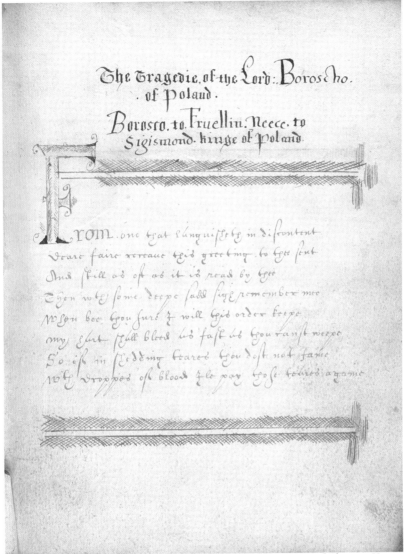

Figure 4.8   R. Kellie, *The Tragedie of Lord Boroscho of Poland*: University of Glasgow, Hunter MS U.8.27.

The printing-room is long and rectangular with compositor's cases, face to face, running three wide in rows along the courtyard side of the room (for natural light), with the presses on the other side. With seven presses, as well as a rolling press for engravings, the room is larger than one that would have housed two–three presses, but even so the Plantin establishment must have been crowded at full capacity. At the far end of the workshop is a second smaller room housing the other cases of type that were not in use, and pages of typeset material that have been tied up, rather than distributed, in expectation that they will be needed again. To the side of this room, there is a small antechamber and then the room where the corrector could read proof away from the noise of the workshop. There are other rooms, including a parlour, hall, storerooms and, upstairs, living rooms, the type foundry, and the library.

Distributed between the rooms, are various books, manuscripts, and other materials from the archives and library: medieval manuscripts and incunabula as well as other important items illustrating the history of the book; various portraits by Rubens and others of the family, and another of Seneca painted from a bust now in the Rubenshuis; an autograph manuscript by Justus Lipsius marked up for composition; a rough draft of a title-page; bills for type; ledgers of book sales; a finished drawing (again by Rubens) to be engraved; original woodcuts and copperplates for illustrations placed alongside the books in which they appeared.[44] These are but a few of the many hundreds of items displayed across more than 30 rooms. In the process, what is mapped is every stage possible in the production of a printed book as well as the cultural and economic context of the business. For the London trade, these records were comprehensively destroyed in the Great Fire.

The importance of the Plantin-Moretus Museum goes beyond the integrity of its buildings, materials, and documents: important as these aspects of the display are. It is evident that the curatorial focus provides an account of every aspect of an early modern printing-house at work. What is also evident, and it is a fact often overlooked by more abstract considerations of hand-press book production, is the sheer range of materials to do with manuscript and illustration that are present, and of the volume of written documents present in a printing-house. In almost every room, there is evidence of the connection between the media.

Print obscures manuscript. Faced with important literary texts whose histories have remained a source of speculation, scholars have tended to focus on the end product, the printed book, and so have simplified the processes though which they were produced and the materials that went into their making. The emphasis is often placed upon the presses, chases, type, cases, reglet, ornament stock, sheets, and so on, that were used to make a printed book, whilst 'the manuscript' from which a text

---

[44] See also, K. L. Bowen and D. Imhof, *Christopher Plantin and Engraved Book Illustrations in Sixteenth Century Europe* (Cambridge, 2008).

was set is treated as a necessary adjunct to the discussion. It is sometimes also assumed that any manuscript was destroyed through its use as copy. The first thing to remember, therefore, is that just because something does not survive does not mean that it did not once exist, or that it was discarded as soon as it ceased to be used: the Plantin-Moretus Museum demonstrates that the printed book is the consequence of a complex process of manuscript activity, and that manuscripts, whether for copy or commerce, were vital to the running of such printing-houses and the publishers with whom they sometimes worked.

Patterns of Production

In July 1586, following the decree of the Star Chamber, the Company of Stationers set a limit to the number of printing-houses and presses that were permitted. Up to that point, the printed book-trade had grown over the previous 80 years from the businesses of Wynkyn de Worde and Richard Pynson, to the 25 printing-houses and 53 presses that were accounted for under the new regulations, as well as those in Oxford and Cambridge. Subsequently, there were attempts to limit the number of presses to two for the more important businesses, and one for the remainder. These limits were adjusted from time to time, but they were not repealed (apart from for a short period during the Civil War), until 1695. It is also evident from the records that these limits were observed more in spirit than to the letter as many houses had an extra press, although it should perhaps be assumed that these generally served for proofing and small jobs rather than on a full-time basis.[45]

A London printing-house of the early seventeenth-century was a slightly larger establishment than one might at first expect. The smaller houses might easily employ eight to ten people; the larger houses, like the one run by William Stansby, as many as 15 to 17.[46] As well as the master, compositors, pressmen, apprentices, and a corrector, there would be someone responsible for the warehouse where the sheets were stored and copies made up. It is possible that some printers offered binding as an option for customers, as did some publishers. A larger business might have an overseer as well as the master; and with a smaller business some of the jobs might be performed by the same person. In addition, a cat served to protect the paper from rodents.

---

[45] E. Arber, *A Transcript of the Registers of the Company of Stationers of London 1554–1640 A.D.*, 5 vols. (London, 1875–94), II, 807–12 and V, lii; W. A. Jackson, *Records of the Court of the Stationers' Company 1602 to 1640* (London, 1957), 75; also, McKenzie, 'Printers of the Mind', 54–6.
[46] Bland, 'William Stansby and the Production of *The Workes of Beniamin Jonson*, 1615–16', 6.

The detailed accounts of the Cambridge University Press over the 16-year period 1696–1712 provide a day-to-day picture of a two-press printing-house at work.[47] They reveal a business that was at once more complex and less productive than had commonly been imagined. In his magisterial study, McKenzie analyzed, in detail, the daily work vouchers for pressmen and compositors, as well as all other material including the books that were printed. It was this analysis that led to his seminal article 'Printers of the Mind' that critiqued then-current assumptions about how the work in a printing-house was organised.[48] In the type, equipment, scale of activity, and working practices, Cambridge was not particularly different to the larger London houses (such as the Cross-Keys under Stansby) a century earlier.[49] If anything, the scale of the London trade allowed for greater complexity, not less.

What we now know from the Cambridge press is what an ordinary workman might have been expected to do in the course of a day. The second and third most efficient compositors averaged between 5,600 and 5,700 ens, whilst the average pica quarto sheet varied between 11,520 and 13,376 ens.[50] Hence an experienced compositor would have set half a sheet or one forme a day. Similarly, the average weekly output at the press was 13,200 impressions, with considerable variation, for a full crew of two pressmen.[51] This is equivalent to 22 formes (the equivalent of four compositors) at an average rate of output of 600 impressions, or 11 formes (two compositors) and an average of 1,200 impressions. For general purposes, many items, such as sermons and plays, would have been printed in runs of c.500 copies or a ream a sheet; reprints of godly pocketbooks, psalm-books, and schoolbooks were printed in runs of 1,200–1,500 copies. It should be emphasized that these figures are highly approximate, but they may serve as a useful guide when attempting to estimate the size of a business.

The essential point about the organization of a printing-house is that the distribution of resources will depend on the kinds of publication involved. Some businesses produced large quantities of a few titles, other houses many books with more limited print-runs, and still others a mix of the two. The first kind of establishment would tend to emphasize print-runs and presswork over composition; the second type would tend to require a greater number of compositors for the same volume of

---

[47] See, McKenzie, *The Cambridge University Press 1696–1712*.
[48] McKenzie, 'Printers of the Mind', 1–75.
[49] Bland, 'William Stansby and the Production of *The Workes of Beniamin Jonson*, 1615–16', 1–34.
[50] McKenzie, 'Printers of the Mind', 8–9.
[51] McKenzie, 'Printers of the Mind', 10–11.

presswork. The master's job was to balance all this out, not on a book-by-book basis, but according to the resources required and available.

By 1600, the average printing-house had anywhere from 15 to 25 or more cases of type. The three standard faces were roman, italic, and black-letter. As well as titling fonts, these faces were usually available in double pica (20 lines of text measuring 144 mm in depth), great primer (111–17 mm), english (94 mm), pica (82 mm), and long primer (67 mm). Other common sizes include small pica (72 mm), brevier (54 mm) and pearl (42 mm) for roman and italic. In addition, a printer may have had Greek, normally in a pica or english font, music, and possibly Hebrew or Anglo-Saxon,[52] Of these, the pica and english cases were in regular use, with the great and long primer availed upon with some frequency. Italic was typically used as a support font rather than as the principal face for composition, although there are exceptions. Thus, even if a printer had only one set of cases available per face and size, several compositors could be at work on different books at the same time.

The ability to work by concurrent composition was important for the press because print-runs would differ from one item to another: a small piece of jobbing work or a private commission might be required in only 200 copies, whereas an oft reprinted godly pocketbook might have a run of 1,500. By having more than one project on the go, these differences could be accommodated because a compositor could be reassigned: whether to read proof, or work from another text and case in order to set something else while the previous forme was waiting to be printed off, or else to distribute and sort type. The more cases in use, the more type available in any given size, and the more presses at work, the more complex this pattern of working activity could become.

Before 'Printers of the Mind', it had been assumed that books were produced one at a time, and that printing was organized in order to maximize productivity in relation to each and every book. Thus, calculations were made about how much type could be set in an hour in order to determine the speed with which a book was printed, and print-runs were estimated based on the number of impressions that might be perfected during a day.[53] These theories proved to be wildly inaccurate and far removed from the evidence provided by the Cambridge archives. Whilst Hinman demonstrated that the first Shakespeare folio was set by forme (that is the side of a sheet of paper), many books were assumed to be set seriatim, or page by page. Seriatim setting was then

---

[52] See, Gaskell, *New Introduction*, 9–56 and 108–117. A case weighed c.50 kg (116lbs).
[53] For instance, Hinman, *The Printing and Proof-Reading of the First Folio of Shakespeare*, I: 39–51.

used to explain conspicuous type shortages and other anomalies in the production process.

The advantage of the book-by-book model was its convenience, as it allowed an item to be studied in isolation from the rest of the output, without requiring a thorough investigation of everything produced by the relevant printing-house. Hence conclusions were drawn that, inevitably, reinforced existing assumptions about the popularity of the early modern drama. The problem is that the theory did not reflect the practical day-to-day realities where several items were going through the press at the same time. Of course, some of the analytical methods had their usefulness (for instance, the study of running-titles), but they were often applied without understanding the connections between all the output being produced at a given time. Hence any generalization made from the analysis could not be sustained, such as exact production runs, or in their use as evidence relating to specific stop-press interruptions.

In studying the organization of a printing-house, two sources had informed the traditional model. The first was the first English manual, Moxon's *Mechanick Exercises for the Whole Art of Printing*, published in 1683.[54] Moxon explained how a book was printed, and the activities involved in hand-press production: hence, the *Mechanick Exercises* offers a contemporary account of the practices of the trade, the materials used, and the concerns of the people involved. It is filled with sage advice about best practices. What it does not do is explain how such activities were integrated in a busy daily production schedule, or the variety of responsibilities that any one individual might encompass: composition, presswork, proof correction, oversight, and warehousing were all treated as separate functions of the business.

The second model for book-by-book production was the private press movement of the late nineteenth and early twentieth centuries, which celebrated printing as an artisan craft. The private presses, which set themselves against industrialized mass-market methods, used small-scale methods to publish deluxe volumes of famous texts in limited print-runs: their source of inspiration was William Morris's Kelmscott Press, which in turn had drawn upon fifteenth-century books including those of Nicolas Jenson.[55] The private press hand-printed books remain collector's items and have been studied in their own right, but they were not produced on the same scale, or for the same reasons, as early

[54] See chapter 1, n. 42 (p. 16).
[55] See, W. S. Peterson, *The Kelmscott Press: A History of William Morris's Typographical Adventure* (Oxford, 1991); also, M. Tidcombe, *The Doves Press* (London, 2002); R. Cave and S. Manson, *A History of the Golden Cockerel Press 1920–1960* (London, 2002).

modern texts.[56] What the private press did ensure was the survival of craft knowledge that could be applied in practical ways, and much of the best bibliographical work reflected this. McKenzie, for instance, composed and printed classroom texts for his students at the Wai-te-Ata Press in Wellington.[57] The period of greatest success for the private press, however, coincided both with the advent of journals with an interest in the history of typography, such as *The Dolphin* and *The Fleuron* (the latter edited by Stanley Morison), and the publication, in 1927, of McKerrow's *An Introduction to Bibliography*.

Drawing on Moxon, and practical knowledge, McKerrow explained the activities of an early modern printing-house in simplified terms.[58] His concern was to separate the various aspects of book production in order that students of early modern literature could understand the components of the printing process, and describe what they saw. His primary example for book production was that of a quarto, as many literary texts, such as plays, were printed in this format. He did not, at any point, suggest that books were printed one at a time—that was a later assumption made by Bowers.[59] McKerrow's *Introduction* became the modern Moxon, and focused the definition of bibliography on print, rather than on all forms of textual production. As a consequence, it occluded the connections between manuscript and print.

The kind of flexibility in working practices that is clearly visible in manuscripts prepared by professional scriveners must be equally true of work in a printing-house: there is no reason why one compositor might not take over from another mid-page, mid-line, or mid-word if that was required: all a compositor had to do was pass the composing stick to a colleague, or complete the line and let another take over. Equally, the second compositor might only set a few lines before the first resumed. If two cases of the same type were in use at the same time, then that could lead to the mixing of sorts when the type was redistributed after the forme had been printed and washed. Similarly, while one forme was

---

[56] See, R. Cave, *The Private Press*, 2nd edn. (New York and London, 1983).

[57] The press also issued small volumes of poetry including Bill Manhire's *How to Take Your Clothes Off at a Picnic* and Alan Lonie's *Courting Death*, and published an occasional journal *WORDS*. At that time, it was housed in a garage in Waiteata Rd, just below the library at Victoria University of Wellington. Students in the 'Literary Scholarship' course were taught hand-press book production; a class that McKenzie continued to teach at Oxford.

[58] R. B. McKerrow, *An Introduction to Bibliography for Literary Students* (Oxford, 1927): Bodleian Library, Oxford, 258 d. 352 is the copy of Falconer Madan and James McManaway, with their annotations.

[59] Although not directly stated, it is implied in the discussion of printing-house procedure: see, F. T. Bowers, 'Notes on Running-Titles as Bibliographical Evidence', *The Library*, IV: 19 (1938), 315–38.

opened up for stop-press correction at the press, another might have a proof pulled, so that the corrector could continue with his work. Naturally, the pattern of work one day might be rather different from the next because no two days were exactly the same: a small piece of jobbing work, like a playbill or ballad, might interrupt some other item at the press, or some funeral verses might be needed rather more quickly than the large folio that several of the compositors were working on. These details are almost impossible to reconstruct, particularly as many single-sheet broadsides have not survived.

The survival of the printed evidence is a significant issue because, in truth, we do not know how much has been lost. This is not a mere matter of there being a gap in the record; it makes the reconstruction of printing-house activity inherently less reliable. Sometimes there are clues: reprinted books might state that they are 'the seventh edition', and if they do then a gap in the sequence is suggestive. Many ballads, broadsides, and hornbooks have perished without trace. Schoolbooks and almanacs were reprinted annually, but survive sporadically. These gaps are difficult to place in context. In at least one case, however, we can link a lost pamphlet with another alongside of which it was printed. Owing to the sheets still being wet, an offset image of the title-page *A Proclamation touchinge the K. of Spaine* has left its trace on the back of an account of James VI's entry into Edinburgh with his new wife in 1590. No copy of the offset pamphlet is known to survive (figure 4.9).

If lost output poses one kind of problem for reconstructing the evidence of a printing-house, shared work poses another. Some items were printed for publishers, others were printed for the house, or as a private commission (these can usually be identified by the pagination being within parentheses at the top centre of the page), and some items were shared with other houses to expedite a book. Shared printing is a more common phenomenon than most bibliographers realize and many entries in the main catalogues fail to identify the involvement of printers whose names are not on the title-page.[60] The difficulties that shared printing pose are twofold: first, some of the known output of a press will contain the work of other houses; and second, some of a printer's output will not be identified. This is a problem that will be returned to in the following chapter where the methods of analysis and identification will be described. For now, what it is important to realize is that, day to day, compositors and pressmen may have been at work on more items than the imprints alone might have one expect.

---

[60] P. W. M. Blayney, 'The Prevalence of Shared Printing in the Early Seventeenth Century', *PBSA*, 67 (1973), 437–42.

Figure 4.9 *A proclamation made by the K. of Spaine* (no known copy): offset image from British Library, C.33 b.56, *A ioyfull receiuing of Iames the sixt . . . and Queene Anne his wife* (STC 14425.3; 1590: entered 3 June), A4ᵛ.

Estimation and Casting Off

Before a compositor could begin to set a book in type, it was necessary for an estimate to be made of the length of the text, and then for this figure to be divided by the amount of type that would be required per page (in ens), in order that the quantity of paper required could be calculated. Conventions of page design and layout determined certain things, whilst the size of the platen provided a technological limit as to how great an area of type could be impressed at one time: the standard type faces of 82 mm pica and 94 mm english existed in an approximate relationship of 7:8 (i.e. eight lines of pica set solid had the same depth as seven lines of english). The standard page depth was 36–8 lines of pica (or 31 lines of english) for a quarto, and 48 lines of english for a folio. The width of the measure was adjustable, and normally varied between 40 and 44 ens for quarto, and 58–64 ens for folio. This ability to make small adjustments allowed printers to determine a best fit between the quantity of text to be set and the number of sheets required.

For convenience, the following example will assume that the printer planned to set the text in either pica or english, and that the format was to be quarto. The author or publisher (who may or may not have been the printer) had already been to visit a chaplain at Lambeth Palace to have the text allowed.[61] The manuscript was 100 pages, with c.2,000 ens of text per handwritten page as calculated by selectively sampling and counting sections of text and averaging the result. With an estimate of c.200,000 ens of text, the printer would seek to match the size of the manuscript to the closest number of whole printed sheets. Hence the estimated count was divided by the number of ens per sheet according to various standard layouts. Hence, if 200,000 ens was to be set in pica:

lines ×	width ×	pages =	ens =	sheets
36	40	8	11,520	17.36
36	42	8	12,096	16.53
37	40	8	11,840	16.89
37	42	8	12,432	16.09
37	44	8	13,024	15.35
38	42	8	12,768	15.66
38	44	8	13,376	14.95

---

[61] See, W. W. Greg, *Licensers of the Press, &c. to 1640* (Oxford, 1962); also, P. W. M. Blayney, 'The Publication of Playbooks', in J. D. Cox and D. S. Kastan (eds.), *A New History of the Early English Drama* (New York, 1997), 404 (383–422).

Similarly, if the text was to be set in english, then the calculation is the same, except that an adjustment needs to be made for the greater width of the type: i.e. the body of a letter is not only taller (hence the fewer number of lines per page), every letter is proportionally bigger. As seven lines of english are the same height as eight lines of pica, so the same amount of text can be set in seven pages of pica as in eight pages of english. The strictly correct way to make this calculation is to divide the 20-line pica height by the 20-line height of the other type (e.g. 82 ÷ 67 for brevier, 82 ÷ 94 for english, and 82 ÷ 117 for great primer) and keep the number of pages as standard; however, early modern printers are unlikely to have done complex fractional calculations, but rather would have relied on standard rules of thumb. Thus, a 200,000-en text set in english, rather than pica, would have had more sheets:

lines ×	width ×	pages =	ens	=	sheets
31	40	7	8,680		23.04
31	42	7	9,114		21.94
31	44	7	9,548		20.94

Having determined the layout of the page, the next thing that the printer had to do was cast off copy, not to determine the organization of work, but to confirm that the estimate was accurate. As McKenzie has remarked:

> We must recall too that neither Moxon, Stower, nor any other early grammar mentions casting off as a means of enabling work to be set by formes. In every case it is . . . a device for costing, and for determining the paper required, not for organizing work.[62]

There are 27 examples of manuscript cast-off copy that survive from before 1640, and 100 in all that survive before 1700.[63] Perhaps the most famous of these is the copy for Book V of Richard Hooker's *Ecclesiasticall Politie* from 1597.[64] Just as with these known examples, the printer (or overseer) would have gone through the manuscript counting the

---

[62] McKenzie, 'Printers of the Mind', 46.

[63] J. K. Moore, *Primary Materials Relating to Copy and Print in English Books of the Sixteenth and Seventeenth Centuries* (Oxford, 1992: OBS 24), 11–30.

[64] See, P. Simpson, *Proof-Reading in the Sixteenth, Seventeenth and Eighteenth Centuries* (Oxford, 1935), 76–9; W. S. Hill et al. (eds.). *The Folger Library Edition of the Workes of Richard Hooker* (Cambridge MA and Binghamton NY, 1977–93), I, xiii–xxii, xxix–xxxviii, 359–72 and II, xiii–xliii.

words, averaging the number of words per line, with part lines allowed at the ends of paragraphs until 37 lines of the page had been counted out. The text would then be marked with a closing square parenthesis] and the next signature was written in the margin to indicate where one page ended and the new began. The process was then begun over again until all the text was so divided up. With verse, matters were simpler, as the printer only had to count the number of lines; and with regular stanzas, estimation might be done simply by counting them out.

Let us assume that the printer decided that the text should be set to a measure of 40 ens, a depth of 37 lines, and that the type size was pica roman. The estimate, that the text of the book will occupy 17 sheets, had been confirmed by the casting off. Having made these calculations, the printer allowed a sheet for the preliminaries (title-page, dedication, preface, and associated verse). At this point, the publisher and printer knew that the retail price of the book, at 1/2*d* a sheet stab-stitched but not bound, was 9*d*.[65] If a publisher was supplying the paper, as would normally be the case, the printer had only to estimate the production cost and the time until delivery. If the printer was publishing on his own account, then he had to factor in both printing costs and paper to calculate the break-even point. That subject, the economics of book production, will be resumed in a later chapter.

Once a manuscript had been cast off, any page could, theoretically, be set in any order, and copy could be divided between compositors, or printing-houses. Each page and forme could be set as a self-contained unit without having to set the pages in between: thus pages 1, 4–5, and 8 (the outer forme of a quarto) were typically set first and, once they had been corrected, were printed while pages 2–3 and 6–7 (the inner forme) were set next. Any slight errors in calculation that were not resolved by the division of paragraphs could be fixed during composition by the adjustment of spacing between words. If the text did not fit an exact number of sheets, the final page or leaf might be blank, or used for an errata list if this was not set along with the preliminaries.

Typography, Layout, and Impression

Both Moxon and Gaskell have described the work of compositors and pressmen.[66] Rather than reiterate their focus on processes and

---

[65] See, F. R. Johnson, 'Notes on English Retail Book-Prices, 1550–1640', *The Library*, v: 5 (1950), 83–112; D. J. McKitterick, "Ovid with a Littleton': The Cost of English Books in the Early Seventeenth Century', *TCBS*, XI: 2 (1997), 184–234.
[66] Gaskell, *New Introduction*, 5–141; Moxon, *Mechanick Exercises*, 191–311.

materials, what follows is concerned with how those means were used to achieve specific ends. In particular, Moxon made a number of comments about best practice, such as even setting, and the avoidance of what the trade called 'pigeon holes', that is the excessive spacing between words, and similarly of vertical rivers of space that open up like an internal fracture within a paragraph: tight composition, so long as legibility and word separation were preserved, was encouraged. 'A Good *Compositer*', noted Moxon, 'is ambitious . . . to make the meaning of his *Author* intelligent to the *Reader*, as to make his Work shew graceful to the Eye, and pleasant in Reading'.[67]

To begin with, the appearance of the page was defined by the size (both height and width) of the face chosen for composition, the choice of format, and the width of the measure. Hence, once a book had been cast off, and the compositor had been told what type was to be used and the proportions of the page, work could commence. For a 37-line, 40-en page, the compositor would take a piece of reglet 40 ens long, or five 4–em quads, and place these in a brass composing stick that was fixed on the right and movable on the left (the stick was held in the left hand). The left gauge was then locked into position so that all lines of type would be exactly the same length. The type was set upside down, left to right, so that if one could imagine it flipped through its vertical axis and the paper below the type, the text would then appear as it ought.

The compositor worked from a pair of type cases placed one above the other. The upper case contained the less used sorts such as capitals, small capitals, and numerals. The size of the compartments for each sort (letter or number) was the same. The lower case was different, as the most commonly used letters had larger compartments in the middle of the case: *a*, *e*, *n*, and *d* being in immediate proximity. The compositor memorized the layout of this case and relied as much on tactile sense as visual confirmation that each letter was in the correct compartment, as different letters are of different width.

The formal requirements of the measure, in turn, influenced the spacing used for justification and the layout of the page. When setting, a compositor started with mids (there are two mids to an en, or one thick and one thin to an en), and then adjusted the spaces as required once the line was complete. If a line was slightly too long, the compositor would look for combinations such as 'say once' to replace the mid with a thin between the words; if the line was too short, the spacing was selectively increased by changing mids to thicks where this would be less noticeable.

---

[67] Moxon, *Mechanick Exercises*, 207–11.

Owing to the flexibility of early modern spelling, a compositor might also change such words as 'easy' to 'easie', or '(s)he' to '(s)hee'. In this way, the more obvious pigeon holes could be avoided. If an initial letter was required, either the ornament or a wooden block of the same size was first put in place, and then composition proceeded as usual. After every six-to-eight lines, the text that had been set would be transferred to a galley.

The rigid structure of the page, and the consistency of letterforms introduced a precise and ordered structure to the printed book; whereas, with manuscript, variation was inevitable, even when professional scribes had to write to strict requirements, and they were skilled at adapting their hand to the nature of the text being prepared. The physical characteristics of type also introduced limitations as to what could be done with a text once it had been printed. With a written document, insertion, deletion, contraction, correction, and, to some extent, erasure are straightforward activities. Even for formal codices, uniformity was always more of an ideal than a practice: the written hand is always variable in its use. Further, in manuscript, space involves the absence of the writing instrument from the page. The reverse was true of print: space was a piece of solid type that had to be physically inserted into the line.

The appearance of a book was shaped not only by the design of the type, but by the characteristics of the hand-press. Once type had been transferred to a galley and locked within a forme, the maximum area that could be impressed upon a sheet of paper was not defined by the size of the sheet, but by the pressure that could be applied (in pounds per square inch) on the type, given the mechanism of the screw and the wooden structure of the press, which consequently limited the maximum size of the platen.[68] In practical terms, an area of little more than forty by thirty centimetres was printed at two pulls per forme including the inner margins between the pages of type; normal practice was less cramped, though it was theoretically possible to print up to an area of 49 × 39 cm.[69] The most common paper size for printing was pot (approximately 40 × 31 cm), with the maximum rarely exceeding crown (45 × 35 cm).

It is that consciousness about the visual construction of typography (the way in which a text is filled out and pieced together, rather than filled in) that separates the visual aesthetics of the written and printed word. The principal advantages of type (its legibility, regularity, and re-usability) exposed its inflexibility in other ways. Hence, print developed a new diversity of presentation as compositors manipulated the visual and spatial structure within which they had to work. Typography evolved in

[68] G. Pollard, 'Notes on the Size of the Sheet', *The Library*, IV: 22 (1941), 130–4.
[69] Gaskell, *New Introduction*, 120–4.

response to both the visual appearance of the text and the meaning and purposes to which it would be put. Even the disposition of margins defined the uses of space within and around the text.[70]

To be sure, many early modern books were printed within what, on reflection, are well-established conventions, and these are formats and layouts that must have seemed instinctive to members of the trade. There is no manual of the age that says that a book of godly devotion has to be set in octavo or duo-decimo, or a play in quarto. The trade understood, in ways that now need greater explication, that certain books suited certain formats, and that the more important books might be printed in typesizes and formats that were a size larger than standard practices. At one level, a printer was always aware that a book had to be adaptable and stable in its binding: physical considerations of malleability and structure were primary when considering the object in hand. The specific market for a book, or pamphlet, might equally shape trade attitudes as to the care with which it was produced: a news pamphlet with a lifespan of a week would be treated with less attention to specific detail than the work of an important public figure whose book reflected on the publisher and the trade: it is important for students of literature to realize that c.1600 Shakespeare was not amongst the latter category.[71]

The way in which reception and use shaped format and presentation can be shown by the way in which a text might evolve through informal and formal manuscripts and then to print. The poems of Donne offer one obvious example: they circulated in separates and booklets, and were then copied individually, or in small groups, in commonplace books; or else they might be transcribed as a whole for personal collections. Some of the collections, such as the Dowden and Leconsfield manuscripts, were carefully prepared on special paper.[72] The 1633 *Poems*, on the other hand, is a standard trade publication intended for the mass market, printed as a pot quarto and set in english roman. The book had shifted from being a personal and, in the case of the Dowden or Leconsfield manuscripts, luxurious object, to a mass-produced public possession. The history of the manuscript and print traditions of Donne's poems demonstrate, as well, the way in which the two media were interrelated. Throughout the seventeenth-century, scriptoria existed in competition with the press, particularly for small-scale production and special needs.[73] Just as Henry

---

[70] A. W. Pollard, 'Margins', *The Dolphin*, 1 (1933), 67–80.
[71] See, Bland, 'The London Book-Trade in 1600', 450–63.
[72] Bodleian Library, MS Eng. Poet. e.99, and Cambridge University, Add MS. 8467. See also, P. Beal, *Index of English Literary Manuscripts: Volume I, 1450–1625*, 1, 243–564 and 566–8.
[73] See, H. Love, *Scribal Publication in Seventeenth-Century England*, 126–34.

Olney offered the editorial integrity of his perfect copy as the prime reason for having the *Essayes* of Sir William Cornwallis printed, so Donne used the scribal medium as a means for publishing his poems.[74]

If the link between manuscript and print is one way of understanding the evolution of a text through the media of production, then another is to consider the changes from edition to edition. Camden's *Britannia*, for instance, was regularly revised and enlarged by the author. The first edition (STC 4503) was entered in the Stationers' Register on 23 February 1586. Letters from that time indicate both Camden's anticipation of the book going to press and his frustration at the quality of the typography.[75] Printed by the Eliot's Court Press, it was a 35½-sheet pot octavo set in long primer roman to a measure of 36 ens and a depth of 40 lines.

Camden continued to work on *Britannia* throughout the following 24 years. The second edition of 1587 (STC 4504) was a 43-sheet pot octavo printed once more in long primer roman. By the third edition of 1590 (STC 4505), the book had expanded to a 50-sheet demy octavo, and the typesize was increased to pica roman. The format was unusual but, compared to the width and page-depth of a pica pot quarto, halved the paper required, though demy was more expensive than pot. A German edition was also printed during 1590. The next revision of 1594 (STC 4506) was a 94½-sheet pot quarto in eights. A sixth edition (STC 4507) was published in 1600 as a 114-sheet pot quarto in eights. Both these editions were again set in pica roman. The final Latin edition of 1607 (STC 4508) took this gradual enlargement to its logical conclusion. The book is a 233½-sheet crown folio, with large paper copies printed on demy, set in english roman to a measure of 70 ens and a depth of 55 lines.

The evolution of the *Britannia* through its various formats and types reflects both the labour of the author and the transformation of the book into a classic of its age. Between 1586 and 1607, the text became nearly four and a half times longer and used more than six and a half times as much paper, the type had increased in size by a third, and Camden had quoted as evidence more than eight times as many inscriptions. Similarly the cost had risen from 2s6d in 1586, to 5s in 1594, whilst the edition of 1607 could scarcely have cost less than £1.[76]

---

[74] Olney claimed that 'hauing in my hands a perfect Copy', he was obliged to see them through the press, as the *Essayes* 'might haue beene by a mercenary hand fowly corrupted and altered in sence, and both in his absence and mine, deliuered to some Printer, who to make present gaine, would haue published them vnpolished, and deformed without any correction': W. Cornwallis, *Essayes* (STC 5775, 1600), A2ʳ⁻ᵛ.

[75] Camden to Jacob Ortelius, 3 February 1586 and undated, MS Smith 74, ff.2–3; see also, Bland, 'The Appearance of the Text', 104.

[76] F. R. Johnson, 'Notes on English Retail Book-prices, 1550–1640', 98.

The skill of the compositor lay not with the accuracy of the text alone, but with even spacing, the selection of appropriate types as well as avoidance of damaged sorts, the avoidance of loose setting that might cause type to drop from the register, and the judicious use of ornament. In particular, a decorative piece of printer's material could be employed to complement the literal concerns of the text whilst, at the same time, helping to stabilize the structure of a page that was only partially set with type. Devices, title-page borders, headpieces, type ornaments, factotums, ornamental initials, rules, and tailpieces were the stock items of decorative material, and were commonly employed with a sense of appropriateness. A well-chosen ornament reflected a degree of elegance and judicious taste on the part of the trade.

In the same way as a compositor wished to make the page pleasing to the eye, so the pressman was concerned to make a fair impression: that is to ensure that a page was evenly and well inked, that the type bit into the paper, and that the alignment of the page was square and consistent on both sides. Loose type might need to be rectified during the run, as the pressure of the platen could cause type to drop or spread. Care was taken to avoid ink in the wrong places (though sometimes a thumbprint might have left its record in the margin). When a printed sheet left a pressman's hands it was as yet untrimmed, with its full margins and deckle edge. Slightly imperfect sheets, and those printed before any stop-press corrections had been introduced, were not discarded but used like any other. Hence, whilst the workmen preferred to have made the proof and revises before printing began in earnest, this was not always possible as sometimes problems were noticed either by them or the author (or that person's representative), once printing had begun.

What the collation of multiple copies of the same book makes evident is that the concerns of compositors and pressmen were not those of a modern textual scholar. The accuracy of the text was not determined by a rigid adherence to the copy before them, but by the requirement that the final printed version could be read and understood: hence, matters of typography, layout, and register were their primary interest. Sometimes stop-press corrections involve nothing more than the adjustment of space, and more fuss could go into those details than ensuring that every last word and punctuation mark were as they ought to be. To the extent that contemporaries still regarded the printed book as a public reiteration of manuscript, what was wrong might easily, if so desired, be later corrected by a pen, as indeed many an author asked the readers to do in their errata.

5 Analysis and Evidence

SOMETIMES, it is necessary to investigate the physical characteristics of a manuscript or printed book with more precision than common descriptive methods alone would require. There are usually two reasons for doing this: either the enquiry is historical (greater clarity is required as to who produced the object, how, and when), or it is textual (an attempt is made to explain perceived deficiencies in the textual record and analyze how they came about). Clearly, these two lines of enquiry may be closely related if the item is a work of particular cultural interest, as with the analysis by Blayney of the 1608 quarto of *King Lear*, and the earlier study of the 1623 *Comedies, Histories, and Tragedies* by Hinman.[1] The association of document and content is not, however, to be assumed as the research might be deployed to resolve such non-textual matters as the date of an item and its place in a historical sequence, or the extent and proportions of shared activity in order to reconstruct the activity of a printing-house or scribe without a specific focus on a text or book. In fact, what the work of Blayney and Hinman illustrates is the risks that are involved when the working assumptions predetermine the results of the analysis. As so often, it is not the methods that are flawed, but the thinking that goes with them. Hence, in this chapter, the focus is on the processes of textual inscription and the traces that are left in the material record, as well as the way in which minor flaws, mistakes, and variant practices might be analyzed for the information that they yield, together with an example of how a simple physical detail can lead to broader questions about the assumptions made concerning a specific text—in this instance, the 1608 quarto of *King Lear*.

Manuscript and Manufacture

Both print and manuscript were prepared by hand: the differences that separate the media lie in the processes and materials involved, and the ways in which these can be read for the information that is latent in their arrangement. Hence, having looked through the page to see the paper, and determined the structure of the object in hand, the bibliographer is interested not only in the presence of ink (including its presence where it ought not to be, as with the image from an offset impression), but in its absence where it ought to be. The distinction that is made is the difference between texture (which records the processes by which

[1] P. W. M. Blayney, *The Texts of* King Lear *and Their Origins: Volume I, Nicholas Okes and the First Quarto* (Cambridge, 1982; Vol. 2 not published); C. Hinman, *The Printing and Proof-Reading of the First Folio of Shakespeare*.

the object was made and the temporal sequence of those events) and the text (which encodes the message or idea that initiated the processes of transmission). It is only once the former has been understood, that its relationship with the latter can be established.

It is, in fact, quite rare for a manuscript or printed text of any length to be prepared in a sequential order by one person for a sustained period of time without any interruption at all; nor should the processes of revision and replication be assumed to be linear and continuous. Yet this fact, which is so obvious from our own experience, is one we are less likely to perceive when possessed of a finished work that can be read from beginning to end. A text might be prepared by two or more different people at the same time, or at different times; or prepared by two or more different people in the same place, or different places. A forme might well be printed on one press, and the sheet then perfected on another.[2] To compound the matter, sometimes these differences are invisible, whilst on other occasions seeming differences are nothing of the kind. As a consequence, working assumptions need to be open to being revised with a frank recognition that, even when there is copious secondary information, any reconstruction will fail to anticipate fully the random and the irrecoverable variations that were woven through a daily routine. As McKenzie remarked, 'a narrow range of theories is less likely to embrace the complex possibilities of organisation within even quite a small printing-house'; or for that matter, one might add, the working arrangements of a scrivener, or secretary.[3]

The important thing to remember with manuscript and print is the human presence in their making: the difference between the media lies in the transparency and regularity of the signs. What is obvious in manuscript may be disguised by the processes of manufacture in print because of the apparent similarity of the materials used; whilst what might seem irregular in manuscript, such as the presence of two hands and therefore of two people, might be nothing more than one person with several hands, as with Sir George Buc, the Master of the Revels.[4]

[2] A modern analogy might be made with film production: when we watch a film, the work of the make-up artist, camera-hand, and film editor, as well as the rest of the crew who stand just outside the frame, are all usually invisible when the component parts are assembled and finished. When the production processes are intrusive, it typically involves a deliberate statement about the relationship between the art and its materials.

[3] McKenzie, 'Printers of the Mind', 61.

[4] See, W. W. Greg, 'Three Manuscript Notes by Sir George Buc', *Collected Papers*, 226–38; also, R. C. Bald, 'The *Locrine* and *George-a-Greene* Title-Page Inscriptions', *The Library*, IV: 15 (1935), 295–305. Buc was responsible for both the Bridgwater manuscript of the poems of Donne (Huntington Library, MS El 6893), which he wrote in a consistent single (and rather feminine) hand, and for British Library, Harley MS 3910, a verse miscellany which he prepared in a diversity of scripts.

Questionable Characters

It is not uncommon for manuscripts to be prepared in stages: sometimes these stages, and the relationship between the parts, are visually striking and can be identified as separate units; although the exact order of the parts, and the intervals between the sequences, may not be as obvious or as easy to determine as the differences are to recognize. Hence, the palaeographical evidence needs to be read alongside other physical details, such as changes in paper stock, the presence of stab-holes from an earlier sewing in one part of the manuscript and not another, or the presence of wormholes in one or more sections that are not extant throughout the manuscript as a whole. In essence, one is comparing information about the structure of the document with the sequences of the writing. When doing so, it should be borne in mind that the original block of material from which the manuscript evolved may not be at the beginning, with later additions then proceeding in a logical manner, but rather it may be surrounded by this later material.

Some of the examples cited elsewhere in this book illustrate the variety of ways in which a manuscript might have been prepared, and these range from the straightforward to the highly complex. Bodleian Library, Rawlinson Poetry MS 31, for instance, is a seven-quire, 26-sheet manuscript, on a single stock of paper, with twin watermarks written in a single professional hand (that of the Feathery scribe) from beginning to end over a relatively short duration.[5] Analytically, it would be very difficult to divide the stints for the work on this manuscript with any accuracy (changes in the intensity of the ink, for instance, may be owing to the quill being dipped afresh), and any reconstruction would be nothing else than imaginative guesswork. On the other hand, the fact that the scribe was a professional means that any associated manuscripts that share the same grape watermarks (figure 2.2; p. 33) would have been copied at much the same time. Hence, via the paper stocks, one would be able to get a sense of what other texts Feathery was working upon at the time that he copied the miscellany, and hence the work on that manuscript could be placed within the broader context of the business.[6]

The verse miscellany that is part of British Library Lansdowne MS 740 tells a very different story to that of the Rawlinson manuscript. Once again, it is copied in a single hand, but here there is more sense of the stages through which the manuscript evolved. The miscellany is copied on multiple paper stocks and there are subtle yet distinctive changes in the script. The earliest group of paper is to be found at ff.74–81, 87–91,

[5] The collation is given on p.69 above.
[6] See, Beal, *In Praise of Scribes*, 58–108 and 211–68.

and 94–7: these three sections consist of Overbury's *Wife* from c.1601–2 (the Lansdowne copy is also the earliest version of the first state of the poem), the Elizabethan libel 'Bashe', and a small group of poems that include two attacks on the marriage of Bishop Fletcher by Sir John Davies from 1595, Donne's 'The Storme' and 'The Calme' from 1596, and the elegy 'Marry and Love thy Flavia'.[7] The 'If' that begins the first poem on Fletcher has some decorative flourishes, which suggests that f.94 may have been the original opening leaf of the manuscript. Overall, these sections suggest greater care in the writing. Interleaved before, between, and after the three sections are other poems, particularly by Donne and Sir John Roe that have been added in at two or more later stages on different paper. Hence, the combination of evidence suggests that the manuscript evolved in several stages over a number of years before work ceased. Eventually, the remaining blanks were removed when the manuscript was bound as part of the sammelbände c.1680.

A third manuscript, British Library Harley, MS 4064 (which is related to Rawlinson Poetry MS 31 via an earlier state of the underlying papers), involves the work of two copyists: scribe A has an elegant secretary hand; scribe B one that is much more rough-hewn and which is clearly not professional. Scribe A is responsible for the first 23 poems; scribe B then copies the title of the next poem and the first 28 lines (figure 4.5, p. 102) before A resumes to copy the remainder of the poem and a further sequence of 22 poems; B then copied the remaining 45 items—it is these poems that are predominantly by Donne. In this case the first interruption looks like a matter of a few minutes: A is called away, and B takes over; when B resumes work later on, however, it is less evident whether this represents a continuation or a separate later stage. Scribe A finally paginated the manuscript when it was finished.

In comparison with the Harley manuscript, the work on Huntington Library HM 198 part 2, which may also be the product of a secretariat, looks as if it was much more complex, as it would appear to combine elements of separate preparation alongside concurrent activity. The manuscript can be divided into four subgroups with a single leaf of indeterminate relationship, and it involves the presence of five different scribes, one of whom (B) is responsible for organizing the collection as whole. In particular, B undertook all the work on the second sequence of papers (ff.57–79), which contain an early version of the poems of Dudley, Lord North, except for a short stint on f.63^{r-v} in the hand of A. Equally hand C writes across the two stocks of paper in the first section (ff.1–56), indicating that the paper does not represent different stages of

---

[7] The manuscript and the textual history of Overbury's *Wife* are discussed at length in Bland, *Jonson and Donne*.

the process. It seems possible that B was therefore at work on some of the North poems (figure 5.1) whilst other material was being copied by A and the others.[8] Equally, however, the final section of the manuscript seems to belong to a different stage of the transcription process than the other material. In general, the nature of the texts being copied indicates that whoever was responsible for its organization, and the material that the manuscript contains, had a relationship with the Inner Temple, which might explain why several people are involved (the hands may be those of law clerks).

The nature of manuscript, with its patterns of scribal activity, allows at least some understanding of the relationship between different hands and parts to emerge from a close study of a document. It is evident that the organization of activity could be as various as the work on any printed book: one or more people might be involved over a sustained period, or at different intervals, working concurrently or sequentially. There are issues, as well, about how far this information might be reconstructed to provide a certain narrative about the order of events, and the time over which they took place. For all that we may be able to point to some distinguishing features as being obvious, there remains much about even the most visible of differences that must be simply irrecoverable. With print, we lay over manuscript the opaque uniformity of type which erases the character of the underlying document, and we introduce a further layer of process that may complicate the material evidence. Not all things beneath the surface are always as they seem.

Lasting Impressions

With a manuscript, the script reveals whether we are working with an author's draft, with a fair or corrected copy, the work of an amanuensis, or with a later copy. With a printed book, unless it is otherwise stated in the prefatory materials, or the errata, that information is not evident, and we know little about the working conditions under which most texts were set and printed. Hence, differences in type and ornament have sometimes been studied in order to establish specific details about the production of a book, from the work on the composition and printing, to the relationship between different formes, and between different books at the press. By measuring type and counting sheets of paper, we can gain a sense of the scale of a business. These insights are no more than piecing together fragments from a damaged fresco.

---

[8] See also, M. Bland, 'Francis Beaumont's Verse Letters to Ben Jonson and "The Mermaid Club"', *English Manuscript Studies*, 12 (2005), 157–8 (139–79), and 159 for Hand A.

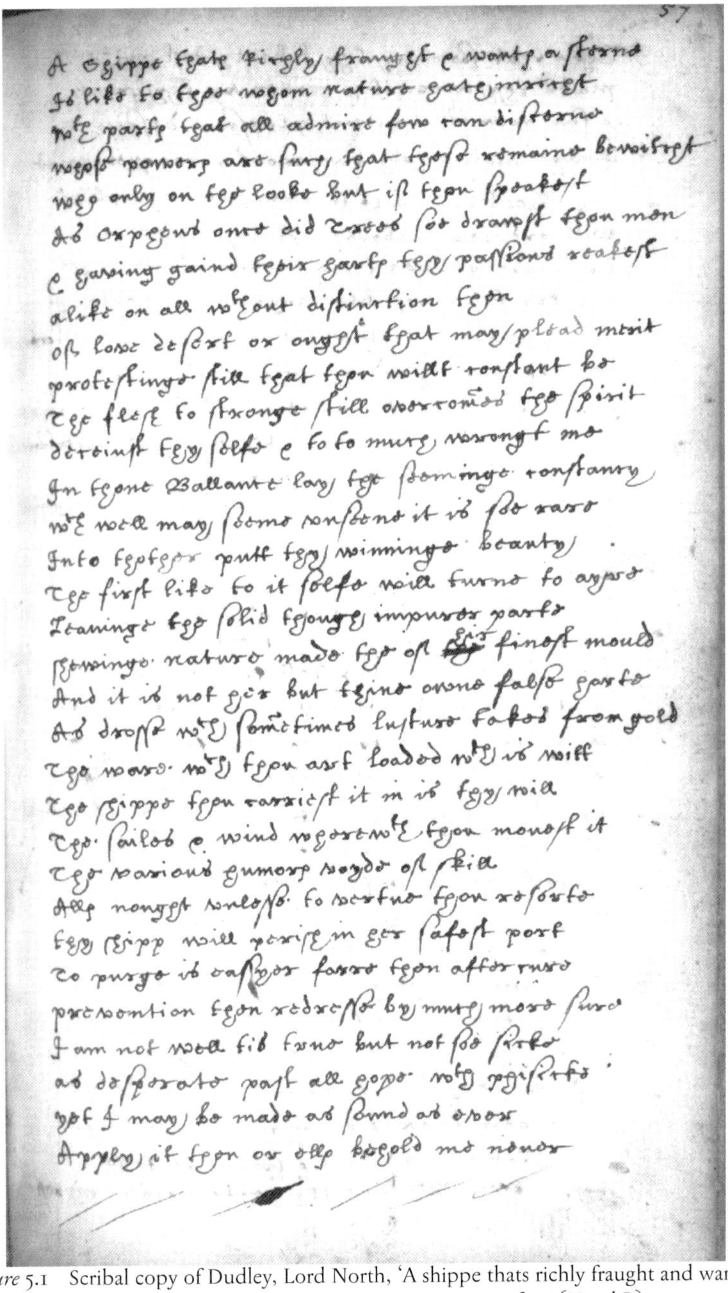

57

A shippe thats richly fraught & wants a sterne
Is like to thee whom nature hath inrichd
wth partes that all admire few can discerne
whose powers are such that these remaine bewitchd
who only on thy looke but iff thou speakest
As orpheus once did trees soe drawest thou men
& having gaind their hartes thy passions reakest
alike on all wthout distinction then
of love desert or ought that may plead merit
professinge still that thou wilt constant be
The flesh so stronge still overcomes the spirit
deceivest thy selfe & so so much wrongst me
In thone ballance lay the seeminge constancy
wch well may seeme consent it is so rare
Into thother putt thy winninge beauty
The first like to it selfe will turne to ayre
leavinge the solid though impurer parte
shewinge nature made the of her finest mould
And it is not her but thine owne false harte
As drosse wch sometimes lusture takes from gold
The ware wch thou art loaded wth is wit
The shippe thou carriest it in is thy will
The sailes & wind wherewth thou movest it
The various humors voyde of skill
All nought unlesse to vertue thou resorte
thy shipp will perish in her safest port
To purge is easier farre then after cure
prevention then redresse by much more sure
I am not well fitt true but not so sicke
as desperate past all hope wch physicke
yet I may be made as sound as ever
Apply it then or else behold me never

Figure 5.1 Scribal copy of Dudley, Lord North, 'A shippe thats richly fraught and wants a sterne': Huntington Library, San Marino, MS HM 198, part 2, f.57r (Hand B).

The analysis of early printed books must take account of the archival records: dates of entry, the dates of prefaces, court records, notes of purchase, correspondence, and so on: these details help to fix a temporal range within which to situate the study of paper, type, and ornament for the information they yield. What cannot be proven from the differences in type fonts, type and ornament damage, running-titles, pagination sequences, and so on, are issues such as edition size, or the rates of composition and presswork: usually any estimates have to be made according to a best guess based on what is known from other sources, such as the Cambridge records combined with what is known via the archival sources. Further, any attempt at reconstruction must also identify any printing that had been shared with another house, which means that the output of the entire trade has to be checked for the relevant period. Further, whilst many practices were common to the trade, the arrangements for the production of a given book cannot be assumed to be true of every book produced by that business, or for every printing-house.[9]

The material record is to be found as an image upon, as well as an image within the paper. The methods of mechanical reproduction mean that everything ought to be the same; hence, it is the minor flaws and differences that have significance. When a piece of type or an ornament is first cast, it is the same as all the other letters and ornaments cast from the same mould. With time, pieces of type and ornament stock become unique and we can trace the history of this through their use and the impressions left on paper: a dent, a hairline fracture, a bent kern, or any other damage that makes one piece of printer's material different from those that are similar, is all that is required to establish the repetition of that piece in the history of a book or across different books. Further, the damage may increase with time, so that it is possible to trace the use of a damaged sort or ornament through its various states.

There are other kinds of typographical trace that may leave evidence of interrelationships: pagination errors in running-titles may relate to a previous forme that was printed, blind impressions left by load-bearing type (i.e. type that was not inked, but used to stabilize the structure of a page because it was not completely set with text) may reveal type taken from another forme or book, offsets from different sheets of output will indicate that they were being worked on at the same time, changes in the relationship between running-titles may indicate they have been removed from the chase, and the misallocation

---

[9] For an extended treatment of analysis and inference, see F. T. Bowers, *Bibliography and Textual Criticism* (Oxford, 1964).

of space within the page may indicate a gap between the printing of one forme and the composition of another as the presswork of the first must have begun before the composition of the second. Indeed, any kind of physical evidence that establishes ruptures in the patterns of activity, or which clarifies the relationship between different pieces of output, is potentially significant. The problem then becomes what one does with this information once it has been established.

Ultimately, the reason for doing detailed analytical work on a book or printing-house must go beyond the facts of sequence and precedence in textual production. Usually, the close bibliographical examination of a book is done with a view to resolving textual issues that have arisen in the study of a work of some literary or historical importance. However, these insights are useful only to the extent that they help explain otherwise irrecoverable details that bear upon the history of the book or house under investigation. Hence, whilst it is necessary that the facts should be right, getting them right requires that the investigation start from the point of what the facts can establish given the evidence that survives, not a prior assumption of what they might show. That caveat must be weighed before embarking on a line of research that could well make the angels tremble at its threshold. Research of this kind needs to concentrate clearly on fact rather than conjecture, and be focused upon resolvable issues.

Materials and Identification

Both Gaskell and Moxon have described, at length, the processes and equipment involved in composition and presswork.[10] Some of the materials employed were purely functional: chases to contain the pages, quoins to lock them in place, composing sticks in which the type was set, galleys to hold the type before it was locked up as well as after it had been printed off and was ready to distribute, and mallets to secure things tight; whilst, at the press, the frisket and tympan ensured that only the area to be printed received an impression of ink, and protected the paper from the surface of the platen. In addition, a printing-house had a great deal of other material that was not type but constituted part of the resources that might be utilised: copper-engraved title-pages and plates, woodcut illustrations and diagrams, headpieces, tailpieces, arabesques, flowers, factotums, initial letters, ornamental borders, brass rules, and printer's devices (block illustrations that were applied on title-pages and

---

[10] Gaskell, *New Introduction*, 40–56 and 118–41; Moxon, *Mechanick Exercises*, 10–44 (type and materials), 45–96 (the press and equipment), 191–246 (composition), 252–311 (presswork).

particular to a house). Some of this material was made from wood, and some might be cast from metal. Any of it might be used, often in combination, in a particular book. To the extent that plays were printed with little more than a device, and perhaps rules, they are the exception to the practices of the trade which viewed a judicious use of ornament as being pleasing to the eye—especially if it could be matched in ways that were appropriate to the work.

A printer's ornament stock was accumulated over time, and from a variety of sources; it was not always bought new. Sometimes type and ornament passed along with a business, as when the house of Thomas Vautrollier passed to Richard Field, or when William Stansby succeeded John Windet. Sometimes it was acquired when another member of the trade ceased to operate. Hence, Windet acquired some of his early material from the estate of Henry Bynneman, at much the same time as John Wolfe acquired material from John Day. Later, Wolfe divided his materials between Windet and Robert Bourne (who was soon after succeeded by Adam Islip), and from late 1590 Wolfe acted as a publisher not a printer although his publications read 'Printed by Iohn Wolfe'.[11] Stansby was later to make much use of Day's Anglo-Saxon type, even though Windet only used it once in a piece of unidentified shared printing,[12] and Wolfe did not use it at all. Understanding the lines of association is a prerequisite for work on printing-house identification.

The ornament stock of a printing-house is normally distinctive. Initial letters may either have a theme (A is Abraham, C is for Cain), or else be cut with a floral or sculptural background. Sizes varied significantly depending on the type it was to feature with, and the format of the page, as one would want to choose a smaller initial for an octavo volume than for a folio. Arabesques could be shaped like diamonds, triangles, ovals, squares, rectangles, or stars; or else be set from smaller units in blocks. Headpieces and tailpieces typically had some kind of symbolic content: cornucopias, archers, birds, fruits, plants, faces, cupids, and so on, like a painted ornamental frieze. The ornaments had their historical roots in the decorative embellishments made to medieval manuscripts as well as some of the earliest printed books, and they can serve for identification alongside the evidence provided by the type.

The importance of Gutenberg's original invention was not that he created the press, but that he found a way to manufacture movable type:

---

[11] Wolfe has been the subject of fairly regular attention: see, C. C. Huffman, *Elizabethan Impressions: John Wolfe and His Press* (New York, 1998); for Windet, Bland, *Jonson, Stansby and English Typography 1579–1623*, I, 121–2 and 125n (Bynneman), and 135–9, 145, 149 (Wolfe).
[12] This is quire 5G of the 1597 reprint of Foxe's *Actes and monuments* (STC 11226).

that is letters that were exactly the same as each other and that could be reused once they had been distributed back into the case. Type was the single most important resource that a printer possessed: it was available in different sizes and faces, including the exotic and special fonts that some, but not all, printers acquired or inherited. The skill of the craft lay not only with the ability to set type, but through the arrangement and deployment of all the resources available to their greatest utility and effect.

Every letter, punctuation mark, or space for a printed page was made from pieces of type. Type was made by first cutting a steel punch about 45 mm long, and then hammering the punch into copper. This piece of copper, or matrix, ensured the uniformity of cast type. The matrix was locked in a hand-held mould into which a mixture of lead with a little tin and antinomy was poured. The mould was shaken, then opened and the type discarded. If it was flawed, it was thrown back into the molten metal; if it was true, the shank was broken off, and the piece filed down to a standard height between 24 and 27.5 mm. Spaces were made in the same way, except that they were blank and shorter than the other type. Across the bottom edge of the sort was a nick that helped a compositor determine by touch the lower side of the letter when setting.[13]

The cutting of the punch was a highly skilled job. The first typecutters were goldsmiths; later it became a specialized craft. Every letter has a mid-section that is level with the line, and some have ascenders (b, d, f, h, k, l, ſ, t), or descenders (g, j, p, q, y). Further, f and ſ were cast as ligatures, either as doubles, or with i, l, and t, because the kern (the front curve of the letter which lipped over the edge of the sort) could easily be damaged when two sorts were combined. All the letters shared the same x-height (the height of x defining the height of the mid-section of a letter). Further, the matrices required exact matching of the strikes, so that each letter would sit in perfect alignment. Overall, the letters had to be able to combine with each other in a way that ensured semantic coherency and sustained legibility, as a gap in the wrong place might imply word separation where it was not intended, whilst confusion in design and height might make the text unreadable.[14]

From a broad historical perspective, changes in typeface have altered the physical appearance of the book over time. Until the twentieth-century, type served as an index of contemporary aesthetic preferences both in its appearance and its relationship to literary style and content.

---

[13] Gaskell, *New Introduction*, 9–12; A. F. Johnson, *A History of the Old English Letter Foundries* (London, 1952), 97–113, with illustrations; H. Carter, *A View of Early Typography up to about 1600* (Oxford, 1969), 5–22.
[14] Carter, *A View of Early Typography*, 93–116.

The primary assumption of good design is that the face is invisible to the reader.[15] Each font is based on a relationship between the vertical and horizontal emphasis of the whole and whether the visual line between letters is weighted to the top or bottom of the x-height as it carries the eye along the page. Subtle adjustments to the weight, width, x-height, and emphasis can be traced across the fonts of different type foundries in the books of the sixteenth and seventeenth centuries.[16]

The visible distinctions that render as obvious the work of different foundries over time may be observed in rather finer detail between the fonts owned by each printing-house. In the first half of the sixteenth-century, English printers acquired their type material from abroad; but by the 1580s there were at least four type foundries operating in London with French and Dutch connections.[17] Printers acquired their type at different times from each other, and not always from the same source: thus, the x-height of one printer's pica or the cut of the g or M, could be different to that of a neighbour. As a consequence, it is often possible to identify the types associated with individual houses.[18]

Printing-house identification is one of the more awkward issues in bibliographical analysis because a mistaken assumption will obviate any reconstruction of a business, or the account of printing a text. For many books, the statement 'Printed by John Jones', or 'Printed by John Jones for George Smith', is accurate; sometimes, as with 'Printed for George Smith', the publisher and not the printer is named. Most attributions are based on the device, border, or ornament on a title-page;[19] when that is not helpful, the ornament stock is next examined for identification. Provided there are no further complications, these details usually pinpoint the printer involved and this can be confirmed by examining the type. There remain, however, a group of books for which these methods are not sufficient owing to lack of ornament, or because shared printing or borrowing are involved. Hence, the ability to distinguish the type of one printing-house from another is helpful for two reasons: first, a direct

---

[15] S. A. Morison, *First Principles of Typography*, 2nd edn. (Cambridge, 1967).

[16] See, Gaskell, *New Introduction*, 21–9.

[17] Johnson, *A History of the Old English Letter Foundries*, 96.

[18] W. C. Ferguson, *Pica Roman Type in Elizabethan England* (Aldershot, 1989); A. Weiss, 'Font Analysis as a Bibliographical Method: The Elizabethan Play-Quarto Printers and Compositors', *Studies in Bibliography*, 43 (1990), 95–164; —, 'Bibliographical Methods for Identifying Unknown Printers in Elizabethan/Jacobean Books', *Studies in Bibliography*, 44 (1991), 183–228.

[19] See, for instance, R. B. McKerrow, *Printers' and Publishers' Devices in England and Scotland 1485–1640* (London, 1949); R. B. McKerrow and F. S. Ferguson, *Title-Page Borders Used in England and Scotland 1485–1640* (London, 1932).

comparison of types in the size and face across all the houses will serve to identify those items for which no printer is known; second, the comparison of fonts between sheets within a book or pamphlet will indicate instances where two or more printing-houses have worked together on the same volume—a practice known as shared printing.

If one identifies shared printing in a particular book, then from a practical perspective, it is possible to construct a database of books produced at that time in the same font by taking the items listed in the chronological indices of the short-title catalogues and then using this information to undertake an initial survey. This can be done via *Early English Books Online (EEBO)*, provided the proper scale is used and any doubtful items are listed for physical inspection.[20] This is particularly true for small-format books where the digital image can be deceptive. Once a list of relevant items is made, the best method is to inspect and measure a physical copy of all the output set in the same size and face of type. This can be done by measuring 20 lines of type to confirm the size of the font; the differences can then be examined in detail. While doing this, it is instructive to carry out spot checks between sheets to ensure that shared printing in the comparison copy is not involved, for the easiest mistake is to attribute a book to the wrong printer by comparing it with only one sample of type from another book that has been shared.

Having determined which printers employed which fonts, and compared the samples with the unidentified output, most books will be able to be removed from further consideration. Then, either there will be one printer whose font is the same; or, if two or three alternatives present themselves, the type should be reinspected both for minor differences and for damage. Taking a sample of damaged types from the item to be identified, it is then possible to look at the output of the alternatives to see if they occur elsewhere in the unidentified items. A comparison of paper may also provide further corroborative, if circumstantial, linkage between the comparative witnesses.

Damage: A History

Damage was caused to type and other material owing to the presence of grit or other stray matter at the press whilst it was being worked, or by loose type being driven under pressure in ways that might damage a

---

[20] Access to *EEBO* is usually possible via university or library databases: the website is http://eebo.chadwyck.com. Unfortunately there is no equivalent site for continental imprints. Any items not available via *EEBO* can be located via the appendices to the standard bibliographical catalogues (*STC* and Wing).

kern. During presswork, the pressure of the platen, as it pressed against the type and paper at c.2.25 kg/cm^2, could easily cause foreign objects to bend or nick the type—lead being a heavy and soft metal, which is why tin and antimony were added to harden it.[21] Each time a piece of type was used, it might be pressed 500–2,000 times, and depending on how much type there was, how many sheets there were in the book, and how often the type was distributed, it could be employed from several to many times in the same publication, as well as repeatedly in different publications over time. It was inevitable that eventually wear or damage would render the type unsatisfactory.

Damaged type has been used by bibliographers in two main ways to trace aspects of printing-house activity. Both Hinman and Blayney analyzed evidence from damaged type to reconstruct the order in which formes were composed, printed, and distributed.[22] This was possible because the books concerned were set exclusively from cases that were not in concurrent use with other items at the press. This kind of reconstruction becomes infinitely more complex when several cases and books in the same type are linked, as the damaged sorts could potentially move between different volumes, especially if they were large folios and there was a plentiful supply of type.

With running-titles, damaged type is the quickest and easiest way to establish the relationship between skeleton formes. Most books were printed using a pair of, or sometimes four or six, skeleton formes. The skeleton was that part of the forme that did not change from sheet to sheet except for the pagination. The running-titles were often set in italic which, owing to the kerning, was more prone to damage. This material was left in place within the chase to ensure that the positioning of the pages was the same, and because running-titles did not require frequent resetting. What should be looked for are breaks in the regular patterns of use owing to interruption, or sometimes added urgency.

The easiest way to trace the movement of running-titles from sheet to sheet is to record the damage as it appears in each title and its place within the signature (1^r, 1^v, etc), and then unfold the paper so that the locations of the damaged type on the inner and outer formes can be seen. If a pair of skeleton formes was used in rotation, then all the outer formes will share one set of damage, and the inner formes the other, and the position of the damage will always be the same, or be rotated 180 degrees. If this sequence is broken then something has occurred.

---

[21] Gaskell, *New Introduction*, 125: the pressure is equal to 31.64 lbs per square inch.
[22] Hinman, *Printing and Proof-Reading*, 1: 52–138; P. W. M. Blayney, *The Texts of* King Lear, 89–150 and 504–39.

There are several possible permutations to the ways in which a set of running-titles might change sequence. First, the sequence of rotation between the inner and outer forme may be switched so that the skeleton of, say, the outer forme recurs immediately: if this is so, then the type may have been removed from both formes before setting continued. This indicates some kind of interruption, most probably a small piece of job printing for which the press was required but not necessarily the chase with the skeleton forme. Second, the placement of the running-titles on one or both sides of the forme may have shifted in a way that cannot be explained by rotation (as when one-half of an octavo is spun around but the other side remains as it is). When this happens, the skeleton must have been taken out of the chase, which suggests that the chase was required for another job. Third, the running-titles may be divided and the number of skeletons in use increased. Finally, two completely different sets of skeleton formes may be present, usually with a clear point of division. This either indicates that work was suspended and the skeleton formes distributed, or that the printing was shared.

Within the running-titles, there is one further piece of information that can be informative: pagination was the only part of the skeleton forme that ought to have been changed every time. In some cases, mistakes in the sequence will have been caused by the wrong sorts being in the wrong box, and sometimes they will be caused by a compositor forgetting to change the number, perhaps owing to a minor distraction. In the latter case, the number will belong to the forme that was previously used, and be from the same position in the forme or the same position rotated 180 degrees. Thus, if a quarto book is printed by using alternating formes, page 41 ($F1^r$) would retain the pagination of $E1^r$ (33) or $E3^r$ (37). If the pagination for $F1^r$ read 25, and the pagination for $E1^r$ was correct, then the skeleton would have belonged to that used for outer D and more than one pair of skeleton formes would be in operation.

Donne's *Psevdo-Martyr* (STC 7048; 1612) is, for instance, an example of a book with a change in the sequence of running-titles and a significant pagination error. It is a 54-sheet crown quarto, printed by Stansby, set in great-primer roman, and entered to Walter Burre in the Stationers' Register on 2 December 1609. It was presented to King James seven and a half weeks later on 24 January 1610, despite the Christmas period.[23] In 'An Advertisement to the Reader', Donne stated that he had been 'willing to giue the Booke a hasty dispatch' and it has been described by Keynes as 'very carelessly printed'.[24] However, Bald suggested that 'the entry was

---

[23] G. Keynes, *A Bibliography of Dr. John Donne*, 4 and 9.
[24] J. Donne, *Psevdo-martyr*, ¶1ᵛ; Keynes, *Bibliography*, 7.

probably made when the printing was well along'.[25] What the evidence of the running-titles suggests, however, is that Stansby printed the book more quickly than Bald realized.

The most serious errors in pagination occur in sheet Y. The outer forme of Y was set with two of the running-titles taken from outer V, and two from inner X which, unchanged, created the mis-pagination. Until inner X, a pair of running-titles had been employed in rotation; in order to set outer Y, the two other skeletons were broken up. Outer X also has a new set of running-titles and must have been in use when the new skeleton for outer Y was created. Further, outer X introduces a faulty *V* that then recurs in outer Z, inner 2B, outer 2D, outer 2F, inner 2H, inner 2K, outer 2M, inner 2O, inner 2Q, inner 2S, inner 2V, outer 2Y, inner 3A, outer 3B, outer 3D, and inner 3F. What this irregular pattern shows is that at least two of the skeleton formes were stripped of their type at any one time, and that the work was divided between several workmen, and probably more than one press. This suggests that additional urgency was taken, and that, in order for the presswork to proceed the compositors set the text more quickly than had previously been the case. In other words, the running-titles suggest that Donne's 'hasty dispatch' is perhaps a more accurate statement than had been supposed.

If the pagination of a book is completely out of kilter and repeats or omits numbers in a sequence, then either a sheet from later in the book was printed before those that preceded it; or, once again, it is a sign of shared printing. Most items where the printing has been shared will have clearly divisible sections between the two houses involved. Let us assume that Jones printed A–D and Smith E–G. The evidence for that claim will be cumulative, including differences in type, and the fact that the running-titles belong to different skeletons. Several further signs also confirm shared printing: first, that there is a disruption to the signature and/or pagination sequence because the second printer thought he was starting from a different point relative to the other house; second, there may be changes in the layout which usually can be measured by differences in the width of the compositor's measure and, perhaps, the number of lines to a page (as in one more or less, consistently); third, an ornament or initial may be present that can be traced to a particular printing-house (not common in plays, but likely to happen in books with chapters, or that have been divided into 'books'); and fourth, through the use of rules that have been bent in distinctive ways.[26]

[25] R. C. Bald, 'Dr. Donne and the Booksellers', *Studies in Bibliography*, 18 (1965), 77.
[26] A. Weiss, 'Bibliographical Methods for Identifying Unknown Printers in Elizabethan/Jacobean Books', *Studies in Bibliography*, 44 (1991), 183–228.

In some cases, shared printing can be difficult to spot. The title-page of Francis Godwin's *Annales of England* (STC 11947–7.5; 1630) states that it was 'Printed by A. Islip, and W. Stansby', as do both the sub-title-pages; nevertheless, the editors of the *Short Title Catalogue* remarked that 'Although entered to both pr[inter]s, the whole book was app[arently] pr[inted] by Stansby.' This is because the printing was not shared in the usual way by dividing parts of the book in sections but was spread throughout the whole, to the extent that the final sheet printed (2V2.5) was divided not by forme, but by leaf, with Islip printing 2V2 on both sides, and Stansby 2V5 in the same way. The tell-tale sign is that Islip's great-primer is slightly larger (116 mm/20) than that employed by Stansby (112 mm/20), but this is less obvious because the two alternate. In all, Islip was responsible for a quarter of the book.[27]

Godwin's *Annales* is a useful reminder that the primary motive of an early modern printer was not profit alone, but the sustained viability of the business. Whilst materials were acquired as needed, larger shifts in capital structure happened on an irregular basis and owing to specific circumstances, such as the division of John Wolfe's resources between Windet and Bourne in late 1590, or the new type and other materials that Stansby purchased when he took over from Windet in 1609–10.[28] Few printers aggressively reinvested profits in order to expand their business constantly; their primary concern was sustainability.

All too often, arguments about the market for books assume that a printer or publisher would maximize production and income, and that this drove the organization of work in hand. Trade practices tell a different story: concurrent production and shared printing ensured that the organization of activity was consistent in volume, and flexible in its use of materials, thus avoiding erratic fluctuations in staff caused by shortages of work in hand. Cash-flow was maintained because the money would come in as the projects were completed. Less obvious, but as important, were the social and familial links that glued many business relationships together. It is friendship, not logic or profit, that led to the work being shared for the *Annales* in the way that it was.

Measuring Output

In most instances, the study of a printing-house is likely to emphasize the scale of business and its social networks, rather than specific material

---

[27] The *Annales* collates: §⁴ A-2I⁴ 2K⁶ 2L-2O⁴ 2P⁴(+2P1.1) 2Q-2T⁴ 2V⁶. Islip printed F-K2.3, S1.4, T2.3, V1.4, X-2A2.3, 2F-2I2.3, 2K3.4, 2M2.3, 2P-2R2.3, 2V1 (2V6 is blank), and 2V2.

[28] Bland, *Jonson, Stansby and English Typography 1579–1623*, I: 184.

evidence; however, shared and unidentified printing has to be included in order to estimate output. Output is best measured by en-count combined with a record of the number of edition sheets set. The number of edition sheets is a less reliable indicator than the en-count because a larger font will require less composition for the same area of a page, and a smaller font more; and because we do not know the average print-run to establish the volume of presswork, so that all that can be measured with some understatement is composition.[29]

The method of calculating composition by ens requires that all fonts be converted to their pica equivalent. Hence why the height of a font over 20 lines set solid matters, for while the number of lines per page will differ according to the height of the type, the differences in letter width need to be accounted for and converted to a standard measure. This can be done by dividing pica height by the font used to give the correct ratio (e.g. 82/94), and then multiplying by measure and page depth to give ens per page in the same way as was described for estimating and casting-off copy (pp. 114–6 above). As an example, *Harwards Phlebotomy* (STC 12922; 1601) is a 9½-sheet octavo, set in pica roman to a measure of 36 ens and a depth of 34 lines. The calculation is: $(82/82) \times 36 \times 34 \times 16 \times 9.5 =$ 186,048 ens. Samuel Daniel's *Certain Small Workes* (STC 6242; 1611) is a duo-decimo that collates $A–P^{12} Q^{4}$ and is set in 67 mm long primer. The calculation for this text is: $(82/67) \times 30 \times 35 \times 24 \times 15.3 = 471,879$ ens. Likewise the *Workes of Benjamin Jonson* (STC 14751–2; 1616) is a 257-sheet folio set in english roman to a measure of 58 ens and a depth of 45 lines, or $(82/94) \times 58 \times 45 \times 4 \times 257 = 2,240,559$ ens.

Once the en composition figures have been established, it is possible to take them and calculate from the average Cambridge rates of 5,600–5,700 ens per day roughly how many compositors would have been working in a given establishment over the course of a year with a fairly accurate sense of the proportions of different types used. Indicatively, in 1606–08, the balance of composition at the printing-house of John Windet was approximately 48 per cent in pica and 22 per cent in english, with nearly 9 per cent set as music, 8½ per cent (quarto and octavo psalmbooks) set in brevier, and nearly 8 per cent in long-primer. Non-pareil and great-primer roman were the next most commonly used types and then small pica and a small-bodied pica inherited from John Wolfe. The balance between the various faces was a little more than 44 per cent black-letter and 44 per cent roman, with italic accounting for less than 3 per cent and music the remainder. In terms of ens set, the various

---

[29] See also, D. L. Gants, 'A Quantitative Analysis of the London Book-Trade 1614–1618', *Studies in Bibliography*, 55 ([2004 for] 2002), 185–213. John Pitcher and Andy Boyle's study of Simon Waterson will be the first to examine fully a publisher's business by en-count.

psalm-books in their differing types accounted for approximately 30 per cent of the compositors' activity and probably a greater percentage of the pressmen's time. The figures suggest that Windet could have employed at least three compositors full-time. He probably had four pressmen. Five years later, the volume of composition under his successor William Stansby had increased sufficiently for there to be work for six compositors.[30]

Invisible Hands

With a manuscript, it is usually evident when one scribe has taken over from another, even when there is an attempt to blend seamlessly the work of those involved. Only rarely does one encounter a manuscript where the scribal habits of a single person suggest multiple identities. With print, type erases the visual distinctions and the activity of different workmen is particularly difficult to separate. At the documentary level, we know from the records when various members of the trade were apprenticed and made free, and from the parish records we often know when they were married and when they died. What we do not know is whether 'Fingers Finnegan' was setting type on 27 August or, once he was made free, whether he worked for the same house. From the output data we know approximately how many employees a business is likely to have had and this can be compared with the life records to see if they are broadly in agreement. From there, it is is possible to make a tentative list of the likely names of the invisible hands at work.

At the time of its publication, one of the principal achievements of Hinman's work on the 1623 Shakespeare folio was felt to be his attempt to assign different sections of work on the text to different compositors (known as A, B, and so on) based on cumulative differences in spelling habits between the workmen. In the years since, this work has been refined and modified, and it is still broadly accepted as being the best assessment we have of the interrelationship between workmen on the composition of a text.[31] In its scope, ambition, and attention to detail, it was a work of great imaginative courage, particularly given the diverse nature of the copy from which the compositors set their text. In lesser hands, compositor studies have been far less convincing.

There are five main issues with compositor identification that need to be resolved or satisfied before an attempt is made at identification. First, the copy from which the text was set must have been neutral and

---

[30] Bland, *Jonson, Stansby and English Typography 1579–1623*, I: 173 and 199–200.
[31] For a revised attribution, see: P. Blayney, 'Addendum to the Textual Introduction', C. Hinman (comp.), *The First Folio of Shakespeare*, 2nd edn. (New York, 1996), xxxiv–xxxvii.

consistent as any underlying scribal variation may influence the analysis and suggest differing practices where none exist. Second, the work of one of the compositors must be sufficiently distinct as to be genuinely separable from the remainder of the text. If the habits of two workmen are essentially the same then any attempt to separate their work will be meaningless. Third, if the right margin is justified (i.e. the text is prose) then all spelling variants that might be used for the purposes of justification must be removed from the analysis (e.g. she/shee, manie/many, learn/learne), because a compositor will vary spelling to fit the line. Fourth, the analysis needs to be carried out line by line, not page by page, because one compositor can take over from another at any point. Finally, the type being used must be studied in detail to establish whether two cases are in service, and attention needs to be paid to any differences in the layout of the page and the accuracy of the setting.

Experience suggests that the habits of scribes and compositors were always, to some extent, inconsistent and to formulate an analysis based on uniformity of practice is conceptually mistaken. Adopting arbitrary criteria and applying them with reductive simplicity will produce an answer that bears no relation to actual practice: a fact McKenzie was able to demonstrate by comparing the method of analysis to the payments for the same book in the Cambridge records.[32] In most instances, and particularly in a larger printing-house, any attempt at compositor analysis is likely to be an object rare and high conceived, in Marvell's phrase, by 'despair upon impossibility'. One needs to be confident that the results of the analysis will serve a genuine purpose and use.

One example of how compositor studies can be helpful is provided by Blayney's analysis of the compositors of the first quarto of *King Lear*.[33] He demonstrated that two different cases of type were in operation, and that the compositors had distinct spelling preferences. This combination of detail is more useful as the play is a mixture of prose and verse. It would appear, as well, that one compositor may have been less experienced: all the surviving stop-press corrections relate to his work. Further, the copy would appear to have been a neutral manuscript written in secretary hand. Blayney's analysis of the *Lear* quarto is exacting in its rigour and comprehensive in its approach. One can therefore be confident that his methodology was careful and his conclusions as accurate as we are likely to be able to establish. In what follows, his study of the compositors will serve to clarify other issues to do with Okes and *Lear*.

---

[32] D. F. McKenzie, 'Stretching a Point: Or, The Case of the Spaced-Out Comps', *Studies in Bibliography*, 37 (1984), 333–65.
[33] Blayney, *The Texts of* King Lear, 148–87.

Okes, King Lear, *and* The Masque of Queenes

Blayney established that the quarto text of *Lear* was set seriatim (one page after another), rather than by formes, and this led him to a number of conclusions about the organization of the printing-house, including the fact that he believed the order of printing to be sequential (one book after another) rather than concurrent. Hence, Blayney suggested that the evidence from the printing-house was contrary to that supplied in exhaustive detail by the Cambridge records, and that the kind of material Okes printed meant that production had to be organized to maximize income. Okes was, according to Blayney, the exception.

For the remainder of this chapter, the discussion will focus on the claim that the Okes' house operated in a significantly different manner to the Cambridge press and it will critique the analysis and evidence to place that assumption under scrutiny. There is no intention to question Blayney's analysis of the physical details to do with the printing of *Lear*, for that is a work of great thoroughness. However, the assertion that Okes was an exception to the rest of the trade is sufficiently important that it should not go unquestioned, as it has a direct bearing on our understanding of early modern book production and the account of that which has been given here. As an example of the primary issues that arise in the use and interpretation of evidence, it will also serve its turn.

There can be no doubt, given the type evidence, that *Lear* was set seriatim, but that does not mean that all of the books printed by Okes were so set—in fact, as Blayney acknowledges, 'Okes's norm is likely to have been setting by formes';[34] nor does the fact that he observed a type shortage in the pica roman cases mean that concurrent production was not the norm—Okes had cases of pica black-letter and english roman. The rationale for claiming that production was organized in a sequential order is, therefore, based on an argument of urgency, and the need for rapid turnover and cash-flow. There are several stages to Blayney's argument, the first of which is to offer an assessment of Okes's work:

> It is true that *some* of his books are quite creditable pieces of work in the rather low-grade context of Jacobean London, but the majority are not. There were printers whose worst was worse than Okes's—but not very many, and not *much* worse. His average standard was good enough to allow him to compete for low-priced work, but was nevertheless poor.[35]

---

[34] Blayney, *The Texts of* King Lear, 150.
[35] Blayney, *The Texts of* King Lear, 29: the italics are present in the original.

It is true that the standards of the London trade were not those of the Plantin establishment in Antwerp, or of a celebrated university press, but then the publishing of scholarly editions was not a primary concern. It was a commercial trade, and it is worth remembering that few books look now as when they were sold: over time they become discoloured, used, cropped, and rebound. The phrase 'low-grade' is pejorative and its purpose is to portray Okes in the least flattering light. Further, there really is no such thing as 'low-priced work' as the Stationers' Company regulated the retail price for books (at a halfpenny a sheet of pica roman) and the cost of paper was the same for everyone. There were longer books and shorter books: between 1607 and 1609 the average book that Okes printed in its entirety and that survives is a little over ten sheets;[36] he did not print a folio until the translation of Lucan by Sir Arthur Gorges (STC 16884) and his share in *The History of Lewis the Eleventh* (STC 17662), both published in 1614. As for the sixpence books, it is inevitable that some will not have survived.

The fact that a book is scarce does not mean that its contents were without merit, it means that it was read. Okes printed books that were read, which is why their survival rate is low. His output includes such items as Theodore Beza's *Houshold Prayers* (STC 2024–4.3; 1607–8), and John Pelling's *A Sermon on the Providence of God* (STC 19567; 1607), both of which went through the press at much the same time as *Lear*. In Okes's case, Blayney argues:

> There were . . . printers who specialized in ephemeral books, and they may have needed to evolve specialized methods. . . . a concurrent system might have rather less appeal for a printer to whom deadlines were frequent and necessary evils associated with the kinds of books he *preferred* to print. [emphasis mine][37]

To describe such items as sermons and godly pocketbooks as ephemera is misleading, and there is throughout an element of false reasoning involved. The larger a printing-house, and the more books it produced, the more frequent were the 'necessary evils' of deadlines, yet this did not change the methods of production, and there is very little evidence that the kinds of books that Okes produced were of the kind that were wanted 'yesterday'. For instance, *The Cobler of Canterburie* (STC 4580; 1608), again printed at the same time as *Lear*, survives as a unique copy. It was first printed in 1590 and then entered in 1600. At the time that Blayney wrote, the 1600 edition was not known to survive, but a single

---

[36] The figures for Okes were compiled from Blayney, *The Texts of* King Lear, 334–428.
[37] Blayney, *The Texts of* King Lear, 48–9.

copy has since emerged in the library of the Polish Academy of Sciences in Gdansk (STC 4579.5; Appendix, vol. 3) as part of a sammelbände with several other unique items.[38] A book that was reprinted every eight-to-ten years is scarcely urgent, and there is no particular reason why a publisher might specify a delivery date equivalent to more than a couple of sheets a week: most books were produced more slowly than that.[39] In fact, what mattered were the trade relationships between the publisher and printer. Unless the printer commissioned work on his own account, it was the publisher who decided what to offer the printer, both in terms of the nature of the content and the length of the text: Okes may have *preferred* to print books of 30 sheets or less (such claims can only be speculation), but it was the publisher who decided what to offer him, and if he was needing work he would sooner have shared a book than lose a contract.

The idea that a printer needed to 'evolve specialized methods' by, in effect, reverting to the simplest and least efficient method of operation has as little foundation as the 'necessary evils' of deadlines. Even Wynkyn de Worde, a century earlier, used cases of different type concurrently. There is an implicit assumption being made that somehow concurrent production is slower, less cash-generative, than sequential printing. Hence Blayney goes on to claim that:

> Concurrent printing provides flexibility, and therefore efficiency, at the expense of individual production rates.[40]

This may seem obvious, but in fact it is not: it depends entirely on how many cases of a given type are available and how many compositors there are available to set text. If a printer has two cases of pica roman and two compositors then this is true; if a printer has three compositors and two cases of pica roman then the third will have to set from another case, such as pica black-letter, whether the other compositors work in tandem or not. Further, if urgency was the primary rationale for organizing work, then in a two-compositor business an analysis of type would always demonstrate two cases being used concurrently on the

[38] Biblioteka Gdanska PAN, Di 3552 (8°), item 8. The edition was printed by Valentine Simmes, and the first sheet was folded inside out by accident. The volume is bound in contemporary vellum and belonged first to 'Georgius Melchman à Mùlbach Hæres in Luckoczin es czarlin 1634', with the later stamp of the Danzig State Library.

[39] McKenzie, 'Printers of the Mind', 15: as McKenzie observes, of 36 books printed at Cambridge between 1698 and 1705 of ten sheets or more, seven were produced at a rate of more than two sheets a week, 14 at a rate of between one and two sheets a week, and the remaining 15 at a rate of less than one sheet a week.

[40] Blayney, *The Texts of* King Lear, 55.

same book. In fact, in *Lear*, compositor B set B–G and most of H before compositor C (there is no compositor A), joined him.[41] Presumably compositor C was busy doing something else. As McKenzie observed:

> It was unusual for a compositor to work for any long period on one book to the exclusion of all others—usually he would be setting type for two or three books concurrently.[42]

If concurrent organization is best for the operation of the business, it has financial advantages as well. Each book may take longer to print, but it would be rare for two books to be completed at exactly the same time. Hence, there is a regular cash-flow that is sustaining work in hand. The argument for sequential printing on the other hand holds that on every given occasion a new contract will be urgent and has to be given priority over existing work. Blayney formulated this working model:

> Suppose that stock work is being undertaken on book A in the absence of other orders. Suppose further that a publisher brings in a small book B, and requests early delivery. The purpose of stock work being what it is, book A is interrupted so that book B can be produced in a short time.[43]

A little reflection might suggest that if a printer were to operate in this manner the results could be financially disastrous. Assume book A is a 20-sheet volume and that Okes has set three formes before a new six-sheet book comes to the press, which he then prints before managing to set another four formes of A, when another eight-sheet book is taken on and needs to be printed urgently, and so on. The production of A, and payment for the work, would stretch out to the edge of doom. Further, even the work for a 'stock' book would have been agreed at some convenient rate such as a sheet or two a week, and if Okes could not reasonably keep to that he might not get any further work from that publisher. No London printer would have agreed to a rate of delivery that would have left them unable to balance their workflows. Trade relationships were based as much on friendships and family associations as they were on financial self-interest.

It is now time to look at the relationship between output and activity a little more closely. In his 'Checklist of Books' in Appendix II, Blayney

---

[41] Blayney, *The Texts of* King Lear, 149.
[42] McKenzie, 'Printers of the Mind'; 18.
[43] Blayney, *The Texts of* King Lear, 53.

lists the output for Okes's predecessors and for Okes in 1607–9.[44] As Okes was first a partner in the business from 27 January 1607 (with all imprints bearing his name),[45] and then in full control three months later, the volume of output for the year does not need to be adjusted, as all but one sheet has his imprint. In 1607, Okes printed 19 items totalling 142½ sheets, with nine of those items being shared; in 1608, he printed 21 items totalling 205½ sheets, with six items shared; and, in 1609, he printed 28 items totalling 276 sheets, of which seven items were shared.

At first glance, this looks like a rapidly growing business, but the figures are deceptive. As Blayney's reconstruction of the printing-house activity suggests, in the third quarter of 1607 Okes apparently printed almost nothing. Two of the most likely reasons for this are an outbreak of the plague, or lost output.[46] Of these alternatives, it is possible that Okes left London owing to the plague, but if he did so he cannot have been particularly concerned about his cash-flow. Between 19 June and 3 July 1607, Windet's house fell victim to the plague, and within two weeks he had lost his apprentice George Vokes, two other workmen (one possibly a nephew), and his wife.[47] Nevertheless Windet continued to work and his output for 1607 is not noticeably lower than average. If the plague is the reason for the low output, then we might assume an adjusted figure of c.200 sheets for 1607 if conditions had been normal.

The most likely reason for a low total, however, remains lost output: as Blayney acknowledges, 'What survives . . . is unlikely to be all that ever existed'; nevertheless, he discounts this by adding that 'The surviving books will thus be assumed to represent (for the sake of hypothesis) a substantial percentage of the total output.'[48] Later, he goes on to add that 'if the losses involved several books it seems unlikely they would have been confined to a single period, and a 40-sheet single book would be more likely to survive'.[49] This may seem to be true but, as the example from an earlier chapter might suggest (p. 65), it is not always so: the 102-sheet fifth edition of Blundevile's *Exercises*, printed by Stansby some time in 1617–18, does not survive. Likewise, the loss rate from Bynneman's press has been estimated as between 17 and 19 per cent.[50] It is

---

[44] Blayney, *The Texts of* King Lear, 334–428.

[45] Blayney, *The Texts of* King Lear, 24.

[46] Blayney, *The Texts of* King Lear, 69–70. Blayney also suggests that Okes may have either been in prison, though not what for, or setting up his new printing-house.

[47] Guildhall, MS 5721/1, f.82ʳ.

[48] Blayney, *The Texts of* King Lear, 37 and 39.

[49] Blayney, *The Texts of* King Lear, 70.

[50] J. Barnard and M. Bell, 'The Inventory of Henry Bynneman (1583) A Preliminary Survey', *Publishing History*, 29 (1991), 5 (5–46).

quite easy to imagine that, during the plague months of 1607, Okes printed a godly pocketbook or two that long ago were read to pieces.

Let us assume, therefore, that Okes's rate of output was 200–40 sheets a year (the total for 1609 probably includes some material printed in 1608), or four to five sheets a week. Bear in mind that the second and third most competent compositors at Cambridge set 5,600–5,700 ens a day, or approximately a forme, with many of their colleagues producing less, and that in the midwinter composition would have been lower owing to poor light.[51] Remember as well that the type evidence shows that compositor B set sheets B–G and most of H before compositor C joined him. If we accept the sequential-printing argument that means a single compositor, who would have set at most two–three sheets a week, did so for at least two–three weeks and that Okes either produced only half his average output during that time, or that the edition was a very large one. If any further evidence were needed that *Lear* was produced in concurrent production, then it simply remains to observe that the four books that Blayney identifies as being produced at the same time as *Lear* were not set from the same cases: two are primarily set in pica black-letter, and two are set in english roman. That difference is significant.[52]

There is one last detail that is of some interest: early in 1609, Okes printed Jonson's *The Masque of Queenes* (STC 14778; figure 5.2). Unlike *Lear*, this text was well produced, with only a single stop-press correction, except for one serious miscalculation. When estimating, a wrong assumption was made about the size of type required for the sidenotes, with the consequence that they occupied much less space than was expected. Now, if *Queenes* had been set seriatim there would have been no problem about closing up the pigeon holes that mar B2^r, B3^v, and B4^r, and the text would have collated as it was first meant to do, A–E^4, not A^4($\pm$A2) B–E^4 F^2(–F2). In the process, fully a page would have been saved in the setting of the text; therefore, *Queenes* must have been set by formes. Further before the inner forme was set, presswork on the outer forme of B must have begun. Thus, outer B had been set, corrected prior to machining, and was well along at the press, if not fully printed, before the compositor began work on inner B: he had to have been busy with something else. It was only when the compositor began to set the sidenotes for B2^r that the error would have become obvious, and for the same reason: the text had to be spaced generously for B3^v and B4^r as well. These blocks of space had to be put in place and they were the only way in which the compositor could have corrected the error.

[51] McKenzie, 'Printers of the Mind', 9.
[52] *Pelling* and *Friendship* were set in 94 mm/20 roman; *Beza* and *Cobler* were set in 82 mm/20 black-letter (see Blayney, *The Texts of* King Lear, 79; App. II. items 31, 49, 21, and 43).

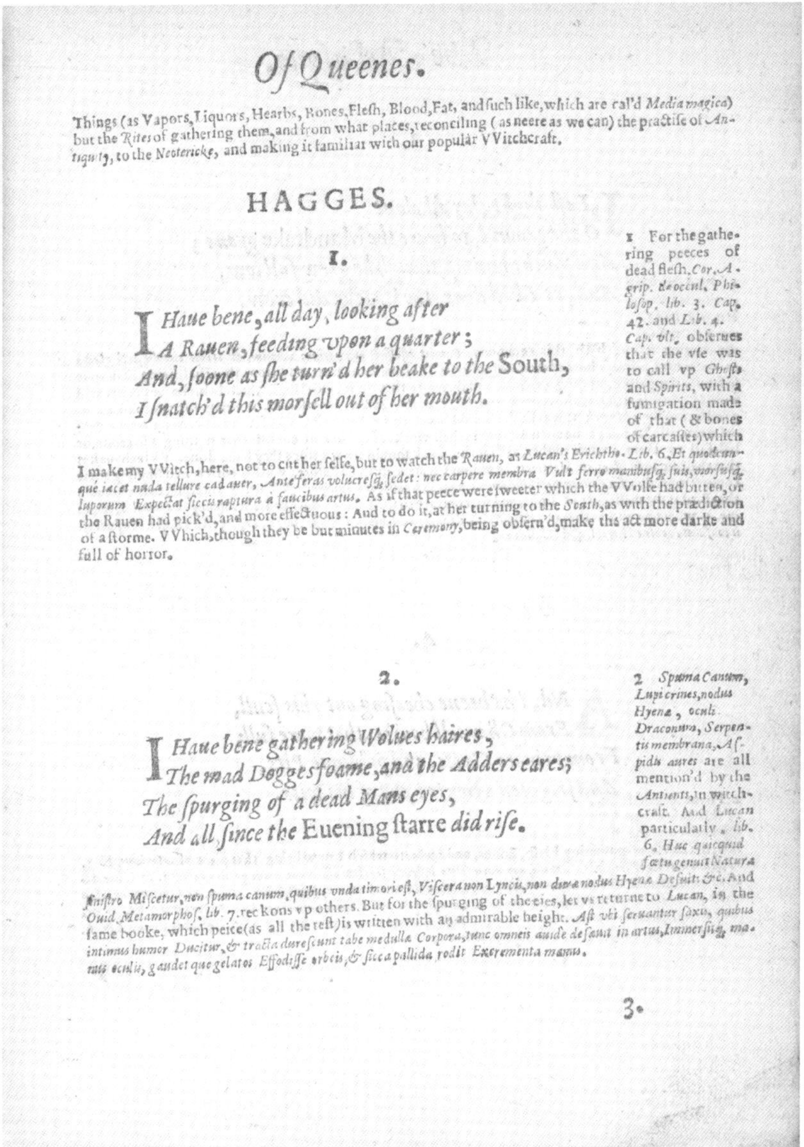

Of Queenes.

Things (as Vapors, Liquors, Hearbs, Bones, Flesh, Blood, Fat, and such like, which are cal'd *Media magica*) but the *Rites* of gathering them, and from what places, reconciling (as neere as we can) the practise of *Antiquity*, to the *Neotericks*, and making it familiar with our popular VVitchcraft.

HAGGES.

I.

I Haue bene, all day, looking after
A *Rauen*, feeding vpon a quarter;
And, soone as she turn'd her beake to the South,
I snatch'd this morsell out of her mouth.

1 For the gathering peeces of dead flesh. *Cor. A-grip. de occul. Phi-losop. lib. 3. Cap.* 42. and *Lib.* 4. *Cap. vlt.* obserues that the vse was to call vp *Ghosts* and *Spirits*, with a fumigation made of that (& bones of carcasses) which

I make my VVitch, here, not to cut her selfe, but to watch the *Rauen*, as *Lucan's* Erichtho. *Lib.* 6. *Et quodcun-que iacet nuda tellure cadauer, Ante feras volucresq; sedet: nec carpere membra Vult ferro manibusq; suis, morsusq; luporum Expectat siccu raptura à faucibus artus.* As if that peece were sweeter which the VVolfe had bitten, or the Rauen had pick'd, and more effectuous: And to do it, at her turning to the *South*, as with the prædiction of a storme. VVhich, though they be but minutes in *Ceremony*, being obseru'd, make the act more darke and full of horror.

2.

I Haue bene gathering VVolues haires,
The mad Dogges foame, and the Adders eares;
The spurging of a dead Mans eyes,
And all since the Euening starre did rise.

2 *Spuma Canum, Lupi crimes, nodus Hyena,* ocnli *Draconum, Serpen-tis membrana.* *Aspidis aures* are all mention'd by the *Antients*, in witch-craft. And *Lucan* particularly, *lib.* 6, *Huc quicquid fœtu genuit Natura sinistro Miscetur, non spuma canum, quibus vnda timori est, Viscera non Lyncis, non dura nodus Hyenæ Defuit. &c.* And *Ouid. Metamorphos. lib. 7.* reckons vp others. But for the spurging of the eies, let vs returne to *Lucan*, in the same booke, which peice (as all the rest) is written with an admirable height. *Ast vbi seruantur saxis, quibus intimus humor Ducitur, & trocla durescunt tabe medulla Corpora, tunc omnes auide desaeui in artus, Immersig;, matati oculis, gaudet quæ gelatos Effodisse orbeis, & sicca pallida rodit Excrementa manus.*

3.

Figure 5.2 B. Jonson, *The Masque of Queenes* (STC 14778; 1609), B4ʳ: Huntington Library, San Marino, RB 62067, the Arundel-Royal Society copy.

If *Queenes* was set by formes and concurrently with other work, then the fact that *Lear* was set seriatim makes it something of an exception.

There are at least three details from Blayney's analysis that might be looked at differently. First, Blayney records that a partial distribution of sheet E took place to assist with the completion of F, yet he also demonstrates that a second compositor appears at sheet H with a new case.[53] If we do have some missing output, therefore, it may be that the second compositor was setting from these other cases of pica italic and roman before he commenced work on *Lear*. Otherwise B could simply have raided the sorts from these cases when small shortages occurred. Second, whilst we only have evidence for stop-press corrections from eight formes out of 21, all this material relates to work set by B: it is an inference only, but one textual error suggests that the compositor may have been an apprentice about two years in the trade (II.ii.47/52), which would point to Thomas Corneforth.[54] That the apprentice set the text may explain why *Lear* was set seriatim. Third, the paper evidence suggests that *Lear* may have been finished in February.[55]

Faced with an outraged modern scholar demanding to know why *Lear* was set by an apprentice, Okes might well have looked in blank astonishment and reminded the scholar that his friend Simon Waterson, for whom he regularly printed, was the leading London literary publisher of the day, whose most important author was Samuel Daniel, and that *Delia* had been reprinted many times. Okes rapidly became Waterson's most important London printer, and for a while was second only in importance to John Legate of Cambridge, who was Waterson's brother-in-law. The fact that Okes was employed by as reputable a publisher as Waterson, whose family business extended back to the late 1550s and had passed through his stepfather Francis Coldock and stepbrother-in-law William Ponsonby, might give one reason to pause before slighting the repute in which he was held by the trade.[56]

If there is a more general point to be made from the example of *Lear*, it is that sometimes the information that is accumulated through the study of bibliographical detail is more securely employed in exposing false assumptions than in revealing the mysteries of the page. McKenzie, in 'Printers of the Mind' expressed a need for greater humility in the face of the erasure of so much quotidian detail: the fragments that survive flatter us and, for the lack of other pieces, we close the space around them and assume they are the picture.

[53] Blayney, *The Texts of* King Lear, 115, 149, and 156.
[54] Blayney, *The Texts of* King Lear, 17 and 26: see p.161 below.
[55] Blayney, *The Texts of* King Lear, 99–101.
[56] I would like to thank John Pitcher and Andy Boyle for providing me advance access to, and involving me with, their work on Waterson and Daniel, which is forthcoming,

6 Making Variants

THE idea that every copy of a book will be the same as another is an illusion that has been made more plausible by machine methods of production. In modern books, different impressions from the same stereotype plates may be variant;[1] whilst recent digital technologies can either be used to create absolute uniformity from one edition to the next, or to modify and recreate texts in multiple forms, both textually and visually, and generate differences analogous to those found in the sixteenth and seventeenth centuries. Before mechanized typesetting in the late nineteenth-century, the standardization of print could only ever be partial;[2] and with manuscript, exact replication of a source document was rarely considered essential. Before the mid-eighteenth-century, variant spellings offered scribes and compositors a means for adjusting the layout of the page that was preferable to the use of hyphens, contractions, and unwanted space. At all times, the function that a copy was intended to serve could have consequences for the methods and materials of replication. This chapter is concerned with the analysis of textual differences between copies and versions, with the generation of corrupt readings and the causes that gave rise to them, and with the broader significance of those issues for textual scholarship.

Sometimes variants are described as errors that reveal specific stages in the mediation of a text; whether as lapses of vigilance, or as active (and often mistaken) attempts to fix corrupt readings: but the truth is more complex than there being an archetype from which all copies descend via a combination of scribal or compositorial mistakes. That is a very simple model of what is possible given the diverse permutations of versions and copies that can exist. In many cases, variants do represent errors of one kind or another; but texts may also be subject to revision and emendation in ways that complicate the patterns of recension, as well as the idea of an original document: Herrick, for instance, often returned to his source papers to modify unresolved lines in a poem, generating a second version, rather than working from his previous revision, and thus reworking the same lines in quite different ways.[3]

All variants are the result of human acts that have left their trace in the text through the processes and sources that shaped each witness.

---

[1] For instance, volume 7 of Herford and Simpson's Oxford edition of Jonson (the *Masques and Entertainments*) was reissued with page corrections by Simpson: see his letter to Sir Walter Greg, 3 September 1951; Trinity College, Cambridge, MS Greg 1, letter 82.
[2] McKitterick, *Print, Manuscript and the Search for Order*, 80.
[3] See, T. Cain (ed.), *The Poems of Robert Herrick* (Oxford, forthcoming).

Thus, we cannot understand whether a variant is significant until we have determined its cause, and the purposes that informed those people responsible for making the documents. (How we apply such an insight is yet another matter, and beyond the scope of the present discussion).[4] Each variant between witnesses will be the result of one or more factors (whether it be a misreading, an attempted correction, and so on), and the reason why one variant occurred may differ from that for other variants in the same document. As a consequence, each difference needs to be analyzed and understood on its own terms in order that the genesis and evolution of a text can be differentiated from the history of its reception and use. This is why, in so far as is possible, it is helpful to determine the circumstances under which any document may have been created, and to analyze the materials that were involved, as it is the combination of the analytical and the textual details that can help to determine the order of witnesses in a given sequence. First assumptions about bibliographical relationships do not always prove correct.

Critical decisions about why variants or versions are significant, and how they ought to be recorded, will depend on the text being edited and the range of evidence that survives: both the treatment and the presentation of the evidence require a balance of precision and clarity. Although, as Peter Shillingsburg remarked, 'Textual criticism does not tell anyone what to do with their texts',[5] it does demonstrate the relationship between, and the reasons for, variants and establishes their importance. There can be no universal rule of what is appropriate with regard to the method for recording these details for all texts, as the organization and interpretation of variants requires an understanding of authorial processes; of the ways in which these have been mediated through the methods of replication; of the forms of social and political influence, and the financial constraints, that may have influenced the making and distribution of a copy or edition; and it requires a judgment about how these factors coalesce and are best represented. Every witness to a text is a fragment because each document encodes in its materials, signs, and structure, the history from its creation to its use. The variant is, therefore, of interest beyond its existence as a fact, as it is always informative of something other than itself: there is always a reason for it being as it is, whether that is cultural or individual, a result of mundane carelessness or deliberate forethought.

---

[4] For a survey and analysis of the issues, see: D. C. Greetham, *Theories of the Text* (Oxford, 1999).
[5] P. L. Shillingsburg, *Resisting Texts: Authority and Submission in Constructions of Meaning* (Ann Arbor MI, 1997), 4.

Original Documents

For bibliographical purposes, an author is the person or group who originates a text and first decides its content. Authors may intervene in the communication of a text at later stages and to various ends, alter content, tone, or structure, and respond to suggestions by others about specific details or issues that are raised. What defines the authorial role, however, is the relationship to, and responsibility for, a work: it is for this that payment (in cash or kind) is commonly made, and for which consequences may be suffered ranging from private rejection to ostracism, exile, mutilation, imprisonment, or death. These non-textual occurrences have influenced biographical accounts of identity, and narratives about the role of the author, or of a document, in the history of reception; but identity and influence are quite separate issues (ones of motive and consequence) to that of origination, and are open to historical (re)interpretation as well as misunderstanding.[6]

It ought to be axiomatic that all accounts that seek to interpret authorial acts ought to be based on a precise textual history of the relevant documents, but that rarely happens: the fire in Jonson's desk where he lost various manuscript materials, for instance, is often spun into a conflagration of his library without awareness of the revisions he made to 'An Execration upon Vulcan', the lack of evidence relating to the fire in the books that he once owned that would have been in his library at that time, the existence of the manuscript that he borrowed from Sir Robert Cotton to write *Henry V* with his marginalia, or the financial accounts of Gresham College where he resided at the time of the fire.[7] In establishing the history of a text and its associated materials, authorial identity (where this is known) matters in so much as it helps to explain the origins of specific documents and the relationship between one witness to a text and another.

All texts have pretexts and contexts: they do not exist in perfect isolation from one another. The act of their creation may be the result of a commission; be owing to patronage, payment, or suggestion; or have as its cause a response to an event. The text will have been shaped and influenced by other words, written, spoken, or sung, as well as lived experience. Yet neither the cause that gives rise to a text, nor the influences upon it, involve that act of making it with an infusion of eloquence and intellectual content that seeks to enable understanding.

---

[6] See, in particular, H. Love, *Attributing Authorship* (Cambridge, 2002), 32–50.
[7] For instance, see C. I. E. Donaldson, *Jonson's Magic Houses: Essays in Interpretation* (Oxford, 1997), 198–216.

There can be complications to the history of authorship. More than one person might be involved in the act of first making; or a text may be issued by a group or body such as the Privy Council, or the Corporation of London.[8] Some texts are anonymous because they were copied without formal attribution, and we do not now know who was responsible for their creation, and for putting them into circulation.[9] Some texts were reattributed to other authors by well-meaning near-contemporaries who associated them with someone more famous, such as the poems of Hare and Roe that were associated with Donne, the various poems (including 'The Goodwife's Ale' by Sir Thomas Jay) that were attributed to Jonson, and others linked to Ralegh.[10] Texts that survive with initials attached may also be difficult to identify, especially 'W. S.' (usually William Skipwith, William Strode, or some seventeenth-century author other than Shakespeare).[11] Sometimes, a person might preserve (with permission or otherwise) the spoken words of another, such as the comments made by Jonson to Drummond.[12] Such complications may affect the processes of textual transmission, and our sense of who was responsible for the text that we have.

The traditional study of variants, as developed in the nineteenth-century by Lachmann, starts out with the idea of a source text from which all else flows. In general, this model could be applied to ancient authors because the paucity of early evidence meant that there were few issues concerning the origins of the texts that required explanation: in many cases, as with the Greek dramatists, most of what has come down to us is fragmentary. Thus, one could assume texts were transmitted broadly as intended (there being no autographs to complicate analysis), and that corrupt readings would demonstrate the relationship between later witnesses. This method of Aristotelian categorization was used to group manuscript families in order that palaeographical and philological methods could then be applied to the differences between the traditions. Specific exceptions, where more than one archetype can be shown to have existed, could then be dealt with, normally as evidence

---

[8] Modern library cataloguing practice has tried to distinguish carefully between the various forms of responsibility for texts: see, www.aacr2.org.

[9] See, M. L. North, *The Anonymous Renaissance: Cultures of Discretion in Tudor-Stuart England* (Chicago, 2003).

[10] See, M. Ruddick (ed.), *The Poems of Sir Walter Raleigh: A Historical Edition* (Tempe, 1999).

[11] Similarly the 'E. S.' responsible for 'A View of the Present State of Ireland' might not be Edmund Spenser, as so often assumed, but Edward Strange who was admitted to Lincoln's Inn at the behest of Sir Thomas Egerton in 1591.

[12] See, M. B. Bland, 'Further Information: Drummond's *Democritie, A Labyrinth of Delight* and His "Certain Informations and Manners of Ben Jonson"', *TEXT*, 17 (2005), 145–86.

of revision—as with Martial's *Epigrams* where Book X (first published in 95; reissued in 98) was revised after the assassination of Domitian in September 96.[13] Such a view of creativity was inherently inflexible, and simplified the processes of writing and the way in which these have been transmitted: it was this predeterminative quality that Foucault and others challenged by insisting on the malleability of authorship.

With the advent of systematic editing for Shakespeare and other non-classical authors, the Lachmannian method was applied to a new range of texts. For Greg, it opened up the possibility of establishing 'the very autograph' of the author behind the typographic page, and thus the 'ideal copy' from which to edit a text.[14] At first, this theory seemed to suit the editing of Shakespeare (as well as Jonson), where half the plays exist only in a single version and most of the other texts exist in either two or, at most, three states (the exception being Jonson's poems, which were edited by Simpson from printed sources in order to avoid the issue of their complicated manuscript history). As some of Shakespeare's quarto texts were highly variant to those in the *Comedies, Histories, and Tragedies* published in 1623 (STC 22273), the differences were held to be a consequence of post-authorial activity (mercenary actors and nefarious printers with an eye to a quick profit), preserving the notion of a stable original text.[15] As with the classics, there were no literary documents in Shakespeare's hand (there are some signatures) except, perhaps, Hand D in the collaborative manuscript of *Sir Thomas More*.[16] Thus, in order to peer behind the texts, the working practices of early modern printers were studied, so that textual scholars could understand the confluence of palaeographical and printing-house errors that gave rise to the issues that perplexed them.

The move away from categorization towards some notion of perfect form (the text as a kind of Platonic shadow), as proposed by Greg, was first taken as a principle, and then subject to much criticism as it became apparent that there were authors whose textual remains proved more varied and complicated than the unitary theory of origins supposed. Daniel's intervention in the printing history of his texts at multiple stages might serve as one example, the complicated manuscript history

---

[13] For a survey of the surviving evidence relating to Latin authors, see L. D. Reynolds (ed.), *Texts and Transmission: A Survey of the Latin Classics*, rev. edn. (Oxford, 1986).

[14] Greg, *Collected Papers*, 251 and 374–91.

[15] See, L. E. Maguire, *Shakespeare's Suspect Texts: The 'Bad' Quartos and Their Contexts* (Cambridge, 1996).

[16] See, T. H. Howard-Hill (ed.), *Shakespeare and 'Sir Thomas More': Essays on the Play and Its Shakespearean Interest* (Cambridge, 1989); V. Cabrieli and G. Melchiori (eds.), *Sir Thomas More: A Play by Anthony Munday and Others* (Manchester, 1990).

of Donne's poems as another. One answer to this problem was to posit the idea of final intention: that it did not matter what the author did in the process of writing (first drafts, revisions, and so on), what mattered was the final version as it was made public, with the obvious caveat that errors by compositors or scribes ought to be emended. The crucial point that needed to be established, for this to be determined, was the order of the versions where more then one survives. The theory of final intention thus reasserted a unitary theory of origin: the best text represents the latest point of intersection between the creative process of the author and the production history of the primary documents.[17]

The problem with the fixed notions of an original source and a final intention is not that they locate responsibility for authorship, but the rigid structure they impose on the fluid and complex activity of textual creation. The idea that the act of writing can only lead to a single version is an obvious fallacy, and one that will lead to false conclusions in the analysis of variants. A text may be begun in oral or written form; there may be drafts, notes jotted down on separate sheets of paper, or in margins and notebooks; revisions may involve both new changes and the reversion to earlier ideas; fair copies may not be autograph, but corrected by the author; and complete versions may exist in different states, with texts adapted to specific circumstances. A rigorously determined authorial text is only one possible outcome of this process. A play, in contrast, might be sketched out, expanded, reimagined, and revised. A copy, with more than was required for performance, might then be prepared for approval and publication, as would appear to be the case with the second quarto of *Hamlet*. In rehearsal, further changes could be made to adjust the pace of the action on the stage with music, costume, gesture, and delivery all becoming part of the text. A performance for a different audience might prompt revisions, new scenes, and changes in emphasis, as well as the addition or deletion of speeches and characters. Further, an author, such as Shakespeare, might not use the fair copy to prepare this new version but, like Herrick, revert to an earlier draft and rewrite the text in a new way. *King Lear* is an example of this process at work, with the 1608 quarto representing the public performance, and the 1623 folio text a court performance that drew upon new, as well as possibly earlier, material.[18]

[17] See, J. McLaverty, 'The Concept of Authorial Intention in Textual Criticism', *The Library*, vi: 6 (1984), 121–38.
[18] Blayney, *The Texts of* King Lear, as before; S. Urkowitz, *Shakespeare's Revision of* King Lear (Princeton NJ, 1980); M. J. Warren and G. Taylor, *The Division of the Kingdoms: Shakespeare's Two Versions of* King Lear (Oxford, 1983).

Once the role of the author is freed from the idea that all copies of a text must derive from a single source, or an original and final revised version, and the variety of human activity is allowed, then Lachmann's method of identifying families can be employed to describe the permutations that underlie all extant documents, both manuscript and printed. The single or binary model of composition is simply not true for many authors: Jonson's 'An Execration upon Vulcan' exists in three states, with the 1640 Benson piracy descending from a combination of a manuscript and stolen sheets of the, as yet unpublished, 1640 *Workes*; the same is true for the piracy of 'Upon My Picture Left in Scotland', which had four stages of composition and revision; whilst Overbury's *A Wife* circulated as five variant texts, with the first, second, and seventh printed editions deriving from different manuscript groups.[19] Familial relationships are similarly important for the later seventeenth-century: the plays and poems of Buckingham, Rochester, and Dorset can only be established by abandoning authorship as the prime criterion for analysis. These authors pose difficult questions concerning the genesis of their work and their relationship to what survives in their name.[20]

In the sixteenth and seventeenth centuries, it is unusual to be able to watch an author at work, from draft to fair copy. In some cases, as with Drummond and Clarendon,[21] we do have extensive autograph papers; otherwise, most of the evidence relating to working practices involves either reading or note-taking (i.e. marginalia in a book the author owned), or the scribal and printed versions of later revisions.[22] A few examples, however, of such things do survive, including a sonnet by King James, written in January 1616 (figures 6.1 and 6.2). The poem is about the king being unable to hunt owing to the severe winter. What the transition from draft to fair copy illustrates is the complexity of the relationship between composition, transmission, and the normalization of authorial language. A further scribal manuscript survives, in the hand of Thomas Carew, in the British Library (Additional MS 24195).

The manuscripts show that James began the process of composition by writing out half a dozen lines of 'thoughts', that were then crossed through once they had been reused in the poem:

---

[19] The evidence for the stages of revision and the piracy will be presented in Bland (ed.), *The Poems of Ben Jonson*.

[20] H. Love (ed.), *The Works of John Wilmot, Earl of Rochester* (Oxford, 1999); R. D. Hume and H. Love (eds.), *Plays, Poems and Miscellaneous Writings Associated with George Villiers, Second Duke of Buckingham*, 2 vols. (Oxford, 2007). Dorset awaits a similar edition.

[21] National Library of Scotland, MSS 2060–7; Bodleian Library, Oxford, Clarendon MSS.

[22] For a conspectus of materials relating to print, see, Moore, *Primary Materials Relating to Copy and Print*.

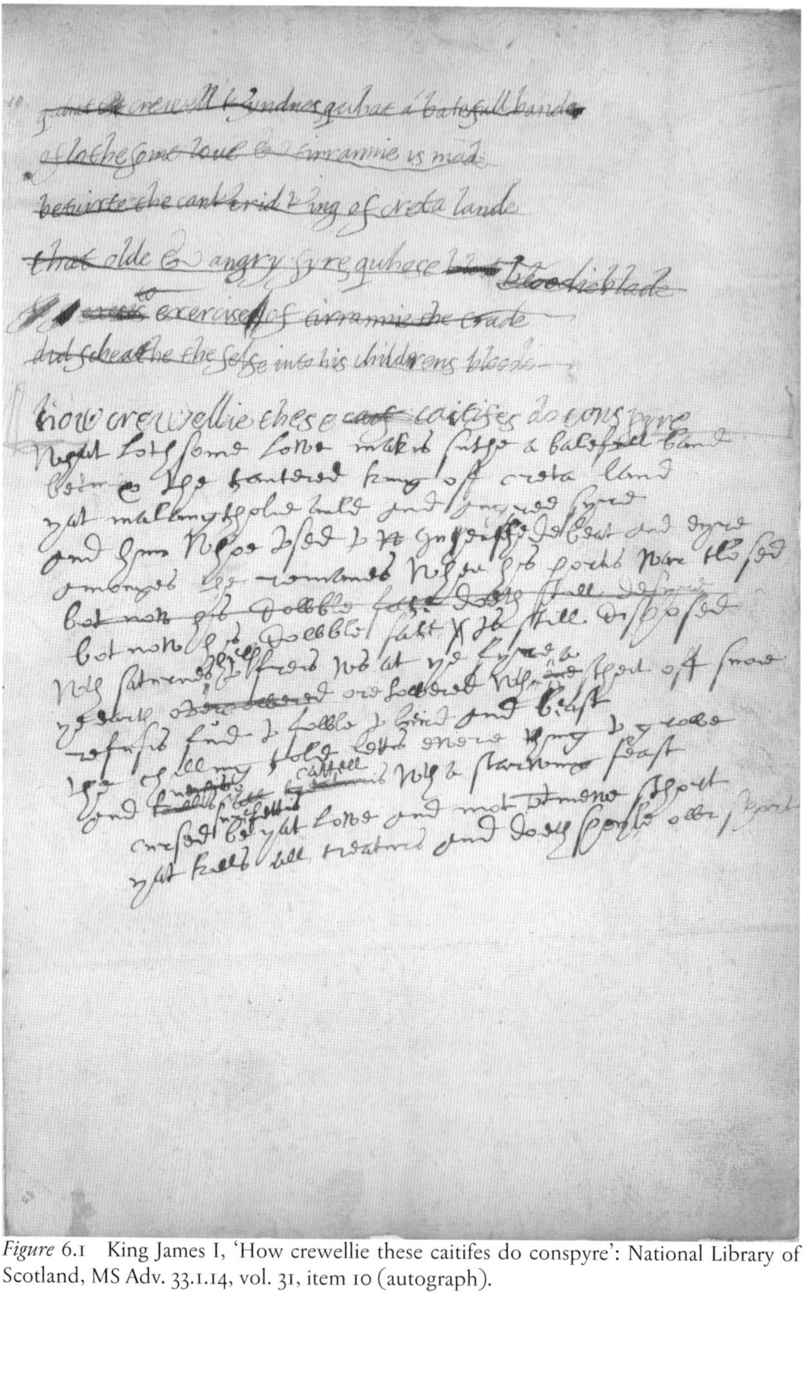

Figure 6.1 King James I, 'How crewellie these caitifes do conspyre': National Library of Scotland, MS Adv. 33.1.14, vol. 31, item 10 (autograph).

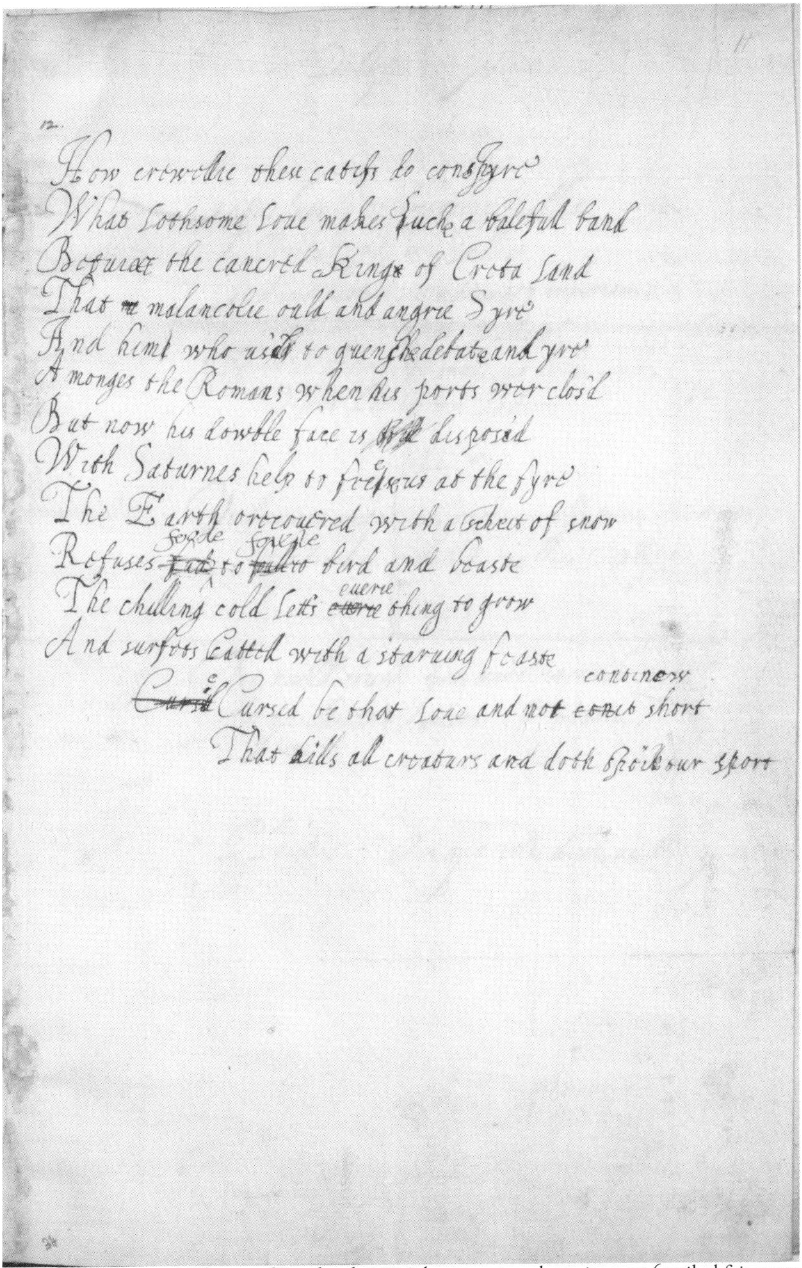

12.

How crewellie then catifs to conspyre
What lothsome loue makes such a balefull band
Bequeat the cancred Kings of Creta land
That ~~ne~~ malancolie ould and angrie Syre
And hemt who usd to quenche debate and yre
Amonges the Romans when his ports wor closd
But now his dowble face is ~~still~~ disposd
With Saturnes help to freizes at the fyre
The Earth orecouered with a sheet of snow
Refuses ~~fatts~~ *foode foode* bird and beaste
The chilling cold letts ~~euere~~ *euerie* thing to grow
And surfets Catted with a starving feasse
                                                    consumes
~~Cursd~~ Cursed be that loue and not ~~comes~~ short
That kills all creaturs and doth spoile our sport

Figure 6.2   National Library of Scotland, MS Adv. 33.1.14, vol. 31, item 12 (scribal fair copy with autograph corrections).

> quhat crewell kyndnes, quhat a balefull bande
> of lothesome loue & tirranie is mad
> betwixte the cankerid King of creta lande
> that olde & angry syre, quhose ~~blood~~ bloodieblade
> ~~to execis~~ to exercises of tirranie the trade
> did scheat the selfe into his childrens blood

These notes have a number of distinct Scottish spellings, particularly 'quhat' and 'scheat'. However, when James then prepared a draft of the full sonnet, he started to anglicize his language, although his text retains distinctive spellings such as 'malangcholie' and 'ws', with 'w' commonly used instead of u/v. Such traits are common in other Scottish authors such as Drummond.[23] The full draft of the poem reads:

> How crewellie these ~~caif~~ caitifes do conspyre
> What lothsome lowe makes suche a balefull band
> betwixt the cankered king of creta land
> that malangcholie ould and angree syre
> and him whoe vsed to ~~w~~ quhenshe debeat and eyre
> amonges the romanes when his ports were closed
> ~~bot now his dowble face doeth still desyre~~
> bot now his dowble face ~~s~~ is still disposed
> W^th saturnes ^help to freis ws at ye fyre
> ye earth ~~overcowered~~ ore cowered w^th ^ane ^a scheit off snoue
> refusis fūd to fowle to bird and beast
> the chilling cold lettis ewere thing to growe
> and ~~kills~~ [del] ^ro ~~all~~ surfettis ~~creaturis~~ cattell wth a starwing feast
> cursed be yat lowe and not continewe short
> yat kills all creaturis and doeth spoyle owr sport

This version of the poem is on pot paper and is clearly intended to be a draft. When the fair copy was made in an italic hand (figure 6.2), Italian flag paper was used. This is significant: it seems likely that this version was initially meant to be made available for others as a source document for their own transcript but, as is often the case, a fresh clear text led to further revision, whilst the fact that it was a scribal copy served to distance the king from his own processes of writing. James, in other words, did not circulate his poems in royal autograph (given his hand that is perhaps as well), rather he made them available via a high-quality secretarial copy. This preliminary fair copy is anglicized further by both the secretary and the king who made some final adjustments, including altering 'fud' to 'foode':

---

[23] Drummond, for instance, introduced Scottish spelling into Jonson's poem 'That Women are but Mens Shaddowes' (*For.* VII): National Library of Scotland, MS 2060. f.238^r.

> How crewellie these catifs do conspyre
> What lothsome loue makes ^s^ouch~e~ a balefull band
> Betwixt the cancred King of Creta land
> That ~~m~~ malancolie ould and angrie Syre
> And him~e~ whoe us'de to quen~s~che debate and yre
> Amonges the Romans when his ports wer clos'd
> But now his dowble face is ~~still~~ dispose'd
> With Saturnes help to fre^c^ise us at the fyre
> The Earth orecouered with a scheit of snow
> Refuses ~~fud~~ ^foode^ to ~~foull~~ ^fowle^ to bird and beaste
> The chilling cold lett's ~~euorie~~ ^euerie^ thing to grow
> And surfets ~~e~~Cattell with a staruing feaste
>   ~~Curs'^°^d~~ Cursed be that loue and not ~~conit~~ continew short
>   That kills all creaturs and doth spoyle our sport

From this corrected secretarial copy, it is likely that a final transcript was made, and that some remaining idiosyncrasies were removed with implicit consent. In a more elaborate way, the same relationship between secretary and author is apparent in the manuscripts of Dudley, Lord North.[24] Secretarial transcription was, in cases such as this, a highly important link between the author and the circulation of the text in its presently finished form. What the example demonstrates is a shift from draft to fair copy, from autograph to scribal copy, from private jottings to public circulation, and from regional to standardized spelling, all within two sheets of paper. From the scribal copy, the poem could be disseminated through the court and beyond, with each subsequent copy giving rise to a unique combination of differences. From that stage onwards, the variants would no longer be the result of revision, or made with implicit authorial consent, but would rather reflect the social history of the text as it was received and (mis)understood. Variants in scribally circulated texts are different in their causes to those in the original documents with which an author is involved.

Visible Signs

Every textual scholar usually has to deal with the presence in the text of agents other than the author who have interpreted what is before them. The problem is that when someone copies a text, they will introduce

---

[24] North's poems can be found in their earliest (scribal) state in Huntington, HM 198 part 2, ff.57^r^–79^r^. Autograph corrected scribal copies include: Bodleian Library, Oxford, North MS e.1 and North MS e.2; and Rosenbach Library, Philadelphia, MS 240/1. Although begun in 1598, North's poems were not published until 1645, when they appeared as *A Forest of Varieties* (Wing N1283).

variations to the text, partly owing to alternate practices, partly to human fallibility, and these differences need to be assessed for the information that they yield. Sometimes the changes have been accepted as without consequence—at least at the time. In the sixteenth and seventeenth centuries, 'she' and 'shee', 'beauty' and 'beautie', 'logic', 'logick', and 'logicke', were all accepted as being the same for all intents and purposes. This fluidity of lexical form was further subject to formal variation through the coexistence of secretarial and italic script, and a tendency in personal script to mix the two alphabets in idiosyncratic ways, with the consequence that both letters and words could change visual form from one copy to another.

The problem with copying a text is that we tend to do so more often in haste than with the exacting care of a public inscription. The motto of the Aldine printing-house, *festina lente*, is an expression of this conflict between speed and accuracy. Owing to the technical aspects of both writing, and setting type, when speed is applied to the process specific kinds of variants occur, sometimes in combination with one another. Thus, most types of variant are generic because they can be explained as being the consequence of one or another particular act, however different each variant is as an example of its kind. In order to clarify how they occur, Dearing has listed 14 main kinds of variant: that discussion has shaped what follows.[25] Dearing's list is conceived with scribal practices in mind, and there are some other issues that relate to printing-house practice that need to be taken into account, as printed variants may arise from the setting, correcting, and distribution of type, or derive from the same scribal issues that arise from communicating a prior manuscript copy.

With printed books for which manuscript copy does not exist (and that is most of them), a recognition of the common patterns of scribal confusion that give rise to a reading may often help to resolve textual cruces. In almost all cases, the simplest explanation is the most likely. All printed books derive from an antecedent document: if the book is a reprint then the source copy would generally (but not always) have been a prior printed edition; in the first instance, however, a manuscript had to be used, whether in the author's hand or prepared by another with, or without, the author's consent. A compositor was, therefore, faced with the same potential problems in setting what was before him as scribe in making a copy: he was capable of misreading exactly as a scribe might, as capable of making unintentional and sometimes deliberate

---

[25] V. A. Dearing, *Principles and Practice of Textual Analysis* (Berkeley CA, 1974), 44–53.

variants, and as potentially subject to working from a copy that was less than satisfactory. What is important, however, is not just the kinds of variant that are possible, but how one recognizes the particular kind of alteration that has occurred: part of the art is being able to understand what happened at an earlier stage than survives.

The simplest form of misreading is the confusion of one letter, or group of letters, for another. This is known as the 'minim' problem, as the even strokes of those letters up and down can make it very difficult to discern the letters intended, and it is possible for there to be two equally valid alternatives. Earlier (p. 89 above), it was noted that with secretary hand, *h* can be confused with *y*, *a* with *u*, and *o* with *e*. These letters, and the possibility of a confusion between them, appear in *King Lear* at II.ii.47/52. Scholars have agreed that the correct reading is 'yeares' rather than 'houres' because, in Greg's words, 'This is sober sense: Shakespeare knew that art is long.' If we accept that the textual difference was an error and not intentional, then it must have had a cause. Hence, what is wrong in Greg's subsequent reasoning is his explanation for why the confusion occurred:

> For the actor and the groundling two years seems an age: so the quarto substitutes 'two hours', which is absurd.[26]

Strictly speaking, the quarto is an inanimate object: what Greg meant is that he believed the quarto to be a piracy and, therefore, that the 'actors' responsible for the text changed one word to suit contemporary notions of theatrical performance. Elsewhere, Greg had argued for the primacy of bibliographical facts over this kind of meta-critical reasoning.[27] In this instance, a misreading of 'yeares' as 'houres' can be explained by something as simple as 'yea' being confused with 'hou'. If there is another reason for the change, then it may be of some consequence, as Blayney demonstrated, that there was a single compositor responsible for setting most of *Lear* and that it was set seriatim.[28] It has already been suggested that this person was Thomas Corneforth, who had been bound as an apprentice to Okes's predecessor in September 1605, some two years previously.[29] Perhaps Corneforth held a higher estimate of his competency than scholarship has subsequently allowed him, and so he read 'yeares' as 'houres'. If the palaeographical similarity is sufficient in

[26] W. W. Greg, *The Editorial Problem in Shakespeare*, 3rd edn. (Oxford, 1951), 91. References to the text, for convenience, are to the Cambridge editions.

[27] Greg, 'Bibliography—An Apologia', 253.

[28] Blayney, *The Texts of* King Lear, 78–84 and 89–150; see also, pp. 141–48 above.

[29] Blayney, *The Texts of* King Lear, 17.

itself to account for the variant readings, the biographical detail of who might have been responsible is suggestive.

A second kind of letter substitution occurs because of the lay of a compositor's case, which was placed on an angle and organized rather like a modern keyboard.[30] With lower-case letters, the most commonly used types (*a*, *e*, *n*, and *d*) were placed as a group on the centre-left of the case. There are a great many words, apart from 'end' and 'and' that end with, or contain, those letters. Unlike 'with' where the sorts are of different widths, 'end' and 'and' have letters of the same width, and are without kerns. Thus, when the individual sorts were distributed back to their slots in the case, it would have been easy for a sort to spill out of a full box into a neighbour, or for the compositor to distribute a sort to the wrong slot and subsequently set one letter for another.

Usually, a compositor did not examine each letter before placing it in the stick: certainly, if a 'w' had dropped into the 'i' box, it would have been noticed from touch that the wrong sort was in the hand, but this would not happen for two sorts of the same width. The fact that 'n' and 'd' are adjacent in the case probably explains another variant in *King Lear*: at II.iv.234/57, the quarto reads 'O reason not the deed', the folio reads 'need'. Editors have argued that 'need' is the correct reading but have not noticed that a misdistribution of type is the most probable cause of 'deed' in the quarto text. What such a variant indicates is that the quarto version was not read against copy, as was best practice, but simply from proof, with the copy only checked if the text did not make sense and in a way that could not be easily fixed.

A third reason for letter substitution involved a combination of loose type and faulty proof correction. When a compositor set type in the composing stick, the letters and spacing had to form a rigid rectangle otherwise the letters could work loose under the pressure of the platen.[31] Thus, it was imperative that loose type be fixed immediately as a single dropped letter might cause an entire page to drop from the forme, with the result that not only would all the composition have to be done again, but all the letters would have to be resorted from the pied heap. As a consequence, loose type was fixed before presswork began in earnest at the time when an early pre-production proof was pulled. If type worked loose during presswork, the typical signs are that some letters have been driven up the edge of the page, or dropped from the register. When loose type was fixed before presswork began, the nature of the variant is what usually indicates the problem.

[30] P. Gaskell, 'The Lay of the Case', *Studies in Bibliography*, 22 (1969), 125–42.
[31] Moxon, *Mechanick Exercises*, 207 and 231–5.

In printed books, the miscorrection of a dropped letter may result in it being substituted for another. For instance, the quarto of *Richard III* reads at I.i.13 'the lasciuious pleasing of a loue' whereas the folio reads 'lute'. As with *Lear*, scholars have preferred the folio on the basis that it is clearly the superior reading, but have not explained the mechanics of the problem. In fact, the cause of the variant is likely to have been a dropped letter rather than, for instance, scribal confusion. As the forme of the quarto was locked into place, the thin 't' probably dropped from the page leaving the reading 'lue' and a slight disturbance of the type: when the proof was read before the printing began, the mistake would have been obvious, but the solution less so, with 'liue', 'loue', 'lure' and 'lute' all possible alternatives. Whilst 'liue' and 'lure' do not make sense in the context, 'loue' can easily be lasciuious and is a more obvious quick fix than 'lute'. It is only because we know the folio variant that we can perceive what the compositor probably did.

It is more unusual to be able to watch a section of type collapse owing to a correction, but this is what happens with the marginal note at III.ii.124 in Jonson's *The Staple of Newes*. The correct text ought to read 'I. Cuft. | A *fhe* Ana- | baptist', but a stop-press correction loosened the type in the marginal column. None of the copies that Simpson had seen had this reading, but the variant was present in a copy owned by Greg who informed Simpson of it. Simpson wrote back:

> None of the 11 copies I collated have the reading <u>A</u> <u>she</u> Ana-/I can't explain it: as the type was deranged at that point it may have been the original reading, or it may have been a correction.[32]

Simpson was, in fact, very fortunate to have located all three variants in only 12 copies. When he finally came to issue volume IX of the Oxford edition, he had made a decision about the order of the three variants and it was a telling one: the most correct reading had to be the last. This order ignored the fact that the type was, in Simpson's word 'deranged', or rather that the 'ft.' of 'Cuft.' had shifted down the page in gradual stages: this is the most common state of the text. He therefore proposed an order that went 'A *fhe* | baptist' (with type movement), 'A *fhe* An- | baptist', and then 'A *fhe* Ana- | baptist'.[33] That this is self-evidently wrong should on reflection be obvious, but it is worth explaining why and exactly what did happen.

---

[32] The note is loosely inserted at Fi^r in Greg's copy of the 1631 plays, now Bodleian Library, Oxford shelfmark: Gibson 519. The second state is also to be found in the copy now at the Peabody Library, Baltimore, shelfmark P820.J81.1616.v.2.RB.

[33] H&S, IX, 123.

There is one variant on Fɪʳ that neither Simpson nor Riddell noticed, where 'idle and laborious,' was corrected to 'idle, and laborious,'.[34] The state of the marginal note that is connected to the first reading is 'A *ſhe* An- | baptist'; all the copies with 'A *ſhe* Ana- | baptist', or type slippage, have the corrected state with the comma. Furthermore, the register of the type on the page in Greg's copy is informative, for the terminal 'a' of 'Ana' is far darker on the page than the capital 'A' indicating that type slippage had already begun to take place. In effect, what happened was that after a few sheets had been printed off, the press was stopped and the corrections made. The result of opening up the marginal sidenotes was that the surrounding quads and other spaces were loosened, and when the page was closed back up again the line was slightly loose. As the forme was then printed off, the pressure of the platen first led 'Ana-' to drop below the level of the other type, so it did not appear, and then as it dropped further for the type in 'Cuſt.' above to collapse gradually down the page.[35]

Similarly, at the opening of *Lear* the quarto reads 'for equalities are so weighed,' whereas the folio reads 'qualities'. In this instance, it is more likely that the folio is in error and the reason, again, is that a letter dropped from the register before a proof was pulled and prior to presswork: this is indicated later in the folio line where the text reads 'weighed , that'. It is uncommon in a printed text of this period for a space to precede the comma and for there to be another after. Further, the space is the same width as the letter 'e'. It is possible, therefore, that the first 'e' of 'equalities' dropped; and that, once again, proof was not checked against copy. When the pull was read, the text would have made sense but a space would have been needed to justify the line and prevent type collapse: and so the compositor inserted a space in a way that did not create an obvious pigeon hole between two words.

A particular form of substitution and omission occurs at the end of words, where a singular may be made plural, a plural singular, or verbs are turned into nouns. This usually occurs because of the similarities in secretary hand between 'e', terminal 's', and the contraction for '-es': the latter like an italic 'e' with a longer tail. A lack of conventions for standard spelling practices only served to compound the problem. Consider, for instance, the words 'writ', 'write', 'writes', and 'writs'.

---

[34] J. A. Riddell, 'Some Notes on the Printing of the Jonson Plays of 1631', *Ben Jonson Journal*, 4 (1997), 65–80.

[35] Strictly speaking, the final state of type collapse is not a variant, as it did not involve a separate stop-press correction; although displaced, 'Ana-' is present if not visible. Some assumed variants are simply nothing more than this: in particular, punctuation marks were apt to shift and a comma might easily register as a full-stop.

Some scribes omitted the final 'e' on various words, so there are several permutations in spelling and understanding that are possible. If, for instance, the original 'he writes' was copied as 'he writs', another person might read 'writs' as we now would do, and so decide that 'he' was a mistake and emend 'he' to 'his'. This is the problem known as the substitution of similar words.

A similar example of a palaeographical misreading leading to a more extensive attempt at emendation occurs in one of Francis Beaumont's verse letters to Jonson, where he disparages the popular taste for several plays including John Marston's *The Fawne* and Edward Sharpham's *The Fleire*. Beaumont remarks that the next play will be called *The Grinne*.[36] Only Huntington, HM198 part 2, a manuscript associated (as was the Beaumont family) with the Inner Temple, records this correctly; the remaining manuscripts have 'geinne', '*Gennie*', and 'ginne': it seems likely that 'geinne' was copied from a manuscript where secretary 'e' and 'r' could be confused, and that what began as a difficulty in reading led to attempts at emendation. What such mangled spellings reveal is a lack of comprehension on the part of those who access the text in its derivative forms. Unusual words, such as 'etiostichs' in Jonson's 'An Execration upon Vulcan', baffled many who copied the poem.

A failure to transcribe the text accurately would cause confusion for those who followed, and has clear antecedents in classical scholarship where the principle of the correctness of the more difficult reading is well established as the more likely alternative. Of course, the analysis of variants must depend on the balance of probabilities, rather than certainty, because we cannot look over the shoulder of those who prepared the text. Variants should be understood as occurring through the processes of textual transmission, and require no broader meta-critical theory than an insight as to what scribes and compositors did. This is exactly what Greg thought bibliographers ought to be able to demonstrate, but in practice he failed to apply the methodological rigour that he advocated in principle.[37] Thus, the level at which each variant must be understood is the variant itself, not all the variants in a text with their separate and distinct causes. Only once there is an irreducible number of variants that have no mechanical cause can the real differences between alternate versions of a text be identified. This is

[36] Jonson shared Beaumont's contempt for these plays and said as much to Drummond. For an analysis of the textual tradition of Beaumont's letters, see my 'Francis Beaumont's Verse Letters to Ben Jonson and "The Mermaid Club"', *English Manuscript Studies*, 12 (2005), 139–78.
[37] Greg, 'Bibliography—An Apologia', 259.

the bibliographical equivalent of the principle established by William of Ockham: the simplest explanation is almost always the correct one.

Similar words could be substituted for several reasons other than an attempt to rectify the meaning or spelling of a source document, and such substitutions can seem like particular acts of carelessness: thus, all the miscellany texts of Jonson's epigram 'On Giles and Joan' (*Epig.* XLII) derive from scribal copies of the 1616 *Workes*. One intermediary changed 'free' to 'good' in line 5 giving rise to two other manuscripts with that reading. In order to make better sense, the text of British Library, Sloane MS 1489 has been altered in line 5 from 'By' to 'With'; whilst, in line 3, the text of Folger, MS V.a.339 reads 'ever' rather than 'her'. This is not unusual. All the other copies of the poem have similar substitutions: in Bodleian, Ashmole MS 47 'yearn'd' in line 11 reads 'yeare and'; in Bodleian, MS Don e.6 'sad' is substituted for 'harsh' in line 10, and 'earnd' for 'yearn'd' in line 11; Folger, MS V.a.345 reads 'doe' for 'can' in line 2, and 'to' for 'with' in line 16; whilst the printed miscellany *Wits Interpreter* has 'mome' for 'morne' in line 2, 'comming' for 'turning' in line 8, 'yarnd' for 'yearn'd' in line 11 and 'thing' for 'things' in line 17.[38] The change of 'comming' for 'turning' is a particularly good example of how an inter-mediary might simplify a text with the more obvious word.

Similar words could be substituted owing to memorial transmission: this was particularly true for songs and ballads where music, sometimes now lost, formed a basis through which texts could be communicated and learned. Subsequent scribal copies would then descend from the variant memorial text. Thus, Clerimont's song from *Epicoene*, 'Still to be neat, still to be dressed' (I.i.91–102), survives in at least 22 manuscript copies and three printed miscellanies. Line 9 ('Robes loosely flowing, haire as free,') shows probable signs of having been influenced from memory. In several manuscripts, 'loosely' either reads 'rudely' or 'sweetly'; in other manuscripts 'flowing' is replaced by 'hanging'. Such changes do not have their origin in a mistranscription; rather they reveal an assumed familiarity with the text.

Some substitutions are of a more deliberate nature, and some reflect shared prejudices and attitudes. In *Pseudo-Martyr*, it was almost certainly the compositor, and not a difficulty with the copy, that was responsible for a gender slur on the Pope, whose claim to authority as '*Supreame spiritual Princeſſe*, ouer all Princes' was corrected by Donne in his errata to '*Prince*'.[39] Similarly, Bodleian, Rawlinson Poetry MS 62, a manuscript

[38] Stemmata will be provided for all of Jonson's poems where more than four copies survive in my forthcoming Oxford edition of *The Poems of Ben Jonson*.

[39] J. Donne, *Pseudo-Martyr* (STC 7048; 1610), G2ʳ and ¶2ᵛ.

of Cambridge origin, changed 'A London Cuckold . . .' in 'Cock Lorrell' to read 'An Oxford Cuckold', reflecting the rivalry between the two universities.[40] Fear might also play its part and cause an intermediary to alter a text. In 1621, Robert Jenison, who was in Newcastle, trusted the publication of a sermon to his friend Richard Sibbes, who toned down some of the phrasing after the book had been licensed. Jenison was not best pleased, and wrote to Samuel Ward, Master of Sidney-Sussex College, Cambridge, about the matter, noting that Sibbes had changed 'owne nation' to 'neighbour nations', and 'forbidden marriages with women popishly affected' to 'unfortunate marriages . . .'.[41]

A particular form of substitution is abbreviation, where the idea is communicated but the phrasing simplified. Hence, when Jonson visited William Drummond in Scotland, Drummond preserved fragments of the comments that Jonson had made in two manuscripts. These reported texts are clearly condensed. The principal manuscript was copied by Sir Robert Sibbald around 1700 and probably destroyed in a fire at Penicuik in the late nineteenth-century. The second manuscript repeats a number of the anecdotes from this lost source. It is therefore possible to compare Drummond's text of these stories with Sibbald's transcript, and what is evident is that Sibbald repeatedly substituted a shorter phrase than found in Drummond's version of the text.[42]

As well as word substitution, inaccurate word separation may give rise to variants. The example from 'On Giles and Joan' where 'yearn'd' becomes 'yeare and' illustrates the problem and its consequences. In manuscripts, a momentary lifting of the pen might mislead later readers into thinking that two words were intended rather than one. Similarly, two words might be merged into one. In printed texts, word separation was basic to the justification of the page and so compositors tended to take more care with spacing than they did with the accuracy of their work as a whole. Hence, the only adjustment to the forme that happened during a stop-press correction two-thirds of the way through printing A2^v/A3^r of Jonson's 'Horace his Art of Poetry' in the 1640 *Workes* (STC 14754) was the alteration of the final line of A3^r where 'Andwealth . . . ;and brought' was respaced 'And wealth . . . ; and brought'.

A common form of variation is transposition, which occurs when the order of two words is switched. For instance (and to revert to an earlier

[40] Bodleian Library, Rawlinson Poetry MS 62, f.32^{r-v}.
[41] Bland, 'Invisible Dangers' 165–6. The book was *The height of Israels heathenish idolatorie* (STC 14991; 1621). Jenison's letter, in which he describes the 'timorousness' of Sibbes, is Bodleian Library, MS Tanner 73, f.29.
[42] See, M. B. Bland, 'Further Information', 145–86.

example), one manuscript of Clerimont's song from *Epicoene* ('Still to be neat . . .') records the text as 'Haires looselie flowinge, roabs as free' (Edinburgh University, Laing MS 436) rather than as 'Robes looselie flowing, haire as free'. Once again, this is a sign of a copy influenced by memorial patterns of transmission, or at least a very casual transcript. As with word substitution, transposition is commonly found in texts with musical settings and songs from plays that are sometimes copied. It should not be assumed, however, that the source of the text was a play or performance. In one instance, Jonson must have circulated Karolin's song from *The Sad Shepherd* (I.v.65–80) separately, as the play was incomplete at his death: it survives in 15 manuscript copies and four printed miscellanies. The second line ought to read 'Either what Death, or Love is well', but several scribal copies transpose the middle of the line to read 'Love, or Death'. Compositors also memorized texts in short sections whilst setting type, and so they might transpose words or punctuation marks: hence, on Z2^v of *The Underwood* in Jonson's 1640 *Workes*, the preliminary setting reads '*done? . . . slave:*' (ll. 31, 33) and the revised setting '*done: . . . slave?*'.

A more substantial kind of transposition can occur when two parts of a text are moved in relation to one another. Sometimes this happens when a text has an oral tradition like 'Cock Lorrell' where the order of the stanzas is sometimes rearranged. Other transpositions may occur because the layout of the source document is more complicated than usual. Thus, Jonson's 'An Epitaph . . . on Vincent Corbett' survives in six manuscript copies. The most important of these is the placard prepared for Corbett's funeral (Beinecke Library, Osborn MS fb230), which is laid out in columns and includes poems by John Selden (whose father was a neighbour) and Richard Corbett, Vincent's son.[43] Of the remaining five manuscripts, two start the poem at line 7, and in one case (Pierpont Morgan Library, MS MA1057), lines 1–6 are moved to the end of the epitaph. The other copy is a later version from the same tradition. It seems likely that the complex arrangement of the text had something to do with the displacement, and then loss, of the first six lines.

As well as being prone to the variants of the kind so far outlined, the transmission of the text might be affected by several forms of omission. The last example noticed how a source document might lead to a partial

---

[43] Selden's father was the tenant at Twickenham of Christopher Jonson (see Jonson's will: PROB 11/90, ff.86^r–87^v), the neo-Latin poet, sometime schoolmaster at Winchester, and member of the Royal College of Physicians from the time Donne's stepfather was president. The Seldens and Corbetts lived there along with Francis Bacon and, later, Lucy Countess of Bedford. It is also very near where Donne lived during his years of removal from London. See also, G. J. Toomer, *John Selden: A Life in Scholarship* (Oxford, 2009), 1–8.

loss of text; an earlier example suggested how an absent letter might lead to an attempted resolution of a reading; the next level of omission is that of an absent word, epithet, or phrase; or what is known as simple omission. This is surprisingly common in early modern texts, and the causes range from carelessness and distraction, through an inability to read a document being copied, to deliberate abbreviation, and private or official censorship. We tend to think of the last as affecting entire texts, but a defter hand might simply omit or alter a word or a phrase.

Scribal omission is so common as to affect almost every manuscript tradition of any complexity. Two of the scribal copies of 'On Giles and Joan', for instance, have omissions: Bodleian, Ashmole MS 47 lacks 'neighbours' in line 2, and Folger, MS V.a.345 'repents' in line 3. Once a text is affected like this, it is almost impossible to recover a lost word unless comparison is made with another copy. In some cases, it is possible to see that a scribe was confused by the copy. The transcript of 'Cock Lorrell' in Folger, V.a.345 has a space in the text where 'vp' should be at line 34; earlier at line 18 the last three words 'and greene sauce' are also wanting. Similarly, with 'An Expostulation with Inigo Jones', the copy in University of Nottingham, MS Pw 2V 154 has a space where 'giuing' ought to be in line 75, as in 'giuing his mind that way'. Such spaces suggest either an intention to return to a difficulty in the copy, or an awareness that the source copy itself was deficient at that point.

Printed texts were frequently affected by simple omissions, and might be indicated in the errata. In a number of cases such errata are accompanied by the comments of either the printer or the author. William Stansby (or his corrector) remarked that:

> Some things haue escaped, others beene mistaken, partly by the absence of him who penned this Treatise, partly by the vnleage-ablenesse of his hand in the written coppy; . . .[44]

Authors might equally admit as much. John Sanford excused:

> the faults herein escaped, thorough ouersight of the Printers; my sicknesse at that time, and the distance of place, not giuing me leaue to be always present . . . the compositors omitting, or not well reading the wordes interlined, wherein I sometimes corrected myselfe, haue thrust in their owne coniectures.[45]

---

[44] A. Roberts, *An exposition vpon the hundred and thirtie psalme* (STC 21073; 1610), O4ʳ. See also, Bland, 'William Stansby and the Production of *The Workes of Beniamin Jonson*, 8–10; McKitterick, *Print, Manuscript and the Search for Order 1450–1830*, 97–165.
[45] P. du Moulin, *A defence of the Catholicke faith*, ed. J. Sanford (STC 7322; 1610), A4ᵛ.

Poor handwriting and interlined copy, combined with the absence of the author might easily lead to every form of variant so far described in combination with one another. Even under the best of circumstances, with an author revising the proofs, variants and stop-press corrections were inevitable; and the bigger the book, the more likely it was that the text would have not only misreadings, but omissions. In 1617, Samuel Purchas explained that 'many faults haue passed in many Copies; though I think not so many in the worst, as in the former Edition, by almost a thousand.'[46] Whilst in his translation of Montaigne, John Florio recorded 127 references to classical texts that had been omitted by the compositors. Florio's presentation copy to Sir Thomas Egerton tells another more complex story, being corrected by Florio throughout with many omissions added back in.[47] Once a text had been set, it was very difficult to restore such material if it meant resetting large blocks of text and readjusting formes. If a compositor had to restore text, he worked by adjusting every line before and after the one affected until the text would 'fit'. Another option was to add the missing text as a marginal note: in Jonson's *Discoveries*, for instance, the word *Thiefe* has an asterisk added and in the margin is added 'with a great belly'.[48] This is clearly not a note as such, but an omission in the text. Such methods were usually only enlisted as a measure of the last resort: many an author must have had to accept the loss of a phrase or a word through oversight and only the conscientious or offended would have recorded the slip.[49]

In some cases, it is clear that the omission was deliberate and may have been required by authority. Seventeenth-century texts were usually censored for theological or political reasons, but the more modern issue of explicit sexual description could also cause a poised censorial pen to delete what was perceived as inappropriate. The fact that several of Donne's elegies including 'To his Mistress Going to Bed', did not appear in the 1633 *Poems* is well known. A more subtle example is Jonson's 'Epigram. To my Bookseller' (*Und.* 58): a poem that has no manuscript witnesses. Editors have been perplexed by a space enclosed by square brackets in the middle of line 12:

> Like a rung Beare, or Swine: grunting out wit
>   As if that part lay for a [   ] most fit!

[46] S. Purchas, *Purchas his pilgrimage* (1617), STC 20507, 5D4ᵛ.
[47] M. de Montaigne, *The essayes or morall, politicke and millitarie discourses* (STC 18041; 1603): Huntington Library, shelfmark RB 61889, dated 20 January 1603.
[48] Jonson, *Discoveries*, paragraph 34. The compositor divided the anecdote.
[49] See, Moxon, *Mechanick Exercises*, 235–6.

The omission is an obscenity. Jonson is referring to a Greek pun that is found in Homer, Xenophon, and Aristophanes: χοιριδιον is the word both for piglet and the female genitalia: hence the deletion. The pun was later exploited by Rochester in the song '*Faire Chloris* in a Pigsty lay', as well as explicitly alluded to in 'The Imperfect Enjoyment' where the poet compares present failure with past history, being a man:

> On whom each Whore Relieves her tingling Cunt
> As Hoggs on Gates doe rubb themselves and grunt (ll.64–5).[50]

More substantial omissions might have several causes. When a word or idea is repeated, or similar words occur in close conjunction, then the intervening words or phrases might be omitted owing to 'eyeskip'. Once this has occurred, all subsequent copies that derive from that source will be affected. For instance, Jonson's 'An Execration upon Vulcan' survives in an original version, an early revision in the mid-1620s, and a late revision in the 1630s. Some copies of the early revision have one line affected by an omission. The affected passage reads in full:

> Or fix'd in the *Low-Countryes*, where you might,
>   On both sides, doe your mischiefe with delight;
> Blow vp, and ruine; mine, and countermine;
>   Vse your Petards, and Granads, all your fine
> Engines of Murder, and enioy the praise
>   Of massacring Mankinde, so manie wayes. (ll.203–8)

One of the early copies of the revision omitted two lines, jumping from 'ruine;' halfway through line 205 to 'and enjoy . . .' in line 207. In all, nine of the 20 extant manuscripts derive from this copy, which was the most widely circulated of any version of the text. What is more unusual is that the skip happens in a medial position, where metre could have been affected; slippage of this kind is more common in prose texts.

In verse, it is common to find the omission of standard lengths, often a line or a couplet. Such omissions are usually a consequence of eyeskip and are common in verse. Hence, the anonymous 'Whoso termes Loue a fire' survives in 26 manuscript copies, nine of which omit line 16. Likewise London Metropolitan Archives, MS ACC/1360/528, which attributes 'Variety' to Nicholas Hare, lacks line 64.[51] Three of the

---

[50] Love (ed.), *The Works of John Wilmot Earl of Rochester*, 13–15 and 39–40.
[51] M. B. Bland, 'Nicholas Hare's "Variety" and the Clitherow Miscellany', Baton Rouge, February 2008. The editors of the Donne Variorum have accepted the reattribution.

manuscripts of Francis Beaumont's letter to Jonson, 'The Sunn (which doth the greatest comfort bringe . . .)' omit line 80, and a fourth substitutes a non-authorial line; another group of manuscripts omits lines 71–4.[52] Similarly, the manuscript copies of Jonson's verse letter 'To Sir Robert Wroth' (*Forr.* III), in Bodleian Library, Rawlinson Poetry MS 31 and British Library, Harley MS 4064 reveal that two lines were omitted from that poem in the 1616 *Workes*: the forthcoming Oxford edition will restore them.[53]

The omission of a standard length could involve a large block of text, such as a page, sheet, or quire. This usually happened because part of a source document had gone astray, or two pages were turned over at once. Given such a gap, a later intermediary might, if they could, conflate sources to 'restore' the missing text. Often the person who did this was unaware that distinct textual traditions were being mixed. Authorial statements about lost material, on the other hand, ought to be treated with some circumspection: Jonson's claim to have lost the last part of his 'Epistle. To the Countess of Rutland' (*Forr.* XII) has been shown from manuscript evidence to be a polite fiction. With *Eupheme* (*Und.* 84) there is a note in the text that 'A whole quaternion in the middle of this Poem is lost, containing entirely the three next pieces of it': most of the other poems survive in manuscript, whereas the missing texts do not. It is quite possible that the work was never finished.

As well as omissions, variants can be created through the addition or substitution of material. In texts with a strong oral tradition, such as 'Cock Lorrell', additional stanzas might be added. An editor has to make a decision about the genuineness of such material and therefore its place in the textual tradition. This can be established by determining where the additions come in the history of transmission. With 'Cock Lorrell', five of the 29 manuscripts and at least two printed copies of the 1640 *Workes* with scribal marginalia contain an extra stanza that begins 'Then broil'd and broacht on a butchers pricke . . . .'. The position varies between witnesses, appearing variously as stanza 5, 7, 9, and 14. None of the witnesses is of high authority, and one of them was written in the nineteenth-century by the forger John Payne Collier who added another stanza to the ballad beginning 'A carted whore a forc'd bakemeat was . . . .'.[54] Inevitably, Collier's version of the 'butchers pricke'

---

[52] Bland, 'Francis Beaumont's Verse Letters to Ben Jonson', 139–78.
[53] The lines follow on from l.60 and allude to Ovid, *Metamorphoses*, I.111–12.
[54] One copy of the 1640 *Workes* is at Harvard, the other is in my possession. Collier's forgery is Rosenbach Library, MS 1083/15. The other manuscripts are British Library, Egerton MS 923 and Additional MS 27879, National Library of Wales, MS 12443A and Beinecke Library, Osborn MS 62.

is variant (it begins 'Then brought he stuckt vppon . . .') from the other witnesses, which are broadly contemporary with the ballad and reflect its popularity and social history in the mid-seventeenth-century. In more extreme circumstances, where a text was known to be imperfect, it might be 'rectified' with the addition of material from another source.

Several other kinds of variation are found in texts, although these are less common. For instance, words could be inserted from the margin if a note was not understood to be such. More commonly, a word or phrase might be repeated: this is the reverse of eyeskip. Hence, it was not until the fourth edition of the *Historie of Tithes* (STC 22172.7) that the repeated 'what through constitutions, what through constitutions' on L3^r, was corrected.[55] In a printed text, a compositor may try to rectify that problem by removing the extra text and respacing the line as well as, possibly, those lines before and after. When this happens, the compositor has to be careful not to open up a river of white space through the middle of the page as this impedes reading. On the other hand, a word or phrase may fail to be repeated because the intermediary or compositor thinks that the repetition is redundant, or because it is assumed (as with a chorus) that the text is sufficiently familiar for '&c.' to be satisfactory: Beinecke Library, MS Osborn b62, for instance, records a chorus after each verse of 'Cock Lorrell' as 'Hi downe downe, &c'; the 'chorus' is found in full in another music manuscript, New York Public Library, Drexel MS 4257.

Scribes and compositors might sometimes add an extra syllable into a word, which might or might not make sense. One of the variants in 'Variety', common to several manuscripts, is 'immedicinable' instead of 'immedicable', and similarly the uncorrected state of P1^r line 31 in the 1640 text of the *Discoveries* reads 'Catalumnie' not 'Calumnie'. Similarly extra punctuation marks might be added, especially either hyphens or parenthetical closures; or, again, the parenthesis may be opened but not closed. For those without a knowledge of Greek (or Hebrew), variants might also arise owing to unfamiliarity with the alphabet: most of the manuscripts of 'An Expostulation with Inigo Jones', for instance, get 'Σχηνοποίος' (stagemaker) in line 60 wrong.

Greek ligatures in the early modern period were highly complex and the transition from the Greek to a Roman alphabet could easily result in variant readings.[56] The problem was well known to scholars of classical texts, and it was on this point that Jonson launched his attack on Jones:

---

[55] Bland, 'Invisible Dangers', 170–7 (176).
[56] The essential article on Greek ligatures is W. H. Ingram, 'The Ligatures of Early Printed Greek', *Greek, Roman and Byzantine Studies*, 7 (1966), 371–89.

M^r: Surueyour, you that first beganne
    From Thirty pound, in pipkins, to the man
You are: from them, leap't forth an Architect,
    Able to talke of Euclide! and correct
Both him, and Archimede! Damne Archytas
    The Noblest Inginere, that euer was!
Controll Ctesibius! ouer-bearìnge vs
    With mistooke names, out of Vitruvius! (ll.1–8).

Against 'Ctesibius' in Jonson's copy of *De Architectura*, a contemporary hand has written 'Clesbius. Ar[undel]. passim'. The hand is not that of Marquard Gude, who notes that the copy was collated 'in Anglia' with the Arundel manuscript. Gude was a professor at Schleswig Holstein and a Counsellor at the Danish court in the mid-seventeenth-century. His library was dispersed at auction in Hamburg on 4 August 1706.[57] After the auction, the volume returned to England and was owned by Philip, Lord Hardwicke in the eighteenth-century. The collation with the Arundel manuscript must have taken place before the volume made its way to Denmark during the Civil War.

Jonson's point is that Jones is guilty both of overbearing pedantry and false scholarship. Ctesibius of Alexandria was a third-century B.C. engineer, who sought to regulate wind and water as mechanisms to control power and time. His name occurs in *De Architectura* at the beginning of a discussion about water-clocks (IX.8). What the collation of Barbari's edition with the Arundel manuscript reveals, therefore, is a variant error in an ancient manuscript based on a mistranscription of the Greek. For Jonson, Jones is a charlatan because he relies on his professional status, and the antiquity of a manuscript, as evidence rather than possessing the palaeographical, historical, philological, and textual skills to understand that 'Clesbius' is an early mistranscription.

One of the inevitable consequences of variant texts, especially those that are not understood, or are perceived to be wrong, is that attempts will be made to correct them. Such attempts are almost always in error because the earlier history is irrecoverable to the person making the attempt, or because the source copy was not consulted when the change was made. There are, in addition, variants in printed texts that have been caused as part of the process of proof correction that were other than intended at the time, either because the marginal annotations were

---

[57] [M. Gude], *Bibliotheca Exquisitissimus Libris . . . à Viro Illustri Domino Marquardo Gudio* (Kiel, 1706). The volume is listed under 'Libri cum manuscriptis collati vel notis autographis doctorum virorum illustrati', 3S2^v item 8. It is now in Boston Public Library, shelfmark ***G.401.66.

misunderstood, or because the change necessitated a further adjustment to the line.[58] Jonson's extensive corrections to sheets C and F of *The Fountaine of Selfe-Love* (as *Cynthias Revels* was first called) caused the compositors both textual and spacing problems (which then confused Simpson when he collated the text). Thus at C2ᵛ line 7, the reading 'Gods i'le' was altered to 'Gods il'e'' (instead of 'Gods, il'e' with a comma), because the marginal annotation that was probably meant to indicate a comma was instead misunderstood as an instruction to shift the apostrophe.[59]

Mistakes in proof correction were more common than is usually assumed and need to be taken into consideration as a possible cause of variant texts. Consider I.iv.96–7 in the folio version of *King Lear*, and the same passage in the quarto (the line breaks have been marked):'

> Truth's a dog muſt to kennell, hee muſt bee | whipt out, when theLady Brach may ſtand by'th'fire | and ſtinke. (F: 2q4ᵛ)

> Truth is a dog muſt to kenell, hee muſt bee whipt | out, when Lady oth'e Brach may ſtand by the fire and ſtincke. (Q1: C4ᵛ)

The folio text is unevenly spaced (the compositor made a dog's dinner of setting the text), with three spaces closed up, whilst the quarto is evenly and fully set: at the visual level of workmanship, therefore, the folio looks suspect, although there is clearly an error in the quarto. As a consequence, the phrase 'the Lady brach' has been accepted as correct because 'brach' is a reasonably common word from the period for a bitch-hound. Yet editors have been uneasy: in part, because 'Lady' in the context is redundant; and, in part, because the quarto reading raises other possibilities. Although in error, the 1608 quarto version matters because it has to have derived from a source *manuscript*, however egregious the mistakes made in the *printed* text; whereas the folio copy has been shown to be a mixture of a different manuscript *and* a copy of the quarto (and possibly the second quarto) as well. The first quarto therefore has an independent authority, whereas the folio must in some way be derivative of it.[60]

Instead of accepting the folio text of *Lear* and attempting to resolve the issue through literary means, the first step must be to understand

---

[58] For a list of early modern proof-sheets, see Moore, *Primary Materials*, 65–86; also, P. Simpson, *Proof-reading in the Sixteenth, Seventeenth and Eighteenth Centuries* (Oxford, 1935).

[59] STC 14773, 1601; H&S, IV, 5–17.

[60] As well as the books referred to in footnote 18 above, see T. H. Howard-Hill, 'The Problem of Manuscript Copy for Folio *King Lear*', *The Library*, VI: 4 (1982), 1–24; and, P. W. K. Stone, *The Textual History of King Lear* (London, 1980).

how the quarto text came to read as it did.[61] There are, at least, four explanations that are possible, depending on whether the manuscript copy read 'the Ladie brach' (as found in the folio), 'the Ladie o'the brach', 'the Ladie, or the brach', or 'the Ladie o'the brace'.

If the source copy read 'the Ladie brach', then the compositor must have set 'Ladie brach', in order for the corrector to indicate that the insertion of 'the' was necessary—which the compositor then placed after 'Ladie' rather than before it. Next, either the compositor assumed that a further correction was necessary, or a further revise was pulled and the corrector compounded the error. Either way, one or both of them did not understand that a 'brach' was a bitch-hound and so turned the word into a noun, misinserting *o* with an apostrophe in order to correct 'Ladie the brach'. It is, in other words, quite a difficult process to get from the folio reading to the one found in the quarto.

The second alternative is that the compositor set 'Ladie brach' or 'the Ladie brach' where the copy read 'the Ladie o'the brach'. The meaning would be that the 'Ladie' who stands by the fire is not the bitch-hound but her spoilt daughter. The marginal note instructed the compositor to insert 'o'the' in the line and possibly 'the' before 'Ladie', but the lack of space was a problem; if 'the' was present before 'Ladie', it was pulled out and used for the other part of correction, with the apostrophe then inserted in the wrong place. This is possible, but the indirect role of the bitch-hound does make it the least likely reading as some of the force of the comparison is lost.

The third alternative implies that the compositor set 'Ladie othe brach', or 'the Ladie, or brach', for 'the Ladie, or the brach'. This reading implies direct sarcasm, with the dignity of 'Ladie' immediately undercut by the crudity of 'brach'. In this instance, the corrector might have noted in the margin 'ₓ the r' with an insert mark before 'Ladie' and slash through 'othe'. Unable to insert 'the' before 'Ladie' and realizing that 'other' could not be correct, the compositor assumed 'r' was an apostrophe and inserted it where the slash seemed to indicate. The other alternative is that a slash after 'or' went through the 'r' instead, so that the compositor assumed 'or' should be corrected to 'othe'—or else he was saving space. The assumption would be that 'oth'e' is the garbled result of correction made without reference to copy.

The final version, 'the Ladie o'the brace' involves the most radical emendation and the simplest explanation. If an 'h' had previously been misdistributed to the 'e' box, the compositor would have set 'Ladie

[61] Blayney, *The Texts of* King Lear, 5–8.

othe brach' by accident and omitted the initial 'the' because it did not fit. If this were the case then a corrector would have placed a mark before 'Ladie' to add 'the', a slash through 'othe' with an apostrophe in the margin, and another slash through the 'h' of 'brach' with an 'e' in the margin. When the compositor saw the note 'ₐthe ' e', he ignored the slash in 'brach' and read it as a single instruction to emend the text as 'oth'e brach' rather than 'o'the brace'. No editor has proposed such an emendation because of the status traditionally accorded the folio text.

Depending on the view one takes of the relationship between the quarto and folio versions of *Lear*, and the extent to which one estimates how much of the folio might derive from the quarto, will affect editorial judgment about the likely validity of the alternative explanations. For some, 'the Lady brach' will be the line of least resistance in an attempt to make sense of the apparently corrupt text; whether or not its reading and redundancy are genuine. To start from the quarto text, however, is to open up a range of issues about the ways in which variants occur. Whilst we cannot know the original reading for certain, it is worth understanding the alternatives because only then can all the possibilities be properly assessed: to assert the folio reading without understanding the problem diminishes the value of the critical judgment being made.

The Pursuit of Difference

For textual scholars, variants matter because it is primarily through them that the history of the transmission of a text can be understood: hence the necessity of recording all the differences between each witness; and, therefore, recording the repetition of every difference as this enables one group of documents to be distinguished from the others. In order to determine difference, it is necessary to collate (in so far as possible or reasonable) every copy of a text in manuscript, print, inscription, or other form of extant record. Collation is simply a method of gathering information through the comparison of one witness with another that requires the primary skill of accuracy in the observation of lexical changes, spelling, punctuation, and, sometimes, the arrangement of the text on the page, in all their possible permutations: that information is essential if a full account of the textual history is to be rendered.[62]

---

[62] For a salutary and cautionary view of the value of collation, see J. A. Dane, 'The Notion of the Variant and the Zen of Collation', *The Myth of Print Culture: Essays on Evidence, Textuality, and Bibliographical Method* (Toronto, 2003), 88–113. In practical terms 1:1 plastic transparencies are sufficient for most collation work provided that sample variant copies are checked with a McLeod or Comet collator (which use mirrors to unify the images).

The collation of manuscript and printed texts is based on different approaches, for printed texts will differ from one edition to another, as well as within an edition owing to stop-press correction. The uniformity of print within an edition (except for stop-press variants) enables the direct comparison of copies by comparing images with a collator, or by using a 1:1 transparency from a master copy and placing this over the text being collated. Such methods will reveal any stop-press correction. Differences between manuscripts, on the other hand, as well as between different printed editions, require a complete transcription of the text to be prepared before a comparison can be made.[63] However, once a complete digital record of a text is made, it is then possible to use software to identify the textual differences.

In practical terms, it may be necessary to collate up to 80 copies of a printed edition in order to ensure that every stop-press correction is recorded; the most difficult to locate being the intermediate corrections when the forme was opened up twice to alter a part of the text.[64] Usually intermediate variants indicate something about the production history of the volume and may occur after the large paper copies have been printed. This is because large paper copies of seventeenth-century books did not generally have their margins readjusted, and so presswork could begin immediately after the stop-press corrections had been made. For printed editions where fewer than 80 publicly owned copies are readily accessible, and where the text is of some length, it is useful to collate a sufficient number—that is as many as to suffice that when no further variants have been recorded for 10–12 copies after the last one was found, it is likely that the list of stop-press variants is complete.

Establishing the order of variants (that is the preliminary and later revised states) is often self-evident from the nature of the corrections involved, but not always so. If we were to think of collation in terms of set theory, it might show that five out of 20 copies of a hypothetical text read 'and', and the remainder 'but'; of those five 'and' copies two have 'kind' and 'just', and the other three 'good' and 'wise'. We would then know that within the history of this text there was a group of 'and' witnesses (five), and a larger group of 'but' witnesses (15). If this was a printed text, we would want to know whether the 'but' copies read 'kind' and 'just' or 'good' and 'wise'. Let us assume that the 'but' copies

---

[63] See also, F. T. Bowers, 'Transcription of Manuscripts: The Record of Variants', *Studies in Bibliography*, 29 (1976), 212–64.

[64] The observation is based on my own collations of Jonson's 1616 and 1640 *Workes*: for some parts of the text 40–50 copies would have been satisfactory, for others the last variants were not found until 65–80 copies had been collated.

read 'kind/just'. What we would then know is that the preliminary state of the forme read 'and/good/wise'; about 15 per cent of the way through, the press was stopped and the forme opened up with 'kind/just' substituted for 'good/wise'. Then, about a quarter of the way through, the forme was opened up again with 'but' substituted for 'and'. Thus we would have a preliminary state, a first revise, and a final revise. Three-quarters of all copies would have the fully corrected final state.

So far, so simple; if the edition was the only witness to the text, an editor would draw the conclusion that 'but/kind/just' was the corrected version and proceed accordingly. The information about the first revise would be informative about the printing history, but not have a bearing on editorial decision-making. However if, ten years later, a second edition was printed from a copy of the first edition, then the state of that copy would have a bearing on what happened subsequently. Imagine that the second edition reads 'if/true/wise'. The presence of 'wise' might indicate that a preliminary state of the first edition was used as copy, and that 'if' and 'true' were new revisions of the original setting—in other words, that the text had been revised for a second time in a different way. Or imagine that the second edition read 'and/true/just': the evidence would then suggest that a copy of the first revise had been altered. Such distinctions reveal an added level of complexity to the revision process and present an editor with distinct alternatives. This can happen easily and, perhaps, unwittingly: when Jonson returned to *Sejanus* for the 1616 *Workes*, he worked with an uncorrected forme outer M from the 1605 Quarto, and he revised it in a second different way.[65]

With manuscripts, and with printed texts from different editions, the collation of variants will demonstrate how copies of a text descended from one witness to another. This method of analysis is known as stemmatics. Stemmata work in two directions: the closer one is to the top, the more it is possible to make a pragmatic reconstruction of what the original document(s) looked like. As they proceed downwards and outwards, stemmata map the social history and circulation of the text. In this sense the variant is less significant as an 'error', than as a key to establishing and tracing various networks and relationships. Hence, the use of stemmata for different texts and authors that are present in the same manuscripts may yield information about the origins of some texts and make more specific the history of those documents whose first associations have yet to be identified.

---

[65] See, T. O. Calhoun and T. L. Gravell, 'Paper and Printing in Jonson's *Sejanus* (1605)', *Papers of the Bibliographical Society of America*, 87 (1993), 13–64 esp. 64: there are four states of outer M.

The problem with the use of stemmatics for early modern texts is that it has been impeded by some careless work. Wolf and Leishman, for instance, claimed that stemmatics were ineffective as a tool for the analysis of miscellanies in the period, but their selection of witnesses was partial and incomplete.[66] Wolf studied Walton Poole's 'If shadows be a picture's excellence', but collated barely half of the 68 surviving copies. His conclusion, that the results were too problematic to be meaningful, needs to be revisited in the light of a more complex and informed understanding of the transmission history of that poem.

For the moment, imagine again a textual history where five of the copies read 'and/good/wise/from', five copies 'but/good/wise/of', two copies 'if/kind/wise/that', two copies 'if/kind/wise/in', four copies 'but/true/just/from' and two copies 'but/kind/just/for'. After drawing together the common elements, and separating the distinctive readings, the stemmata would be constructed as follows:

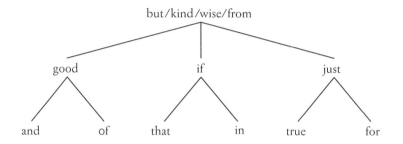

What the diagram demonstrates is that the original reading was 'but/kind/wise/from': ten of the manuscripts read 'good' and of those five have the reading 'and', with five 'of'; four copies read 'if', of which two have 'that', and two 'in'; six copies read 'just', four of which have 'true', and two 'wise'. Hence we can establish that the readings 'but' and 'from' are common to the groups that read 'good' and 'just'; the reading 'kind' is common to the groups that read 'if' and 'just'; and the reading 'wise' is common to the groups that read 'good' and 'if': these must be, therefore, the earlier readings that the other copies descend from, and we would expect further differentiation to occur within each group. What we also know is that each of the three families can be identified by a variant that is common to that line of descent alone.

[66] J. B. Leishman, 'You Meaner Beauties of the Night. A Study in Transmission and Transmogrification', *The Library*, IV: 26 (1945), 99–123; E. Wolf II, '"If shadows be a picture's excellence": An Experiment in Critical Bibliography', *PMLA*, 63 (1948), 831–57.

For most texts, the stemmatic analysis of variants will establish the historical relationship between different witnesses. Unfortunately, if a copy from one line of recension is conflated with that from another group, then contamination of the text will take place when the versions are mixed.[67] Whilst conflation is not always an issue, it can happen and when it does the analysis of the variants will reveal common elements that contradict the remaining evidence. Sometimes, it is possible to identify the source of the conflation, but when a text is anonymous and the direction of the manuscript history is difficult to establish, then contamination between traditions may pose particular problems.

Harold Love, for instance, was particularly interested in restoration satire and libertine verse. For Love, the problem of contamination is compounded by that of direction. In other words, if one does not know what the source text ought to be, then the analysis of the variants and the contamination between independent lines of recension becomes more opaque and much depends upon whether a particular line of recension can be established. Such analysis has to begin with an assumption that a certain version of the text represents a likely point of departure and then see what happens when the collations are prepared. Under such a scenario, it may be possible to construct the stemmata in two or more different ways and to have distinct versions and variations from such a text. This simply points to the other problem with which this chapter began: authors revise, sometimes more than once, and when one analyzes the material, that fact needs to be borne in mind.

Through an understanding of both how error is transmitted and of how copies of a text are related, it becomes possible to establish a list of variants that cannot be readily explained by the processes of scribal or printed transmission. That final irreducible group of variants must then either be the consequence of revision by whoever was responsible for the text, or caused by a later and deliberate intervention in its history. It is the privilege of an author to vary a text as they wish; to return to ideas that were first discarded, and to add or remove material as they see fit. Every author is likely to do this more than once, and in many different ways. Any stemmatic analysis may need to recognize that there was more than one document of origin, and that distinct and separate traditions of transmission exist. Revision has always been part of the creative process.

Sometimes, of course, the difference between an author and a later reviser, or a second hand, is easy to discern; on other occasions, it may

[67] The problem of contamination is particularly frequent in late medieval texts; see also, H. Love, *Scribal Publication in Seventeenth Century England* (Oxford, 1993); —, *English Clandestine Satire 1660–1702* (Oxford, 2004); and his editions of Rochester (Oxford, 1999) and Buckingham (Oxford, 2007: with R. D. Hume).

not be that simple to demonstrate.[68] An original version might be recast in ways that involve truncation, rewriting, or the creation of additional material, as with 'His Parting from Her'.[69] On other occasions, a work may be the product of two or more people working in tandem, and their revisions will have occurred in a concurrent and semi-independent manner. In other words, when faced with genuine independent variants, the permutation of what is possible needs to be borne in mind given the evidence that is available.

One final comment: it is one thing to identify all the variant readings in a text, another to analyze their causes and demonstrate relationships; yet to do this requires that such information be organized in a way that is intelligible for others to use. Every editorial decision about how to use and record this information is always, as Dane has observed, an act of interpretation; and it is one that will shape the response of others to the methods of analysis.[70] Textual analysis is never entirely neutral, nor is the organization of that information without consequence. It is the exercise of editorial judgment, based on the material and textual understanding of alternatives, which must justify the orchestration of the information in the form that it is received. What an editor does is analyze the genesis and history of the relevant documents to achieve that end.

---

[68] For instance, M. P. Jackson, *Defining Shakespeare: Pericles as Test Case* (Oxford 2003); B. Vickers, *Shakespeare, Co-author: A historical Study of Five Collaborative Lays* (Oxford, 2002); —, *Counterfeiting Shakespeare: Evidence, Authorship, and John Ford's Funerall Elegye* (Cambridge, 2002).

[69] G. A. Stringer, et al. (eds.), *The Variorum Edition of the Poetry of John Donne*, 8 vols. (Bloomington IN, 1995—in progress), II: 335–68.

[70] Dane, 'The Notion of the Variant and the Zen of Collation', 88–113.

7 Setting Conditions

IN the previous chapters, the emphasis has been on understanding the material and textual analysis of early modern books and manuscripts. The focus now needs to turn to the other kinds of archival and historical information relating to the book-trade, in particular the commercial and political aspects of the business: the economics of the trade, the forms of regulation, and the role and records of the Scriveners' and Stationers' Companies. These sources describe how the book-trade was organized, and the constraints under which it operated. From a broad perspective, that context is part of an evolving narrative of the history of the book; whilst for analytical purposes, the archival records are essential as they provide details of dates, events, and formal decisions that were made about both books and members—these details act as an important control on speculative impulses and convenient assumptions.

The Companies

By the end of the fourteenth-century, the London book-trade was well established, with scribes, limners (illustrators), and binders plying their related trades.[1] Even at this stage, it was apparent that there were two types of scribes: those who primarily prepared books and longer tracts, and those who prepared legal and other documents using a hierarchy of specialized scripts. It was the former who worked most closely with the limners and the binders. On 12 July 1403 (some 70 years before Caxton), the two groups separated into the Writers of the Court Letter and the Writers of the Text Letter, with the latter joined by the limners.[2] That early division of text production between two different companies had implications for the book-trade that contemporaries could not have foreseen. Thereafter, the companies kept separate statutes, records, members, and apprentices. In the following decades, the Writers of the Text Letter began to use the word 'stationer' to describe their activity, and from 1443, they were known by that term alone.[3]

With the arrival of the printing trade, a number of other companies became involved in book production, including the Drapers, Grocers, and Haberdashers. Whilst the two great successors to Caxton, Pynson

---

[1] For a discussion of manuscript production in the fourteenth-century, see R. Hanna, *London Literature, 1300–1380* (Cambridge, 2005).
[2] P. W. M. Blayney, *The Stationers' Company before the Charter, 1403–1557* (London, 2003), 13; Steer, *Scriveners' Company Common Paper*, ix, as before.
[3] Blayney, *The Stationers' Company before the Charter*, 15–18.

and de Worde, were Stationers (Caxton was a Mercer), the guild was slow to move from manuscript book production to print. To the extent that its members sold printed books, many of these would have been imported from the continent. Indeed, by 1547, only six of the 15 printing-houses in England (not all of them in London) were owned by Stationers.[4] It is probably that lack of dominance that doomed their first attempt at incorporation in 1542.[5]

With the accession of Mary (1553–8), England reverted to Rome and a number of Protestant printers went into hiding. This put the printed trade back in the control of the Stationers who, on 4 May 1557, became a corporation.[6] Their control was further consolidated by the Star Chamber decree of 1586 (which vested powers of search and oversight in the Company and set out the requirements for licensing), although the Drapers continued to dispute the Stationers' exclusive right to print books through the late sixteenth-century.[7] As the Stationers took control of the printed trade, the Writers of the Court Letter evolved into Scriveners, who became a corporation on 28 January 1617.[8]

Broadly speaking, the Stationers and the Scriveners had very similar structures, governance, and responsibilities; and it is clear that Bacon, Montague, and Hobart must have based the Charter for the Scriveners on that of the Stationers.[9] Both companies had a Master, two Wardens, and a Court of Assistants, as well as a Beadle and a Clerk. At the lower levels, a Stationer was first apprenticed, next freed as a yeoman, and then made a member of the livery. As a member of the livery, he had to serve as Junior and Senior Renter-Warden before rising to the Court of Assistants, from which the Master and Wardens were chosen.[10] Some chose not to take this step. In the Scriveners' Company, the junior ranks are referred to as Stewards and Younger Members.[11]

Both companies grew consistently, with the Stationers doing so more substantially. From 1558 to 1567, Gadd noted that 271 apprentices were bound and 119 freed (not all apprentices remained in the trade); from 1681 to 1690, 672 were bound and 467 freed. He estimates the size

---

[4] Blayney, *The Stationers' Company before the Charter*, 45–7.

[5] Blayney, *The Stationers' Company before the Charter*, 41.

[6] Blayney, *The Stationers' Company before the Charter*, 49–53.

[7] G. D. Johnson, 'The Stationers versus the Drapers: Control of the Press in the Late Sixteenth Century', *The Library*, VI: 10 (1988), 1–17.

[8] Steer, *Scriveners' Company Common Paper*, vii.

[9] For the Charter, see Steer, *Scriveners' Company Common Paper*, 92–107.

[10] I. A. Gadd, *Being like a Field: Corporate Identity in the Stationers' Company, 1557–1684* (University of Oxford, MS DPhil c.15604; 1999), 67–83.

[11] Steer, *Scriveners' Company Common Paper*, 125.

of the Company as being 120–50 members in 1557, and some 5–600 in 1684.[12] Comparatively, between 1557 and 1580, the Scriveners made free 141 apprentices, of which one was not expert in the skill; between 1581 and 1604, 168 were made free, of which 11 were described as being not expert; and between 1605 and 1628, 217 were made free, of which 39 were described as being not expert.[13] Once the non-expert members are removed from the figures, the trade shows a consistent growth from 140, to 159, to 178 for each period, or just under an extra apprentice per year. In 1671, the Scriveners had one Master, two Wardens, 21 Assistants, nine Stewards, and 25 Younger Members.[14]

The companies were bodies corporate: this gave them a permanent legal status that was at once inanimate (and therefore free of personal jeopardy and liability), but otherwise equivalent to that of an adult male. A corporation could enter into contract, sue and be sued, purchase and alienate land, and be granted privileges by letters patent.[15] As a consequence, it could act collectively on behalf of its members in the broad defence of their interests, and it could regulate the behaviour of its members in the interests of the greater good. It was both the representative of the trade to society and government, and the guardian of its members' lives. For the members, it was the point of authority that they turned to in order to conduct their business activities.

In his study of the Stationers' Company, Gadd has identified five main areas of corporate responsibility, and these roles apply in much the same way to the Scriveners as well. First, the right to own property meant that a Company could acquire a Hall that served as a focal point both for entertainment and administration. In particular, the Stationers kept such records in the Hall as to who in the trade owned the rights to the copy of any given book, as well as of its role as an arbiter of disputes and manager of trade activities, and it kept records of its financial activities.[16] These documents are of prime importance for understanding the organization of the trade and the activities of its members. Second, the Company had powers of jurisdiction over its members and the ability to regulate their conduct.[17] Some of these powers had been vested in the Company by such instruments as the decree of the Star Chamber from 1586, which allowed for the search and seizure of

[12] Gadd, *Being like a Field*, 23.

[13] Steer, *Scriveners' Company Common Paper*, 28–62.

[14] Steer, *Scriveners' Company Common Paper*, 125.

[15] Gadd, *Being like a Field*, 31–6.

[16] Gadd, *Being like a Field*, 84–8; C. C. Blagden, 'The Accounts of the Wardens of the Stationers' Company', *Studies in Bibliography*, 9 (1957), 69–93.

[17] Gadd, *Being like a Field*, 88–99.

unauthorized books upon 'reasonable cause for suspicion', and the arrest of those involved (including bookbinders).[18] It could also fine members for disorderly conduct (swearing is the most usual foible so punished), or for the failure to present an apprentice in a timely manner. In addition, the Company set limits as to how far any one member could encroach on the interests of the others by setting limits to the number of presses, apprentices, and the quantities of books that could be printed, and by establishing a standard retail price per sheet in order to ensure that members of the trade did not undercut each other to the detriment of all. Third, the Company looked after the social and corporate welfare of its members.[19] It did this primarily through the provision of financial relief to those in distress and, from 1603, through the dividends paid (relative to their rank in the Company) from the English Stock; a joint property arrangement that vested the income from psalm-books and almanacs into a common account shared by the members.[20] Fourth, the Company had civic obligations, not least the storage of grain and arms, the provision of men at times of need, and the attendance of its members at city and royal events. It could also be asked to collect taxes.[21] Fifth, the Company made petitions to the government and City of London on behalf of the trade when it sought redress of grievance, the relief of its members, or the protection of their interests.[22] It is the cumulative aspect of all these roles that allows a picture to be built up of the production and publication of books in their historical context, and for specific events to be related to particular items at the press.

Blagden has sketched out, in a calendar, the typical activities of the Company over a year.[23] Most of the day-to-day detail is about the entry of copy, and the admission and freedom of apprentices. This however, is interspersed with the other matters that arose from time to time: disputes, regulatory activities, a petition, and the corporate dinner. This suggests that, while other issues would impinge from time to time, what really mattered to the Company was the control of trade assets; that is the people that were employed, and the property of its members. It was precisely those issues that were also the concern of the authorities, and

---

[18] Arber, *A Transcript of the Registers of the Company of Stationers*, ii: 811 (item 6).
[19] Gadd, *Being like a Field*, 99–109.
[20] See, W. C. Ferguson, *The Loan Book of The Stationers' Company with a List of Transactions 1592–1692* (London, 1989); C. C. Blagden, *The Stationers' Company: A History 1403–1959* (London, 1960), 92–109. There were also Irish and Latin Stocks, but these were not as financially lucrative.
[21] Gadd, *Being like a Field*, 109–112.
[22] Gadd, *Being like a Field*, 139–52.
[23] Blagden, *The Stationers' Company*, 47–55.

so in their management there was a confluence of interest that served both, for the most part, conveniently.

Allowance, Licence, and Entry

After 1586, there were two stages that a printed book had to go through once a publisher had decided that there was a sufficient market for it to be viable. First of all, the book had to be allowed; that is, a copy of the manuscript had to be approved for publication by the ecclesiastical authorities. Second, the copy that had been allowed was then presented to the Stationers' Company to be licensed by the Master and one of the Wardens. This was a formal protocol that demonstrated that the proper procedures had been followed. It was precisely the failure to gain allowance, or the misuse of copy through the introduction of substantial alterations, that got those concerned into the most trouble. A printer, therefore, might begin work on a book before it had been properly licensed so long as it had been allowed. Nevertheless, before a book was published, those involved made sure that it was licensed, not because of the formal approval, but because it demonstrated that the book was their commercial property. Once these two conditions had been met, a third stage was possible. If the publisher (who might also be, but was not necessarily, the printer) wanted to protect their copy from infringement by others, they might request that it was entered into the Register by the Clerk, for which they paid sixpence. Entry provided a permanent record of the right to copy that the Company could turn to in the event of a dispute but, before the second Star Chamber decree of 1637, it was not a necessity.[24]

In 1606 the method of licensing was altered for plays. From 1586, they had been allowed, like any other book, by the chaplains; but this meant that they were licensed only for the press with the consequence that things might be performed that otherwise would not be allowed. To remedy the situation, the Master of the Revels allowed plays both for performance and the press, and he charged for the privilege. Buc (the first Master to do so) appears to have treated his office more as a sinecure than a means for stricter regulatory oversight. His successor, Sir Henry Herbert, was more active, and sought to double the fees by requiring that plays be licensed separately for the stage and the press.[25]

[24] See, P. W. M. Blayney, 'The Publication of Playbooks', 396–404.
[25] See, A. R. Dutton, *Mastering the Revels* (Basingstoke, 1991); N. D. Bawcutt, *The Control and Censorship of Caroline Drama: The Records of Sir Henry Herbert, Master of the Revels, 1623–73* (Oxford, 1996).

It is important to realize that manuscript publication was not subject to the same restrictions as print, or the drama, because it could not be monitored in the same way and, therefore, general oversight of the trade was vested with the Scriveners. This does not mean that the authorities were not concerned about what circulated in manuscript; it was rather an implicit admission that it was far more difficult to control, and that its impact was more limited. It was one thing for a manuscript to be copied a dozen times, or even 50, quite another for a book or pamphlet to be issued in anywhere between 500 and 1,500 copies. Furthermore, whilst the Scriveners could oversee the professional trade, private individuals were quite beyond their reach. This does not mean, however, that the ownership and copying of manuscript was without risk.

Censorship

For the early modern authorities, the press was a mixed blessing. It did not take long for it to become an instrument for the projection of power that was used for proclamations, to establish religious orthodoxy, to explain official opinion or policy, and to disseminate official versions of events. The problem was that others equally perceived its usefulness as a vehicle for ideas and beliefs that did not necessarily conform with, or reflect, the values of those who exercised power. Further, the sheer scale of book production and the extent of the growing trade convinced the authorities that some kind of oversight was necessary. After decades of ad hoc measures, the Star Chamber decree of 1586 established a formal system, in which the Archbishop of Canterbury and the Bishop of London were given the responsibility for ensuring that what was printed conformed to the accepted doctrines of Church and State. This responsibility the bishops immediately shared with the chaplains in their households, who undertook most of the work. The temperament of those at the top played its part as well: Whitgift, Bancroft, and Abbott all took a fairly relaxed view of what might require their intervention; whereas Laud was more prone to the exercise of official discretion, and it proved his downfall.[26]

Censorship is an issue of some textual and historical importance that is commonly misunderstood. Some 90,000 books, pamphlets, and broadsides survive that were printed in sixteenth- and seventeenth-century

---

[26] For a comprehensive survey and discussion of censorship practices, see C. S. Clegg, *Press Censorship in Elizabethan England* (Cambridge, 1997); —, *Press Censorship in Jacobean England* (Cambridge, 2001); —, *Press Censorship in Caroline England* (Cambridge, 2008). For Laud and Prynne, see Bland, 'Invisible Dangers', 190–3.

England. Against that broad swathe of material, much of which would never have exercised a licenser's interest beyond the formal requirements of approval, a few notable examples of official heavy-handedness stand in uneasy contrast. It is all too obvious, as well, that the competing claims of divine right and liberty of conscience ended in a convulsive conflict that broke society apart, and that in its midst Milton wrote some of his most compelling prose to argue against official oversight of the press. These political tensions that, in times of anxiety, sometimes focused around books, or libraries, have led some to argue that censorship shaped intellectual and political values among the elite, and even society as a whole, in such a way as to have become 'the central problem of consciousness and communication'.[27]

The truth is more mundane: those who licensed books ranged across a spectrum of opinion, and some were more tolerant than others; in practice, their primary concern was not political except in so much as matters of religion were in dispute.[28] The chaplains were, in this sense, the protectors of the Elizabethan settlement and, in that cause, they had a vested interest. Later, under the commonwealth, the licensers were the guardians of Presbyterian governance and sought to protect its interests accordingly. It would, in fact, be more surprising if those who held such responsibility did not identify with the government they served.

Of course, certain things were not permitted to circulate in print, including discussions of crown finances, or of the rights of the monarch or the Church; and it was not until the 1640s that news-books dealt with domestic political issues (earlier pamphlets that treated of such matters were usually issued, sometimes covertly, by authority).[29] From time to time, other restrictions were also attempted. After 1599, all domestic historical writing was supposed to be vetted by the Privy Council; in practice this did not happen. Daniel was printed with the allowance of Richard Mockett, and at the 'pleasure' of the Archbishop of Canterbury, George Abbott; Camden was printed with the permission of James I; and Bacon was allowed by the Bishop of London, George Montaigne.[30] Similarly, political pamphlets and foreign news were usually licensed by one of the secretaries of state.

---

[27] A. Patterson, *Censorship and Interpretation: The Conditions of Writing and Reading in Early Modern England* (Madison WI, 1984), 17.
[28] See, S. Lambert, 'Richard Montagu, Arminianism and Censorship', *Past and Present*, 124 (1989), 62 and 65; —, 'State Control of the Press in Theory and Practice: The Role of the Stationers' Company before 1640', *Censorship and the Control of Print in England and France 1600–1910* (Winchester, 1992), 1–32.
[29] Bland, 'Invisible Dangers', 159–63.
[30] W. W. Greg, *Licensers of the Press, &c. to 1640* (Oxford, 1962), 68, 51, and 63.

Print glittered. Like a magpie, the authorities noticed: they sought to control what they perceived to be most publicly dangerous or, at least, vicariously unstable. Bodily frankness was acceptable, provided it was neither explicitly obscene nor pornographic—one writer recommended copulation as a means of keeping warm in winter in a book dedicated to his sister-in-law.[31] Samuel Harsnett saw nothing wrong with the advice.[32] *Venus and Adonis* was printed with the allowance of Archbishop Whitgift; whilst one of his secretaries, Michael Murgetrode, sanctioned *Hero and Leander*.[33] What mattered was religious doctrine, and what exercised the authorities most were the non-conformist and Catholic publications that were generally not a product of the London trade. Allison and Rogers, for instance, record that 932 Catholic books were printed in English (mainly at Douai) between 1558 and 1640, with another 1619 publications in languages other than English that were either intended to be distributed there, or which engaged in controversial dispute with the Anglican settlement.[34] These books circulated through recusant networks, as well as the booksellers, and they often were much more difficult to trace than the ordinary stock sold by the Stationers.

For those caught with manuscript material of treasonable intent, it was a serious political offence; however, much circulated in manuscript that could not be printed, including parliamentary speeches, accounts of political trials such as that for Essex, and the more scabrous shades of erotic literature. From the viewpoint of the authorities, manuscript was seen as more a form of replication and preservation for texts, rather than as a medium through which copies proliferated, and it recognized that those who gained access to such texts would have an education and background sufficient to read them in an informed and responsible manner. Provided the texts did not cross into print, therefore, a more benign attitude could be taken to the nature of their contents and their transmission through personal networks.

If oversight was deemed necessary, several factors served to make it less effective than the term might suggest. First, those who licensed books, and those who wrote them, were often connected through personal networks such as the universities. An author therefore might approach a chaplain who was known to be sympathetic to their work:

---

[31] W. Vaughan, *Natural and Artificial Directions for Health* (STC 24612; 1600), D7^v–8^r; see Bland, 'The London Book-Trade in 1600', 455–6.

[32] Greg, *Licensers of the Press, &c. to 1640*, 42.

[33] Greg, *Licensers of the Press, &c. to 1640*, 20 and 70.

[34] A. F. Allison and D. M. Rogers, *The Contemporary Printed Literature of the English Counter-Reformation between 1558 and 1640*, 2 vols. (Aldershot, 1989–94).

hence the fact that the same person could have all his work authorized by a single chaplain, regardless of the publisher. Second, the economic insignificance of book production, combined with the proliferation of print, meant that official reaction to problems was often retrospective. Third, authority was frequently subverted by an intelligent response to its concerns, with readers given scope to draw their own conclusions. The willingness with which writers and publishers took political risks—and equally, the frustrations caused when publishers proved financially risk averse, reveals the extent to which the chaplains were arbiters of the tolerable, rather than enforcers of a particular view. It was, in other words, not censorship that proved to be the problem for the author, but the failure of oversight as a means to control the circulation of ideas that was a problem for the political authorities.

A fruitful way of approaching the subject is to look more closely at the chaplains and their work. For instance, Abraham Hartwell is a name that occurs more often than any other during the years of Whitgift and Elizabeth. He was born in the mid-1550s,[35] and first came under the influence of Whitgift at Trinity College, Cambridge, in the late 1560s as an undergraduate. He later became a fellow, and subsequently joined the staff at Lambeth as Whitgift's secretary by 1584. On 10 November 1586, he licensed his first book (Doleta's *Straunge newes out of Calabria*; STC 6992); and, on 3 June 1588, he was listed as a senior member of the panel of correctors.[36] Between November 1586 and October 1607, he allowed at least 45 books (not all entries for licensed books record the name of the chaplain, and not all books were entered in the Register). These included, Allot's *Englands Parnassus*, Carew's *Tasso*, Drayton's *Idea* and 1606 *Poems*, Florio's *Montaigne*, Kyd's *Spanish Tragedy*, Marston's *The Metamorphosis of Pygmalion's Image* and *The Dutch Courtesan*, as well as works by Greene, Lodge, and Dekker, ballads, and much more. A manuscript on the life of Claudius of Guyse has his imprimatur. He made no alterations to the text.[37] Although Hartwell was collated to the rectory of Toddington in Bedfordshire by Whitgift before 1604, he lived in London and died at Lambeth at the end of 1607.[38]

From 1596 through 1604, Hartwell was joined by William Barlow, later Bishop of Rochester (from 1605) and Lincoln (1608–13); and, from

---

[35] Hartwell is not to be confused with his namesake, the author of *Regina Literata* (STC 12987; 1564), who matriculated at King's, after attending Eton, in 1559. See, J. Venn and J. A. Venn, *Alumni Cantabrigiensis*, 4 vols. (Cambridge, 1922), II, 322.

[36] Greg, *Licensers of the Press, &c. to 1640*, 42–5; W. W. Greg and E. Boswell (eds.), *Records of the Court of the Stationers' Company 1576 to 1602—from Register B* (London, 1930), 29.

[37] British Library, Royal MS 18 B xxix, f.3ʳ; no printed copy is known to survive.

[38] His will is PROB 11/109, f.47ᵛ–9ᵛ.

1600, by Zachariah Pasfield. Barlow went to St John's, Cambridge, and was later a fellow at Trinity Hall, before becoming rector of St Dunstan's in the East between 1597 and 1604, and a prebend of St Paul's from 1601 until 1608, and Westminster from 1601 until his death in 1613. He was a protégé of Richard Cosin, and allowed *Richard III*, *Dr Faustus*, Hall's *Virgidemiarum*, and the anthology *England's Helicon*.[39] Pasfield was even more active. He was Barlow's Cambridge contemporary next door at Trinity College, later a fellow, and then vicar of Trumpington, before moving to East Hanningfield, Asheldam and Bocking in Essex. Like Barlow he was a prebend of St Paul's until his death in 1616. He allowed the *Essaies* of Sir William Cornwallis, *Hamlet*, *The Malcontent*, and Daniel's *Philotas*. Even more tellingly, he was the chaplain preferred by Jonson, approving *Every Man in His Humor*, *Narcissus or the Fountayne of Selfe-Love* (as *Cynthias Revels* was known), *Poetaster*, *King James His Royal Entertainment*, *Sejanus*, and possibly *Hymenaei* although no record for this survives.[40] Only when Sir George Buc took over the regulation of the drama, late in 1606, does Jonson cease to be allowed by Pasfield, whose last book was Donne's *Pseudo-Martyr* in 1609.

In their bare outlines, the careers of these three licensers offer much scope for further research. Pasfield, regrettably, appears not to have written a book, nor do we have any indication of the books that might have been in his library. As with Barlow and Hartwell, however, we have a copy of his will.[41] It shows him to have been a cousin of Dr Timothy Bright, and good friends of several senior ecclesiastics, including Drs Childerley and Dockett, who acted as overseers to his will. Of Barlow, we know rather more. He published a number of sermons, as well as an account of the Hampton Court conference (STC 1446–60, 10321, and 15322). His will shows him to have owned a substantial library of books. To Trinity Hall, he left a complete Plantin Polyglot Bible in eight volumes; the five-volume *Councells* by Binnius and the civil laws in six volumes, as well as a two-volume Plato in Latin and Greek, 'to be placed in their Librarye vppon one deske by them selves and the name of the donor to be set vppon the front of the deske'. The rest of Barlow's books were bequeathed to his sister's son William Johnson 'vppon condition that he be a Scholler at my death' and that he never sell the books.[42]

Hartwell is the most interesting figure of all. As well as his licensing duties, he translated three books out of Italian and one out of French,

---

[39] Greg, *Licensers of the Press*, 9–10.
[40] Greg, *Licensers of the Press*, 75–6.
[41] PROB 11/128, f.465ᵛ–6ᵛ.
[42] PROB 11/122, f.349ᵛ–51ᵛ.

which perhaps explains why he was the licenser for the translations of Tasso and Montaigne. A few of his entries show him to have exercised some control: a ballad *A Belman for England* was to be printed 'leauing out the two staues that are crossed', and *The history of the last troubles of Fraunce* 'leauing out the discourse touching the Quene of Scotts by him crossed out'.[43] On the other hand, he allowed Marston's *Metamorphosis*, although this was later called in and burnt, as was *Willobie's Avisa*. Yet the fact that the authorities overrode his permission does not appear to have been held against him. The image is one of benign tolerance: two staves of a ballad and an obviously sensitive political narrative represent a light hand over a 21-year period. Of course, it is possible that Hartwell changed more than the records indicate, but there are other signs that he was a minimalist in these matters.

In his dedication to Whitgift of Minadoi's *The History of the Warres between the Turkes and the Persians*, Hartwell admitted that it had taken him three years, off and on, and that 'The houres that I haue employed in writing this translation, were stollen from your Graces grauer businesses whereon I should haue attended'.[44] During that period he licensed at least nine books. Even more telling is a subject to which he turned in his next book, a translation of Pigafetta's *A Report of the Kingdon of Congo*. Here he found something offensive, but his impulse was to temporize. His friends, not least Hakluyt, had asked him to do the translation:

> But within two houres conference, I found him nibling at two most honourable Gentlemen of *England*, whome in plaine tearmes he called *Pirates*: so that I had much adoo to hold my hands from renting of him into many mo peeces, then his *Cozen Lopez* the *Doctor* was quartered. Yet δολίτεραι φροντίδες, *My second wits* stayed me, and advised me, that I should peruse all his *Report*, before I would proceed to execution: which in deede I did. And, because I sawe that in all the rest of his behauiour hee contayned himselfe very well and honestly, and that he vsed this lewd speech, not altogether *ex animo*, but rather *ex vitio gentis*, of the now-inveterate hatred, which the *Spanyard* and *Portingall* beare against our *Nation*, I was so bold as to pardon him, and so taught him to speake the *Englishe toung*.[45]

[43] Greg, *Licensers of the Press*, 43 and 44, summarizing Arber.
[44] G. Minadoi, *The History of the Warres between the Turkes and the Persians* (STC 17943; 1595), A4^r.
[45] D. Lopez and F. Pigafetta, *A Report of the Kingdon of Congo* (STC 16805; 1597), *1^r.

It is interesting that what causes Hartwell to react is not a matter of theology, but of national pride. The passage that he appears to refer to is the following:

> But an infortunate end had this *Embassadour*, for he was taken at sea by *Englishmen*, and his shippe also, which being drawen towards *Englande*, when it was neere vnto the Coast, by great misfortune it ranne athwart the shoare, ane there *Don Piedro Antonio* & his sonne were both drowned.[46]

At once, therefore, we can see how Hartwell resolved his difficulty, teaching Pigafetta how 'to speake the *Englishe toung*', while at the same time leaving the original reading present in the work. The text, in effect, remained intact for those who had read the preface.

The example is important because it illustrates how lightly the censor's pen might brush against a text: an offensive word modified, but not the narrative itself: decorum preserved, rather than the story suppressed. In fact, in his preface, Hartwell sets out a very strong claim for preserving the integrity of the original. As a statement, it has significant implications given his work as a licenser:

> I was alwayes of this opinion (and therein do I still dwell) that *Authors* should be published in the same *Order*, in the same *Termes*, & in the same *Stile* which they themselues vsed. For how know I, what moued them to obserue this *Order* or that *Order*, and to make choyce of one word rather then of another? peraduenture the reason of their so doing might proue to be so strong, as I doubt it would not easily be ouerthrowne.[47]

As a defence of the integrity of the original against interference by third parties, this is a quite startling statement from a licenser. Hartwell's first impulse was always, it would seem, to leave well alone; and his second was but to preserve decorum, if absolutely necessary, with the lightest touch. Of course, he may have disagreed with things that he read, but that does not mean that he altered them; and he must have had a considerable knowledge of contemporary literature, which clearly interested him: he owned the copy of Puttenham's *The Arte of English Poesie* (STC 20519.5; 1589) that was subsequently acquired by Jonson.[48]

---

[46] Lopez and Pigafetta, *A Report of the Kingdon of Congo*, Y4ᵛ.
[47] Lopez and Pigafetta, *A Report of the Kingdon of Congo*, *2ʳ.
[48] British Library, shelfmark G.11548.

In his final work of translation, *The Ottoman of Lazaro Soranzo*, Hartwell reveals another aspect of the way in which the publication of books might be affected by contemporary circumstances. Writing once more to Whitgift, he recalls that 'it pleased your Grace in the beginning of Michaelmas terme last [i.e. September 1602], to demand of me a question touching the Bassaes and Visiers belonging to the Turkish Court'. Hartwell goes on:

> wherein although I did for the present satisfie your Grace to your contentment by the small skill & knowledge which I haue in those Turkish affaires: yet bethinking my selfe of this Discourse which . . . had passed the Print, & had lyen by me these two years not published to the viewe of this English world, vpon some speciall considerations, that moued me for the time to conceale the same. I thought it would bee a very acceptable and pleasing matter now to thrust it forth.[49]

Those 'speciall considerations' from two years before are most likely to have had to do with the Essex Rebellion and the execution of Robert Devereux, matters that had contemporary analogies in Turkish affairs.

The passage, however, is remarkable for a number of other reasons. First, the book had sat in Windet's warehouse for two years: Windet, it would appear, had either been left financially harmless by that decision, or was willing to let the sheets remain unsold for other reasons. Second, although the book was put to one side, Hartwell still had it published and let it circulate with the text unchanged, the political reverberations now muted. Third, Whitgift clearly had every confidence in the abilities and judgment of his secretary, and allowed him to translate politically sensitive material that might from time to time prove embarrassing: Hartwell, as a senior licenser, was as aware as anyone involved with the book-trade as to what was acceptable or otherwise.

Hartwell elsewhere in the dedication described this work, like his translation of Minadoi, as one 'performed by starts and at idle houres'.[50] The image is one that gives an added dimension to his other activities, secretary to the archbishop, licenser of literature, translator of exotic histories, antiquarian,[51] and (it seems so inevitable) bibliophile. Hartwell owned copies of both William Tooker's *Charisma siva Donum Sanationis* (STC 24118; 1597), and Richard Harvey's *A Theologicall*

[49] L. Soranzo, *The Ottoman of Lazaro Soranzo* (STC 22931; 1603), ¶2ᵛ.
[50] Soranzo, *The Ottoman of Lazaro Soranzo*, 2¶1ʳ.
[51] See, *Oxford Dictionary of National Biography*, 60 vols. (Oxford, 2004), 51: 523–4.

Discourse of the Lamb of God and his Enemies (STC 12915; 1590), both now
in the Bodleian Library.[52] Like all of Hartwell's publications, and several
more that he licensed, these two volumes were printed by John Windet.
Windet was the cousin of Richard Hooker, and the printer of *Of the Lawes
of Eccliasticall Politie* (STC 13712–2.5; 1593, 1597ff.) He also printed for
Bancroft, Bridges, Bright, and Barlow. He took over the psalm-book
privilege from John Wolfe, and he printed much godly piety in pocketbook formats.

The links between Windet and Lambeth point to the Cross Keys
as being the 'unofficial' press of the Church. Windet, for instance,
printed Barlow's account of the Hampton Court conference, which has
some interesting things to say about the practice of censorship, not least
because it is written by one of the clerics responsible for implementing
that policy. The puritan, John Reynolds, had objected that 'vnlawfull and
seditious bookes, might be suppressed, at least restrained, and imparted
to a few' adding that 'for by the liberty of publishing such bookes, so
commonly, many young schollers, and vnsetled mindes in both
Vniuersities, and through the whole Realme were corrupted, and
peruerted'.[53] The claim, in effect, is that licensing as practised did not
work and the authorities were too tolerant.

The response, as a whole, makes clear what the authorities' concerns
were. First, Richard Bancroft as the bishop most directly responsible
for overseeing the licensers denied that there was any 'such licentious
diuulging of those books, as he imagined or complained of'; next, he
notes that as for imported books only those 'who were supposed, would
confute them, had liberty, by authority, to buy them'—itself an interesting
statement of privilege. Third, Cecil affirms that Bancroft 'had done
therein what might be, for the suppressing of' Catholic books. Then,
after an intervention by the king, who admonished Reynolds for his own
lack of conformity, Cecil argues that certain imported books are tolerated
because their larger argument supports government policy even if some
views are less than acceptable; and finally, Bancroft states that all books
printed in England are either properly licensed or suppressed, and that
the book-trade as a whole is orderly.[54] In other words, the authorities
attempted to do what was possible within practicable limits and with due
respect to the liberty of the subject to write what they would (and accept
the consequences if necessary).

---

[52] Bodleian Library, Oxford, shelfmarks: 4° Th. T8 Seld; Tanner 898.
[53] W. Barlow, *The summe and substance of the conference . . . at Hampton court* (STC 1456; 1604,
et sqq.), G4[v].
[54] Barlow, *The summe and substance of the conference*, G4[v]–H2[r].

There are some examples of how the authorities reacted when faced with a problem that place the more dramatic gestures into a less fraught context. One incident involves the examination of John Peck by the Archbishop of Canterbury on 11 September 1616. Peck was called for an interview to discuss his association with John Traske, a prisoner in Newgate, and a 'scrivener' called Porter.[55] His mistake had been to present a manuscript on Traske's behalf to the king at Bagshot the previous Tuesday (figure 7.1). The archbishop wanted to establish the extent of his involvement and whether he was a non-conformist. The answers reveal a man who is very scared and who is trying to be careful not to implicate himself further. At the end of the interview, Peck is asked to sign a summary of the main points of the conversation, which is then countersigned by the archbishop. In effect, he is given a formal warning.

Peck had met Traske some three years previously, when Traske (who lived nearby at Exminster) had preached a sermon at Hunniton. Over the next few years, Traske began publishing and continued preaching without a licence. He also attended a conventicle, or meeting of non-conformists. For his trouble, he ended up in Newgate, where Peck had visited him some ten times. After considerable evasion, Peck admitted that 'he received the foule Copy at his hands' (i.e. the author's manuscript) and (having first tried to blame the scrivener) that he copied the preface himself, because he did not want the scrivener to see its content. As Peck acknowledged 'hee did dislike it, because the authour dealeth wth the king in so familiar a manner'. In fact, Peck acknowledged that he had asked Traske why he had done this, and Traske had replied that 'the kinge would take no offence at it, because it was the manner of speeche wch was vsed to God himselfe' (Traske had clearly never met James I). With that response, Peck was sufficiently satisfied to present the manuscript to the king.

Peck was a student at the Inner Temple and would have fully realized what the signed document would mean should he ever attempt such folly again. He informed Abbott that he attended divine service at the Temple church, received divine sacrament, and had never been a non-conformist, or sectary. Soon after, Traske would appear to have been moved from Newgate to the Fleet, where he continued to be held until 1620, when he finally published *A treatise of libertie from Iudaisme* (STC 24178), in which he wrote of the reformation of his beliefs. Perhaps, the most striking aspect of his imprisonment was that he was furnished with books to read and paper to write.[56]

---

[55] Porter is not recorded by Steer; he may have been a writing-master of some kind.
[56] Bland, 'Invisible Dangers', 163.

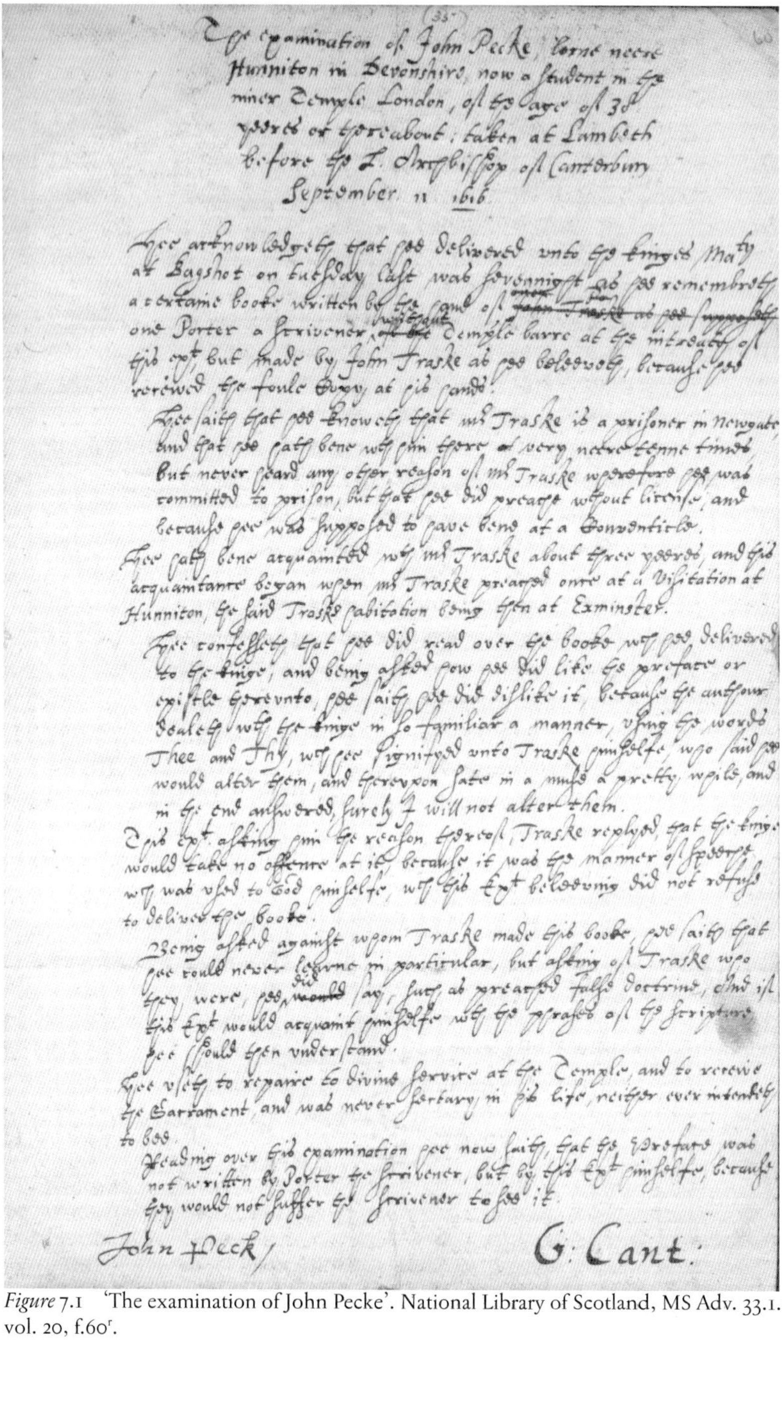
The examination of John Pecke, borne neere
Hunniton in Devonshire, now a student in the
inner Temple London, of the age of 38
yeeres or thereabout; taken at Lambeth
before the L. Archbishop of Canterbury
September 11 1616

Hee acknowledgeth that hee delivered unto the kings Maty
at Bagshot on tuesday last was sevennight as hee remembreth
a certaine booke written by the same of ~~John Traske as hee supposeth~~
one Porter a scrivener, without ~~at the~~ Temple barre at the intreaty of
this ext but made by John Traske as hee beleeveth, because hee
receved the foule copy at his hands.

Hee saith that hee knoweth that Mr Traske is a prisoner in Newgate
and that hee hath bene wth him there very neere tenne times
but never heard any other reason of Mr Traske wherefore hee was
committed to prison, but that hee did preach wthout licence, and
because hee was supposed to have bene at a Conventicle.

Hee hath bene acquainted wth Mr Traske about three yeeres, and this
acquaintance began when Mr Traske preached once at a Visitation at
Hunniton, the said Traskes habitation being then at Exminster.

Hee confesseth that hee did read over the booke wch hee delivered
to the kinge, and being asked how hee did like the preface or
epistle thereunto, hee saith hee did dislike it, because the authour
dealeth wth the kinge in so familiar a manner, using the words
Thee and Thy, wch hee signifyed unto Traske himselfe, who said hee
would alter them, and thereupon sate in a muse a pretty while, and
in the end answered, surely I will not alter them.

This ext asking him the reason thereof, Traske replyed that the kinge
would take no offence at it, because it was the manner of speech
wch was used to God himselfe, wch this ext beleeving did not refuse
to deliver the booke.

Being asked against whom Traske made this booke, hee saith that
hee could never learne in particular, but asking of Traske who
they were, hee did ~~would~~ say, such as preached false doctrine, and if
this ext would acquaint himselfe wth the phrases of the scripture
hee should then understand.

Hee useth to repaire to divine service at the Temple, and to receive
the Sacrament and was never sectary in his life, neither ever intendeth
to bee.

Reading over this examination hee now saith, that the preface was
not written by Porter the scrivener, but by this ext himselfe, because
they would not suffer the scrivener to see it.

John Peck G: Cant:

Figure 7.1 'The examination of John Pecke'. National Library of Scotland, MS Adv. 33.1.6, vol. 20, f.60r.

What the case of Traske and Peck points up is something that is not usually discussed in the study of censorship: Peck presented a *manuscript* to the king, not a printed book; and the secondary person responsible was a *scrivener*, not a printer. Further, it would appear that the primary issue was not the text, but the *preface*. Because print glittered, modern scholars have focused on the examples that are obvious rather than the broad spectrum of the evidence; and they have focused on the formal processes, not the actual practices. Few now read St Augustine in the Latin, or are seduced by his use of *te* in the *Confessions*; Traske apparently was. His offence was that he used the second-person singular to the king: we no longer differentiate, and so are deaf to the *faux pas*. As a religious writer, Traske would not have been taken seriously: his prose, and his grasp of controversy, would scarcely have given the authorities cause to pause. That he was a non-conformist, that he preached without a licence, and that he lacked a patron to protect him, made him an easy target. Peck was the person who worried the authorities because he ought to have known better; they wanted to make sure that he did.

Occasionally mistakes occured, but they reveal a great deal about the ordinary assumptions with which books were treated. In his Lyell Lecture on censorship, McKenzie cited the example of Thomas Fuller, whose *A Sermon. Of Reformation* (Wing F2461; 1643) had been altered by the examiner and licensed in its changed form. Fuller complained and the licenser apologized:

> *I must confesse, had I but knowne you to have been the Authour . . . I should have endeavoured to have satisfied M. Saltmarsh of your good meaning therein, before I had set my hand to his Examination of it. Your other Books made me conceive the Authour some other of your name . . . My licensing the Examination of some passages of your Sermon, was (at most) but on supposition their meaning had been such as some conceited them, and suppositions are no accusations.*[57]

The point here is that the system of personal contacts broke down, as sometimes it must have done. It was, in fact, only those who lacked the contacts, and who were outside of the primary protection of patronage, that were liable to have their texts altered by authority. Yet, despite this, many a book passed unaltered and approved on the commercial reality of the bookstall. Of course, some works of literature did occasionally broach politically sensitive issues (not least those by

[57] D. F. McKenzie, 'Censorship', the third Lyell Lecture, Oxford, May 1988, 22–3. The lecture was not subsequently published; a copy is available on deposit in the Bodleian Library, Oxford.

Shakespeare and Jonson), but the mechanisms of control existed more to assuage official and public concern than to enforce an ideology. The ultimate arbiter of literary success was whether a printer or publisher was willing to finance a subsequent edition; or whether a scrivener was willing to engage in speculative serial copying. In commercial terms, this is what interested the book-trade. It is easy to take something out of context and misrepresent its significance, but a publisher cared little for the meanings and indirections of a text unless it was likely to cost him his livelihood. For such material, there was always unrestricted circulation through manuscript, or publication abroad.

Illicit Books, Piracy, and Surreptitious Printing

There is a particular class of books that poses problems both of material analysis and social history: those that were printed either illicitly or surreptitiously. The incidence of illicit books printed in England is low with the notable exception of the Marprelate tracts which, for a short while, greatly exercised the authorities in their attempt to track down who was responsible. Most illicit books were printed abroad: puritan tracts in the Netherlands, and Catholic books at Douai. They were smuggled into the country and sold under the counter. The authorities did what they could to control this, but only ever with limited success.

From time to time, illegal attempts were made to print books owned by another member of the Company. When this happened, the printing was stayed until the matter had been adjudicated, with any printed sheets reassigned to the person whose copy it was. Usually the material evidence for piracy of this kind is relatively straightforward as there was no conspicuous attempt to hide responsibility—the Pied Bull quartos of Shakespeare, with their false imprints, being an exception. There were, however, occasions when printers pushed their luck a little too far. One such was Thomas Dawson who, for several months in 1614–15, decided to print 10,000 copies of the Book of Common Prayer. This item was the copy of Robert Barker, the king's printer. In itself, piracy was a serious enough offence, but the indictment makes clear that Dawson printed things that were not

> sett forth or appoynted to be soe reade in the booke of Common prayer, and you intend and have given out That you will add other thinges allsoe thereto, to the greate disturbance of the peace of the Church of England and to the evell example of others.[58]

---

[58] Beinecke Library, Yale University, Osborn MS fb24, item 94. See also *STC*, 3: 51.

Dawson was duly prosecuted in the ecclesiastical court for his attempt to reform the order of service, and the edition was suppressed. Dawson, however, continued to print until his death in 1620.

A rather different class of books that 'are not what they seem' include those that were either printed surreptitiously, or which were printed by the authorities for the purposes of disinformation. These were not illegal books, but they were printed with the intent to deceive their audience as to their origins. The authorities did this in the 1580s with the treason trials, as they had used torture to extract confessions.[59] The tone of the pamphlets is that of a gentleman who happens to be aware of the details, and is surprised at the conduct of his acquaintance who had got into such trouble. These pamphlets are a very calculated attempt to manage opinion and justify (as well as minimize) the conduct of the authorities in the pursuit of the truth.

The subject of surreptitious printing has been dealt with extensively by Woodfield.[60] Although four foreign-language books had appeared without an imprint in England before the 1580s, the first genuinely surreptitious books were printed in the 1580s by John Wolfe with the approval of the authorities. These imprints deliberately suggested that the book was printed somewhere in Europe and by someone else. Wolfe, who had worked in Italy in the 1570s, began by printing the *Discorsi* and *Il Prencipe* of Machiavelli, and the *Ragionamenti* of Aretino in 1584. The Aretino is without an imprint, but the Machiavelli is identified as from a press in Palermo. Later imprints would include Leiden, Paris, Monaco, Turin, Venice, and Piacenza.[61] The names he adopts as a printer are similarly suggestive. John Charlewood followed immediately in Wolfe's footsteps, printing Giordano Bruno with Parisian and Venetian imprints. Joseph Barnes at Oxford, Richard Field, and slightly later John Windet on Wolfe's behalf, soon did the same.[62] The practice continued through the seventeenth-century and later: a recently discovered edition of the notorious play *Sodom, or The Gentleman's Instruction* (c.1720) claims to have been printed in the Hague, with the date '1000000'.[63]

The reason for surreptitious imprints was usually commercial, and because the authors were notorious. Both Aretino and Machiavelli had been placed on the *Index Librorum Prohibitorum* and were banned by the Inquisition. Hence, the implication was that, not only did Wolfe have an

[59] Bland, 'Invisible Dangers', 159–63.
[60] D. B. Woodfield, *Surreptitious Printing in England 1550–1640* (New York, 1973).
[61] Woodfield, *Surreptitious Printing in England*, 5–18.
[62] Woodfield, *Surreptitious Printing in England*, 19–45.
[63] Sotheby's, London, 16 December 2004, lot 54.

Italian edition, it was one printed illegally. In Catholic Europe, such a book would get its owner into trouble; but in tolerant England, the salaciousness of Aretino and the cynicism of Machiavelli could be bought and read—provided the purchaser had the Italian to do so.

Commerce

In 1500, the English printed book-trade was confined to a very small group of printers, who have been studied in great detail; by 1700, the press had been freed by the Licensing Act of 1695 and was on the verge of a massive expansion through the eighteenth-century.[64] What was most significant about the Act was the removal of constraint on the number of presses and printers, and this affected the Scriveners because, as print-production costs fell, they became uncompetitive except for legal and financial documents. In between, the printed book-trade grew substantially if inconsistently, to the extent that the forms of oversight that were possible in 1600 were quite unmanageable a century later.

Booksellers, of course, hoped to make money from their work, and many did, but the overall size of the trade was, for a long time, quite modest. Hence, in some respects, its social and intellectual importance was greater than its economic significance. It is likely that Southampton, Egerton, Pembroke, and Cecil each had a greater personal net worth than the asset value of the trade as a whole: that places their relationship with Shakespeare, Donne, Daniel, and Jonson, and their ability to protect them, in a rather different perspective.[65] Printers, publishers, and scriveners, must all have been open to opportunities for immediate work, and even the accumulation of small or large profits, but very few made more than an adequate or comfortable living from their business (scriveners rather more so because some of them acted as moneylenders). Most books made small profits or provided sufficient work and income to tide things over until a better opportunity came along; most authors were paid not with coin, but with books.[66]

The economics of publishing and book production in the sixteenth and seventeenth centuries is difficult to reconstruct in detail, although

---

[64] See, M. Treadwell, 'The Stationers and the Printing Acts at the End of the Seventeenth Century', *The Book in Britain . . . 1557–1695*, 755–6.

[65] Bland, 'The London Book-Trade in 1600'.

[66] William Prynne received 35–6 copies in lieu of payment for *Histrio-mastix* (STC 20464a; 1633): W. W. Greg, *A Companion to Arber* (Oxford, 1967), 85 and 278; Bp. William Bedel to Dr Samuel Ward (on behalf of Dr Gaspar Despotin; no STC entry recorded), 5 April 1622, Bodleian Library, MS Tanner 73, f.140 records that Despotin wished for 40 copies in lieu of payment.

we know the outlines of what books cost to produce and the price that could be charged for them. What we do not know, in many cases, are the size of edition runs, the speed with which they sold, or the extent to which they were sold on to other members of the trade at a discount. Most plays, pamphlets, and sermons were useful as sources of cash-flow and work; capital and profits were generated by larger books and longer print-runs. In the letter to Sibbes cited earlier (p. 167), Jenison specifies that 500 copies of his book were printed.[67] A ream per sheet must have been a very standard arrangement for most first editions, but it is not one that can be applied with any consistency and predictability.

As well as lists of prices, there are a number of booksellers' bills.[68] Among the Stanhope papers in the Osborn Manuscripts at Yale are two further invoices and a receipt for books and other materials supplied by the king's printer, Robert Barker, from 1604, 1610, and 1614.[69] These documents describe the books supplied, the size of the print-run for two proclamations, and the kinds of book-trade-related products that were supplied by the royal printing-house. The first receipt (f.33^v) is endorsed on its recto edge 'Allowanc*es* made to m^r | Barker the King*es* Printer'. It records three transactions, the first of which is crossed through.[70]

20° ffeb: 1609; Anno ~~Mj~~ Jacobi Septimo: To Robᵉte Barker his Ma:^{ties} Printer, for sundrie book*es* by him printed for his Ma:^{ties} vse & service, ————————	CCCx^{li} xiiij^s viij^d
19° Maij <u>1609</u>. More to him for paper bookes deliūed for the vse of the Parliam^t house – lxx^{li} and for printing of privie seales – xxx^{li} – In all	C^{li}
22° Dec: 1610 Anno ~~Mj~~ Iacobi Octavo. More to him for parchem^t, book*es*, &c deliūed for the vse of the vpper house of Parliam^t	lxxviij^{li} ij^s x^d
<u>11 Aprilis 1612.</u> /	Clxxij^{li} xx^d

[67] Bodleian Library, MS Tanner 73, f.29.

[68] See, Johnson, 'Notes on English Retail Book-Prices, 1550–1640', 83–112; McKitterick, '"Ovid with a Littleton" ', 184–234; D. F. McKenzie, 'Two Bills for Printing, 1620–22', *The Library*, v: 15 (1960), 129–32; —; 'Printing and Publishing 1557–1700: Constraints on the London Book Trades', *The Book in Britain . . . 1557–1695*, 553–67.

[69] Beinecke Library, MS Osborn fb159, f.33, f.33, 40 and 41. The Stanhope papers were calendared in HMC, 10th Report, Appendix VI, and were sold at Christies, 23 June 1954, lot 112.

[70] The paper is pot (83 × 22 mm), initials 'PO', chainlines 21 mm.

The first item is substantial and indicates that the 'sundrie bookes' have been printed by Barker. The other two items appear to be for blank books and binding parchment for use by both Houses of Parliament, as well as the printing of the Privy Seals. They show Barker to be a stationer in the more modern sense: someone who supplied blank books and paper—in this case, for official purposes.

The next invoice dated 'April. 4°. 1614' (f.40^r), is endorsed on the verso of its other leaf 'Copia of m^r Barker his | bill delivered vnto mee | 28 october 1614'. It is a more substantial document.

Deliuered for his Maties service: by Rob̄t Barker.
His Maties Printer. as followeth.

1.	Booke of Com̄on Prayer and two testam^{ts}	
	Of the largest volume, wth praiers for ye Parl.	– 2 — 10 — 0
1.	Booke of statutes A°. 1° Elz: Regin. et 3° Iacobi	– 6 — 0 — 0
1.	Poultons Abridgem^{ts}, and Rastalls fayre boun	– 2 — 4 — 0
	Paper & Parchm^t for the vpper house of Parliam^t	– 4 — 16 — 8
1.	Giornall booke fayre bound and gilt	– 0 — 16 — 0
1.	Speedes Chronologie of England fayre bound	– 4 — 0 — 0
	Paper & Parchm^t for the lower howse	– 2 — 16 — 8
1.	largest Bible faire bound & guilt	– 3 — 0 — 0
1.	Hollinsheads Cronicle. 2. Volumes faire bound	– 3 — 6 — 8
1.	Booke of ~~Marty~~ Martyrs fayre bound	– 2 — 13 — 4
1.	Statuts at large for the Parlim^t howse	– 6 — 0 — 0
1	Statute booke. 1°. Elz: 3°. Iacobi, 7°. Iacobi	– 1 — 0 — 0
	Standish and Inkhorne furnisht	– 0 — 8 — 0
	Poulton and Rastall fayre bound	– 2 — 4 — 0
1	large bagg wth Turky leather wth silke stringes	– 2 — 0 — 0
	All the K^s. Speeches in sundry bookes faire bound	– 0 — 6 — 8
6	Proclam. touching the oath of Allegiance	– 0 — 1 — 0
6	Proclam. Concerning Recusantes	– 0 — 1 — 0
100	Procl: and bookes of duelles more	– 10 — 0 — 0
4	Bibles for the King and Qeene, wherof	
	3. very faire bound and guilt all over	– 20 — 0 — 0
1800.	Proclm. For dying and dressing cloth	– 15 — 0 — 0
600.	Proclam. Touching Recusantes in Ireland	– 5 — 0 — 0
1.	Booke of the K^s. Maties Bounty	– 0 — 0 — 8
		———————
Total		– 94 — 18 — 0

Vera copia. ex̄per me | Henry Elsynge | Richard Rosseter.

As a list of materials supplied for the Addled Parliament of 1614, and of the books that were deemed appropriate, this is a particularly interesting invoice. Bibles, books of common prayer, statutes, and legal interpreters form the core of the volumes supplied, but it is noteworthy to see Fox, Holinshed, and Speed in addition, given the antiquarian and historical interests of early Stuart politics. Second, Barker is not only supplying books and paper, but turkey leather, silk ties, and an inkhorn. This kind of material is also to be found in the following bill from ten years earlier. Third, Barker supplied 1,800 copies of one proclamation, 600 copies of another, yet only six each of the proclamations to do with recusants and the oath of allegiance. It is difficult to know whether these are the actual print-runs, though it seems likely and the larger numbers are for what one might expect. If that is the case, however, it is notable that the quantity could vary so widely; the small runs must have been printed with a very specific purpose in mind. Finally, the cost of £20 for four bibles 'very faire bound and guilt all over' for James and Anne is very high and it is clear that much more was spent on the binding than the books.

The final bill (f.41^r) is endorsed by Barker. It is addressed 'To Sr Tho: Smithe Knight: Clarke of ye Vpper Howse of Parliam^{te}', and is dated 'Febr. 10°. 1603' though the context immediately makes clear that the bill is for the first Parliament of James's reign and that legal dating is being used.

Delivered by Robt Barker Printer to the Kings
Matie for his Highnes service   viz

One Statuts at large wth severall parliam^{ts} in 9. Volumes	– 5^{li}	– 0	– 0
The Statuts at large from Magna Charta fayre bounde in two severall Volumes	– 3^{li}	– 6	– 8
Three paper bookes of Large fine Paper §	– 1	– 10	– 0
Three Realmes of fine Paper §	– 1	– 10	– 0
The Abridgemts of Statuts, Polton and Rastell §	– 1	– 4	– 0
Fiftie skinnes of fine Parchmente §	– 3	– 6	– 8
Two books of Computacōn of yeeres §	– 0	– 3	– 0
Three Almanacks bounde in Velame §	– 0	– 2	– 6
A large bagge of Turkie leather with silke strings, for ye Parliam^{te} bills §	– 1	– 10	– 0
One booke of Common Prayer of ye largest Volume with prayers for ye Parliam^{te} inserted §	– 0	– 10	– 0
Two boxes covered with leather, with lockes & keyes to them. to locke in the bills §	– 1	– 0	– 0
One fayre bible. in folio. ————————	– 1	– 10	– 0

Although this invoice is more modest, it helps to clarify some aspects of the previous one. The turkey leather (goatskin) and silk strings are for the parliament bills, and on this occasion Barker supplies two boxes with locks and keys. The fine parchments are presumably intended for the bills, so that they may be permanently preserved. Another interesting item is the three reams of fine paper at £1 10s, or 10s a ream, which suggests that this was the price for Italian paper compared to 3s6d for French pot. The 'fayre bible' in folio, at £1 10s, is far more modest than the average of £5 for the lavishly bound royal copies ten years later. Further, one might note the special prayers for the parliament for the book of common prayer—a small piece of job printing.

Overall, these three documents give an impression of Barker, not just as the king's printer, but of the printing-house at the centre of a network of related activities: binding, stationery, special document boxes, and other occasional work. Other stationers, if not as lavishly, must have done similar things, and that income would have been an important component of their business: the trade was not just about books. Further, the bills illustrate the way in which Barker supplied material printed by other members of the trade by virtue of his privileged position and interests. Finally, the bills give some sense of the scale and value of these activities and what was involved. In particular, they cast a light on the relations between the book-trade and parliament, including the role of the trade in facilitating the materials for reference, and the means for keeping and preserving records.

As well as printer's bills, some inventories survive including those for the London printer Henry Bynneman, who died in 1583, the York bookseller John Foster from 1616,[71] and for the Cambridge printer Thomas Thomas in 1587.[72] Thomas, for instance had £43 16s7½d of printing equipment, £12 19s of paper and parchment books, as well as other skins and boards, and £147 12s10d of stock on hand. His stock included 1,381 copies of a book he had recently printed; other quantities ranged widely: 122, 429, 377, 233, 125, 29, 16, 99, and 147.[73] Bynneman's was a much larger business with £113 12s of equipment, of which £87 7s4d was type. He also had £607 0s1d of stock, mostly valued at cost, of which £258 5s9d was accounted for by 775 copies of a Greek and Latin dictionary (STC 18101) that he had recently finished printing.[74] The

[71] Barnard and Bell, 'The Inventory of Henry Bynneman', 5–46; —, *The Early Seventeenth-Century York Book Trade and John Foster's Inventory of 1616* (Leeds, 1994).
[72] McKitterick, *A History of Cambridge University Press . . . 1534–1698*, 106–7.
[73] McKitterick, *A History of Cambridge University Press . . . 1534–1698*, 84–5, 106–7.
[74] Barnard and Bell, 'The Inventory of Henry Bynneman', 17 and 8.

inventory also affords some insight into what sold and what did not: about 25 per cent of his stock dated from 1570–5, whilst 75 per cent was more recent, and of most things he had between 100 and 300 copies. Nevertheless, he still had 435 copies of Guiciardini's *Houres of recreation* (STC 12465; 1576), and 450 copies of Elviden's *Pesistratus and Cantanea* (STC 7624; 1570?). Comparatively, he had 20 copies of Gesner's *New iewell of health* (STC 11798; 1576), 29 copies of Lupton's *A persuasion from papistrie* (STC 16950; 1581), and 100 copies of Stow's *Chronicles* (STC 23333; 1580).[75] The market for literature was not always profitable.

Whilst not all publishers were printers, most printers did publish books on their own account. When a printer worked for a publisher, it was up to the publisher to assess the commercial risk. When a printer worked for themselves, they would assess the balance between continuity of work, commercial return, the size of the project, and the investment involved. The story of Sir Henry Spelman taking his *Archæologus* (STC 23065; 1626), to the press, must have been familiar to many an author:

> After he had made large Collections, and got tolerable knowledge of the Saxon Tongue; he resolv'd to go on with his undertaking: but because he would not depend altogether upon his own Judgement, he Printed a sheet or two for a Specimen, whereby his Friends might be able to give him their opinion of the design . . . . Upon their encouragement, he prepar'd part of it for the Press, and offer'd the whole Copy to Mr. *Bill* the King's Printer. He was very moderate in his demands; desiring only five pound, in consideration of his labour, and that to be paid him in Books. But Mr. *Bill* absolutely refus'd to meddle with it; knowing it to be upon a subject out of the common road, and not likely to prove a saleable work. So that Sir *Henry* was forc'd to carry it on at his own charge; and in the year 1626. publisht the first part of it, to the end of the Letter *L*. Why he went no farther, I cannot tell; . . . . But I believe, the true reason was this: Printing it at his own charge, he must have laid out a considerable summ upon the first part, and having a large Family, there was no reason why he should venture as much more, without the prospect of a quicker return, than either the coldness of the Bookseller, or the nature of the work gave him. It fell out accordingly; for, eleven years after, the greatest part of the Impression remain'd unsold; till in 1637. two of the *London* Booksellers took it off his hands.[76]

[75] Barnard and Bell, 'The Inventory of Henry Bynneman', 26, 27, 30, 35, and 29.
[76] H. Spelman, *Reliquiæ Spelmannianæ* (Wing S4930; 1698), b3^r-v.

Thus, Spelman had 'Printed a sheet or two for a Specimen' and prepared the copy for the press; his initial desire was for £5 'and that to be paid him in Books', but he was prepared to print the first part of the volume at his own expense. It did not sell, and he eventually sold his copies to the trade at, one presumes, a severely discounted price. Although the printing of a specimen sheet may have been unusual, it is testimony to the degree of authorial care that could be taken when the composition was likely to be difficult. In fact, Spelman had been 'busie about the impression of his Glossary' since at least April 1622.[77] It was, therefore, at least four years in pre-production and printing, and he only got to *L*. The second part was not published until 1664, 23 years after Spelman's death.

Coryate was another author who paid for the printing, as a number of the contributors to the prefatory poems of his *Crudities* remarked.[78] Despite the fact that Coryate paid for the costs of the printing, the book was entered by the publishers and booksellers William Barret and Edmund Blount, however only Stansby's initials appear in the imprint. The role of the publishers, and in particular the extent to which they were responsible for decisions concerning typography and format, is not self-evident. Some authors appear to have worked with one printer and a number of publishers and others appear to have worked with only one publisher and a number of printers: more often the situation was more complex, but the implication is that the relationships between authors and the trade depended on individual arrangements. In some cases, books would only be published if privately funded either by the author or with a subvention from a patron.

Large type, generous spacing, larger or better paper, engraved plates, all had a direct impact on the production costs of a book. If the difference in final costs meant a penny or two on the price of the final book or pamphlet, then a publisher might not be particularly concerned for the right author. If the book was large, and special requirements were desired by the author, the more likely it was that the trade would want some assistance with the costs. A 250-sheet folio, printed in 1,000 copies, would require 500 reams of paper. Add in four or five engraved plates (maps perhaps), an engraved frontispiece, large paper for presentation copies, and the cost of composition, and the publisher was making a substantial investment before a single copy had sold. The risk might be shared with other members of the trade, who each would take a portion of the books

---

[77] R. Parr (ed.), *The Life of . . . James Usher*, Wing P548, 3K4ᵛ: Sir Henry Bourgchier to James Ussher, 16 April 1622.
[78] T. Coryate, *Coryats crudities* (STC 5808; 1611), b1ᵛ, b4ʳ, e5ᵛ and g6ʳ.

produced, but that was not always possible. Stansby sold 20 per cent of the Jonson edition to Richard Meighen, and clearly hoped to find a purchaser for another 25 per cent, but he was not successful.[79] As the *Workes* were set with a shorter than usual page, one might also wonder whether Pembroke or Aubigny helped with the costs. It is possible.

Continental Books

A trip to one of the better London bookshops of the seventeenth-century might surprise those who now work on English literature. As well as the English books, there would have been a substantial quantity of books in Latin and Greek, with French, Italian, and Spanish also to be found. Approximately 90 per cent of the books owned by Selden and Dee were in languages other than English, and the figures for Jonson and Donne are between 70 and 80 per cent. The Latin trade was an important part of the business for at least some of the booksellers, and of the intellectual life of its customers.[80] These were the kind of people who also tended to acquire political and historical manuscripts: they usually had a university education, and frequently acquired substantial libraries over the course of their lives.

Much of the Latin trade relates to theology, or works of scholarship, some of which now seem arcane, and scholarly editions. A glance at the books in Jonson's library suggests what was available, both new and second-hand: not only did he own editions of the classics by scholars such as Scaliger, Casaubon, Lipsius, and Heinsius, but monographs on a vast range of topics. For instance, his library included the *Tactica* of Claudius Aelianus (Antwerp, 1613),[81] the *Antiquae Tabulae Marmorae* of Girolamo Aleandro (Paris, 1617),[82] the *Commentaria Germaniae* by Andreas Althamer (Nuremberg, 1534),[83] the *Syriados* of Pietro Angelio (Florence, 1616),[84] an edition of the *De Re Culinaria* by Coelius Apicius (Basle, 1541),[85] and a copy of *Pericula Poetica* by Valentinus Arithmaeus (Frankfurt, 1613).[86] These are just some of the items by authors whose surname begins with A. We also know that there are many books that Jonson must have owned, but which either have not survived or have

---

[79] Bland, 'William Stansby and *The Workes of Beniamin Jonson*', 18–19.
[80] See, R. J. Roberts, 'The Latin Trade', *The Book in Britain . . . 1557–1695*, 141–73.
[81] Cambridge University Library, shelfmark M.10.32.
[82] Folger Shakespeare Library, shelfmark N5763 A3 Cage.
[83] British Library, shelfmark 587 f.24.
[84] British Library, shelfmark 837 g.43.
[85] British Library, shelfmark 453 d.26.
[86] Huntington Library, San Marino, shelfmark RB 611670.

not been located, including such items as the *De Occultis Philosophia* of Heinrich Cornelius Agrippa ab Nettesheim (probably Lyons, 1600), which he used for *The Masque of Queenes*.

Jonson's interests were wide-ranging, and included some religious materials such as Aquinas, but he was not a particular connoisseur of theological controversy. For clerics of the established Church, this was their primary interest and many parochial, as well as cathedral libraries have collections of this kind of material that were once owned by the clergy.[87] What is apparent from these collections is the sheer scale of the Latin trade. Without an understanding that imported books would have constituted a major portion of any bookseller's stock, our sense of the trade is radically incomplete. Often the number of English books commissioned by a publisher, who did not print, in any given year is quite low, and alone they would certainly not have provided a sufficient income to sustain a business, or an attractive variety of material for a customer to browse. One has to situate the production of the London trade, and its domestic concerns, within the broader context of what was sold by the booksellers, and that was European in scope.

Commerce was really the ultimate form of regulation: it dictated what a bookseller could sell, and that dictated what he was prepared to publish. What was printed in England had to compete with what was available from Europe, and it was not until the late seventeenth-century that Oxford and Cambridge began to compete in a serious way with publishers of Antwerp, Amsterdam, Paris, and Frankfurt in the market for scholarly books. As Britain became more of an empire, it changed from being a net importer, to a net exporter of books. That story belongs to the eighteenth and nineteenth centuries, after licensing had been abolished, and when the commercial and political power of the trade found a consanguinity of interest with the emergence of a new imperial ambition. Such coincidences of time, chance, and power leave their traces most visibly in the book as a witness to that past.

[87] N. R. Ker, rev. M. R. Perkins, *A Directory of the Parochial Libraries of the Church of England and the Church in Wales* (London, 2004)—the Bodleian manuscript with the original report of the parochial holdings is MS Eng misc. c.360; M. S. G. McLeod et al., *The Cathedral Libraries Catalogue: Books Printed before 1701 in the Libraries of the Anglican Cathedrals of England and Wales*, 2 vols. in 3 pts. (London, 1984–8).

8   Last Words

O N 18 June 1940, Greg wrote to John Quincy Adams, the Librarian of the Folger Shakespeare Library:

> Dear Dr Adams
>   Your letter of 3 June has just arrived, with its more than generous references to my very modest qualifications. I value your opinion greatly, however wildly exaggerated it may be.
>   By the time this reaches you, you will be able at least to guess at the magnitude of the disaster that has befallen the cause we have at heart. I cannot speak of it.
> Ever yours
W. W. Greg[1]

The day on which this letter was written is of some consequence. The day before France had surrendered to Germany. In Greg's letter, 'the darkest hour' is captured in the authentic voice, not of a soldier or politician, but of someone who cared for the literary and historical heritage of the book, and the preservation of documentary evidence. In parliament, that same day as Greg wrote to Adams, Churchill spoke of the battle about to commence, upon which 'the survival of Christian civilisation' depended, pitted, as it was, against 'a new Dark Age made more sinister, and perhaps more protracted, by the lights of perverted science'. What the letter reveals is the depths of Greg's despair and, implicitly, the way in which he saw the newly established Folger Shakespeare Library as the institution that would carry forward the preservation of the literature and values that he believed were not simply at risk, but on the brink of destruction.

It is important to realise what Greg so evidently understood: that all books become unique, and there are many stages through which they do so. In the choice of script or type, paper, and format, every document is distinguished from, and connected to, those with which it is most closely related. Then there is the later history of ownership, annotation, and, quite often, rebinding—sometimes as sammelbände, sometimes through breaking up such collections. There may have been efforts to remove the trace of previous owners through washing, scraping, obliteration, or excision. As artefacts, books contain other signs of life and use than the underlining and annotation of an owner, or their signature, bookplate, or stamp on the boards, flyleaves, or title:

[1] Folger Shakespeare Library, MS Y.c.1098 (2).

there are books with the thumbprints of pressmen, the paw prints of a domestic cat,[2] the footprints of a bird,[3] the pen scrawls of a child, tobacco burns, wine stains, remnants of food, pressed flowers, scissors, spectacles, and writing instruments. The history of collecting and of dispersal is part of this material history as well. Each and every book, manuscript or printed, is an historical artefact in its own right.

As well as the books that survive, there are many others that have been destroyed by their owners, or through circumstance: books have been thrown away after reading, used for toilet paper, turned to cinders in accidental or deliberate fire, shot through or blown to pieces in war, twisted and crumpled by earthquake, carbonized by volcanic eruption, lost at sea, suppressed by authority, pulped by librarians, consumed in an explosion while being 'conserved' with the rocket propellant diethyl zinc,[4] used for wrapping paper or lining the dishes for pies,[5] being torn to pieces, or read until their physical structure disintegrates. Some books survive mutilated almost beyond recognition, and certainly use. Other volumes have suffered irreparable damage through mistreatment and neglect including the effects of damp and mould, the damage from insects or bacteria, or being cut up by bibliographers wanting examples of printing-house ornaments.

Compared to the damage and destruction that is regularly done to books, the silence of the shelves is an enlightened Elysium. Yet, for all of our uses of communication, of documents and texts, for all of what libraries preserve as a witness to a society and its civilization, much of what we do and think is lost to posterity. When we treat books and manuscripts simply as texts, we compound the possibilities of not understanding the past because we remove the archaeological evidence that gives the artefacts historical meaning. From this perspective, the damage that we do to libraries by treating literary documents as sites of information is manifold. For all its triumph, in manuscript, in print, and through electronic and recorded resources, the written testament is but

---

[2] Noticed in a copy of Jonson's 1616 *Workes* in the Newberry Library, Chicago, shelfmark Case Y135 J735, 4H4^v–5^r. As the leaves are not conjugate, it is likely that the cat with the muddy paws belonged to an owner rather than to the printing-house; it was, perhaps, the pet of George Rutland of Newcastle, who had the volume rebound in the early nineteenth-century, and who annotated his copy extensively.

[3] Again, noticed in a copy of Jonson's 1616 *Workes*; this time, Folger Shakespeare Library, shelfmark STC 14751 copy 1, H3^r: illustrated in Bland, 'William Stansby and . . . *The Workes of Beniamin Jonson*', 7.

[4] This astonishing story is told by N. Baker, *Double-fold: Libraries and the Assault on Paper* (New York, 2001), 111–34.

[5] See Greg, 'The Bakings of Betsy', *Collected Papers*, 48–74; Jonson also refers to the practice in 'An Execration upon Vulcan', l.54.

a fragment of that larger lost work of the living word, and the history of its preservation.

Libraries are about fragments.[6] Their first lesson, the law of the catalogue, is that no literary document exists in isolation. This is as true of the most simple as the most erudite of witnesses. What we do with these fragments is discover the relationships that exist between them (physical, textual, historical), and from that discovery we construct a pattern of understanding: when we write something down, we distance ourselves from its meaning, and conceive of it as relating to something else. As soon as we understand that all texts have *contexts*—other words, other ideas, against which they exist—we enter into a far more fruitful and complex understanding of the human record. On a higher level, we also discover that all libraries are incomplete, and that each library has its own particular role as a witness to civilization; and as scholars, we need to recognise that our records of their holdings may be incomplete.

Libraries are libraries of libraries, built up from an accumulation of both single volumes, and collections put together by scholars, families, and booksellers. If books have editions, libraries have collections, yet libraries are not simply collections of books, nor are multiple copies of a text historically ever quite the same (for a start, a duplicate is not the original copy acquired and so is present in a collection for another reason than the first); nor may two 'copies' be physically the same. In a more profound sense, all libraries are fragmentary witnesses to the use of the history of the written word.

All libraries are incomplete, and each library that serves the public or a specific community, has its own role as a guardian of the inscriptions, manuscripts, printed books, and, more recently, other media in its trust. Such collections are never haphazard, and their continuing maintenance and development needs to engage fully with the history of their form as well as with their meaning. As a consequence, the practice of analytical and descriptive bibliography is informed with an ethical and historical responsibility towards the preservation and care of printed books, manuscripts, and other documents as artefacts of cultural heritage, by demonstrating that the iconic works of imagination and intellect can only be fully understood in relation to the material and textual histories of those other marginal and mundane items alongside which they were created, consumed, and kept.[7]

---

[6] For a discussion of the importance of literary and historical fragments: G. W. Most (ed.), *Collecting Fragments* (Gottingen, 1998).
[7] For further reflections on the function and responsibilities of a national library, see McKenzie, 'Our Textual Definition of the Future', 277.

The first simple, obvious fact about early modern documents (the manuscripts, books, drawings, letters, accounts, and contracts that all used paper) is that most of the evidence does not survive. In an earlier chapter, it was observed that between 1500 and 1700 almost all paper in England was imported. Certainly, there were elements of a domestic trade, but it was not until after 1700 that it became a significant manufacturing industry in its own right. If we look at the import figures from the viewpoint of establishing a minimum of how much paper was used between 1500 and 1700 (broadly tripling over the course of each century, with any local output being in addition to this), then we are talking about the domestic consumption of, at least, c.6–7 billion sheets of white paper during that 200-year period (the important point is the order of magnitude, not the exact figure), and that does not include the trade in imported books.

As far as domestic book production is concerned, we have c.90,000 entries for pre-1700 books and broadsides printed in Britain, some of which involve minor distinctions such as variant imprints for title-pages. Of these, many items survive as unique copies, and some as fragments; the vast majority of pre-Civil War books are represented by no more than ten copies, with most items there are fewer extant witnesses than that.[8] Even if we were to guess at the quantity of surviving manuscripts, we would have to acknowledge that the vast majority of written texts have been lost. If we were to propose that 3–4 per cent, or even 6–8 per cent of all the paper that was used survives (no-one has counted how much actually does exist), the point would be the same: there is reason to believe that at least c.95 per cent, possibly as much as 98 per cent, of the paper that was used in the sixteenth and seventeenth centuries has perished.

There is nothing particularly surprising about the scale of this loss: the Reformation, Civil War, and Great Fire, all played their part, but the single greatest factor determining the destruction of paper was simply a combination of its temporary use, and the insignificance of the texts as historical documents to those who made or owned them. Paper once used is frequently discarded, and although it is durable (and rag paper especially so), it was used for its convenience, not its permanence. The caveat that follows from this is that any discussion of the uses of books and manuscripts needs to recognize the imperfect and partial nature of the evidence that we have.[9]

---

[8] For an extended review of the completed revision to the pre-1640 *Short Title Catalogue*: P. W. M. Blayney, 'The Numbers Game: Appraising the Revised *STC*', *Papers of the Bibliographical Society of America* (1994), 353–407.

[9] See also, McKenzie, 'Printing and Publishing 1557–1700', 553–67.

Yet, as Glen Dudbridge has remarked, texts can 'exist in a state which is neither full transmission nor full loss'.[10] Quotations, or references to texts that once existed, may be present in other texts; annotations may be present in a book that was used to prepare another; a printed book might exist in its manuscript form but the edition may not have survived; entries in the Stationers' Register indicate that there are books that no longer exist; edition numbers on a title-page, or regular reprinting (such as with almanacs) may reveal other printings that have been lost to posterity; the preparation of stemmata for manuscript traditions will reveal intermediaries in the transmission process that no longer survive, but whose textual variants we can surmise. Such information is useful on three counts. First, it urges prudence about the assumptions we make regarding extant materials and the patterns of production. Second, it helps identify material that might still exist but that has not yet been recorded. Third, it reveals aspects about the histories and uses of texts and documents that we might otherwise overlook. That which remains, that can be known, has been shaped not only by the impulses of creation and preservation, or the structures of understanding and the hierarchies implied by critical judgment and taste, but also by obligations, by the mutability of desires, and by forgetfulness, suppression, erasure, and neglect.

From the books that do survive, there is considerable evidence of the formation of personal libraries,[11] and of how books were read in the early modern period. Hence, a substantial body of work has been done on the libraries of various writers, scholars, and intellectuals. Reading, as Roger Chartier remarked, 'is always a practice embodied in acts, spaces, and habits'.[12] Personal libraries, whether located as separate spaces or as an ordinary room furnished with books, shaped the lives of those who used them, and created shared obligations. Those practices and spaces have been explored recently with some thoughtfulness.[13] Equally, the early modern reader might have access to parochial, cathedral, college and university libraries, or the substantial private collections of individuals such as John Dee, Sir Robert Cotton, and John Selden.

---

[10] G. Dudbridge, *Lost Books of Medieval China* (London, 2000), 27.
[11] See, E. Leedham-Green and D. J. McKitterick, 'Ownership: Private and Public Libraries', *The Book in Britain . . . 1557–1695*, 323–38.
[12] Chartier, *The Order of Books: Readers, Authors and Libraries in Europe between the Fourteenth and Eighteenth Centuries* (Oxford, 1994), 3.
[13] For instance, H. Brayman Hackel, *Reading Materials in Early Modern England: Print, Gender and Literacy* (Cambridge, 2005); K. Sharpe, *Reading Revolutions: The Politics of Reading in Early Modern England* (New Haven CT, 2000); W. H. Sherman, *Used Books: Marking Readers in Renaissance England* (Philadelphia PA, 2008).

The problem with books is that they occupy space, and cumulatively any large collection occupies a lot of space; furthermore, readers require space, and the more books a library has, the more readers there are likely to be. Cumulatively, as well, books are heavy and that means any building that houses them has to be structurally resilient. In the past, these issues were dealt with by building libraries, some magnificent, most with a quiet dignity, to house the collections and cater to those who accessed them.[14] In recent decades, digital technology has seemed to offer an alternative, by compressing the physical space of the book into a digitally encoded form.

There can be no doubt that much manuscript activity, as well as the composition and manufacture of books, has been transformed by digital means. Serious projects for the creation of electronic archives, and the creation of digital scholarly editions, offer the possibility of making texts and their versions available in ways that have not previously been possible. What is, at this stage, less certain is the durability of those methods, of the commitment of universities, publishers, and libraries to house them on a permanent basis, and of the willingness for them to be maintained in such a way that the primary documents are able to cope with evolving technological circumstances. The funding available to develop digital projects is often limited, the technical and archival aspects of the work can be highly complex and the project may take a great deal of time to complete, the standards and methods adopted for different projects have been inconsistent, and the institutional support is usually based on the involvement of specific individuals. Nevertheless, a commitment to the making and maintaining of digital scholarly archives and editions must be part of the future provision of university and library resources as an enhancement to, not as a substitute for, the physical book.

The problem that the digital library creates, as an additional activity, is that it may divert scarce resources away from the maintenance and development of the physical collections. The risk, which now recurs with increasing frequency, is that the digital image is seen as a substitute for the physical artefact and thus, instead of arguing from high moral principle for the provision of adequate funding, those concerned collude in the belief that the book is only a text, that a text is only information, and that the physical copy can be discarded and replaced by a digital image. At the same time, the funding that ought to be devoted to libraries, and the maintenance of the human written record, is instead diverted by governments into projects that seek to gather

---

[14] See, R. Chartier, *The Order of Books*, 61–91; D. J. McKitterick, et al., *The Making of the Wren Library* (Cambridge, 1995).

information of an ever more intrusive nature on the lives of private citizens. The pursuit of information at the expense of knowledge and understanding as represented by considered written discourse, the privileging of political self-interest over a broader ethical responsibility that ought to be at the heart of civilized government, and the claim that such institutions have the assumed right to control the behaviour of others rather than tolerate the liberty of individual conscience, has quietly been pursued by the lights of perverted science.[15]

Scholars and librarians have a responsibility to the history of the book as an artefact that reflects the values of society over time and the use of the human intellect in its material forms. The ability to study a book and read its history in the hand, as well as its text on the page, is to engage in a deeper understanding of the arts of human communication and the ways in which that has evolved. Paper, script, type, structure, the traces left by other texts, the changes that have been made from one copy to another, and the attempts to control what was written are not incidental matters: without them no books or manuscripts would exist as they do. As guardians of those objects that we seek to understand in this way, libraries have an opportunity to celebrate and inform about the rich diversity of physical materials in their possession; to work with scholars to explain the significance of such items, and how these artefacts relate to the beliefs, ideas, and practices of the time in which they were made; and a responsibility to those who come after, and who will use the marginal, the mundane, and the extraordinary materials in their collections, in ways unimagined, to illuminate times present and past: that is a purpose and a pleasure they ought never surrender.

---

[15] Much the same point was long ago made by D. F. McKenzie, 'John Milton, Alexander Turnbull and Kathleen Coleridge', *Turnbull Library Record*, 14 (1981), 111 (106–11): 'As an example of its projective force in the present, one could develop from *Areopagitica* a defence of the physical book—in contrast to the mechanics of information retrieval. Preselected, institutionally controlled, commercially directed and ephemeral "information" is no more accessible to the individual than authority, short-time storage, and sophisticated technology (beyond the means of any individual) will permit. The portability and thought-ful privacy of the physical book, its hospitality (unlike VDU screens) to the formal shaping of consecutively presented though, and even the coarse and publicly overt means required to suppress, censor and frustrate the adequate housing of *physical* books, make it a surer defence against institutional secrecy and its attendant, political tyranny.'

Selected Further Reading

THE following suggestions are intended as guidance to the essential reference materials and some further reading. The lists are selective: the objective is to illustrate the conversations that have taken place in bibliographical scholarship, and to shape an understanding that can be built upon further in more wide-ranging and specialized ways.

Journals

Analytical & Enumerative Bibliography (now defunct).
Bodleian Library Record
Book History
English Manuscript Studies 1100–1700
The Library
Papers of the Bibliographical Society of America (*PBSA*)
Publishing History
Quaerendo
Script & Print (formerly the *Bulletin of the Bibliographical Society of Australia and New Zealand*)
Studies in Bibliography
TEXT/Textual Cultures (since 2006)
Transactions of the Cambridge Bibliographical Society (*TCBS*)

As well as the above, bibliographical and textual articles may be published in author specific periodicals such as the *John Donne Journal*, or journals with a historical literary emphasis, including *English Literary Renaissance*, the *Huntington Library Quarterly*, and the *Review of English Studies*.

Reference Materials

Arber, E. (ed.), *A Transcript of the Registers of the Company of Stationers of London 1554–1640 A.D.*, 5 vols. (London, 1875–94).
Beal, P. (comp.), *Index of English Literary Manuscripts: Volume I, 1450–1625; Volume II, 1625–1700*, 2 vols. in 4 pts. (London, 1980–93).
—, *A Dictionary of English Manuscript Terminology 1450–2000* (Oxford, 2008).
Carter, J., *ABC for Book Collectors* (London, 1952; last revised, 1973; many subsequent editions).
Dawson, G. and L. Kennedy-Skipton, *Elizabethan Handwriting 1500–1650: A Guide to the Reading of Documents and Manuscripts* (London, 1968).

Ferguson, W. C., *The Loan Book of the Stationers' Company with a List of Transactions 1592–1692* (London, 1989).

Greg, W. W. (ed.), *A Bibliography of the English Printed Drama to the Restoration*, 4 vols. (London, 1939–59).

—, *Licensers for the Press, &c. to 1640* (Oxford, 1962).

—, *A Companion to Arber* (Oxford, 1967).

Greg, W. W. and E. Boswell (eds.), *Records of the Court of the Stationers' Company 1576–1602 ~ from Register B* (London, 1930).

Ingram, W. H., 'The Ligatures of Early Printed Greek', *Greek, Roman and Byzantine Studies*, 7 (1966), 371–89.

Jackson, W. A. (ed.), *Records of the Court of the Stationers' Company 1602 to 1640* (London, 1957).

McKenzie, D. F. (ed.), *Stationers' Company Apprentices 1605–1640* (Charlottesville VA, 1961).

—, *Stationers' Company Apprentices 1641–1700* (Oxford, 1974).

—, *Stationers' Company Apprentices 1701–1800* (Oxford, 1978).

McKenzie, D. F. and M. Bell, *A Chronology and Calendar of Documents Relating to the London Book-Trade 1641–1700*, 3 vols. (Oxford, 2005).

McKerrow, R. B., *Printers' and Publishers' Devices in England and Scotland, 1485–1640* (London, 1913).

—, *An Introduction to Bibliography for Literary Students*, 2nd impression with corrections (Oxford, 1928).

McKerrow, R. B. and F. S., Ferguson, *Title-Page Borders Used in England and Scotland 1485–1640* (London, 1932).

McLeod, M. S. G., et al., *The Cathedral Libraries Catalogue: Books Printed before 1701 in the Libraries of the Anglican Cathedrals of England and Wales*, 2 vols. in 3 pts. (London, 1984–8).

Moore, J. K., *Primary Materials Relating to Copy and Print in English Books of the Sixteenth and Seventeenth Centuries* (Oxford, 1992).

Moxon, J., *Mechanick Exercises on the Whole Art of Printing (1683–4)*, ed. H. Davis and H. Carter, 2nd edn., (Oxford, 1962).

Myers, R., *The Stationers' Company Archive 1554–1984* (Winchester, 1990).

Pearson, D., *Provenance Research in Book History: A Handbook* (London, 1994).

Pettegree, A., M. Walsby, and A. Wilkinson (eds.), *French Vernacular Books: Books Published in the French Language before 1601 · Livres vernaculaires français: Livres imprimés en français avant 1601*, 2 vols. (Leiden, 2007).

Plomer, H. R. (ed.), *A Transcript of the Register of the Worshipful Company of Stationers 1640–1708 A.D.*, 3 vols. (London, 1913–14).

Pollard, A. W. and G. W. Redgrave (eds.), *A Short-Title Catalogue of Books Printed in England, Scotland, and Ireland and of English Books Printed Abroad 1475–1640*, 2nd edn. W. A. Jackson, F. S. Ferguson, and K. F. Pantzer, 3 vols. (London, 1976–91).

Ringler, W. A., Jr, *Bibliography and Index of English Verse Printed 1476–1558* (London, 1988).

—, *Bibliography and Index of English Verse in Manuscript, 1501–1558* (London, 1992).

Ringler, W. A. and S. W. May (eds.), *Elizabethan Poetry: A Bibliography and First-line Index of English Verse, 1559–1603* (London and New York, 2004).

Steer, F. W., *Scriveners' Company Common Paper 1357–1628: With a Continuation to 1678* (London, 1968).

Tanselle, G. T., *Introduction to Bibliography: Seminar Syllabus* (Charlottesville VA, 2002).

—, *Introduction to Scholarly Editing: Seminar Syllabus* (Charlottesville VA, 2002).

Williams, F. B. Jr (comp.), *Index of Dedications and Commendatory Verses in English Books before 1641* (London, 1962).

Williams, W. P. (comp.), *Index to the Stationers' Register, 1640–1708* (La Jolla CA, 1980).

Wing, D. (comp.), *Short-Title Catalogue of Books Printed in England, Scotland, Ireland, Wales and British America and of English Books Printed in Other Countries 1641–1700*, rev. and enlarged edn., J. J. Morison, C. W. Nelson, et al., 4 vols. (New York, 1982–98).

Primary Digital Resources

Early English Books Online: http://eebo.chadwyck.com
English Short-Title Catalogue: http://estc/bl.uk

Essential Reading

Cavallo, G. and R. Chartier (eds.), *A History of Reading in the West*, trans. L. G. Cochrane (Oxford, 1999).

Dane, J. A., *The Myth of Print Culture: Essays on Evidence, Textuality, and Bibliographical Method* (Toronto, 2003).

Gaskell, P., *A New Introduction to Bibliography* (Oxford, 1972; rev. 1974).

Greg, W. W., *Collected Papers*, ed. J. C. Maxwell (Oxford, 1966).

McGann, J. J., *A Critique of Modern Textual Criticism* (Chicago, 1983).

McKenzie, D. F., *Bibliography and the Sociology of Texts* (London, 1986; reissued with 'The Sociology of a Text: Orality, Literacy and Print in Early New Zealand': Cambridge, 1999).

—, *Making Meaning: 'Printers of the Mind' and Other Essays* (Amherst MA, 2002).

McKitterick, D. J., *Print, Manuscript and the Search for Order, 1450–1830* (Cambridge, 2003).

Morison, S., *Politics and Script: Aspects of Authority and Freedom in the Development of Graeco-Latin Script from the Sixth Century* B.C. *to the Twentieth Century* A.D. (Oxford, 1972).

Parkes, M. B., *Pause and Effect: Punctuation in the West* (Aldershot, 1993).

Further Reading

Before 1500

Bühler, C. F., *The Fifteenth Century Book: The Scribes · The Printers · The Decorators* (Philadelphia PA, 1960).

Carley, J. P. and C. G. C. Tite (eds.), *Books and Collectors 1200–1700* (London, 1997).

Carruthers, M., *The Book of Memory* (Cambridge, 1990).

Dreyfus, J., 'The Invention of Spectacles and the Advent of Printing', *The Library*, VI: 10 (1988), 93–106.

Gillespie, A. and D. Wakelin, *The Production of Books in England, 1350–1500* (Cambridge, 2011).

Green, D. H., *Women Readers in the Middle Ages* (Cambridge, 2007).

Hanna, R., *Pursuing History: Middle English Manuscripts and Their Texts* (Stanford CA, 1996).

—, *London Literature, 1300–1380* (Cambridge, 2005).

Hellinga, L., *William Caxton and Early Printing in England* (London, 2010).

Jensen, K. (ed.), *Incunabula and Their Readers: Printing, Selling and Using Books in the Fifteenth Century* (London, 2003).

Ker, N. R., *Books, Collectors and Libraries: Studies in Medieval Heritage* (London, [1985]).

Lowry, M., *The World of Aldus Manutius: Business and Scholarship in Renaissance Venice* (Oxford, 1979).

—, *Nicholas Jenson and the Rise of Venetian Publishing in Renaissance Europe* (Oxford, 1991).

McKitterick, R. (ed.), *The Uses of Literacy in Early Medieval Europe* (Cambridge, 1990).

Morgan, R. N. and R. M. Thompson (eds.), *The Cambridge History of the Book in Britain, Volume II 1100–1400* (Cambridge, 2008).

Moulton, I. F. (ed.), *Reading and Literacy in the Middle Ages and Renaissance* (Turnhout, 2004).

Newton, F., *The Scriptorium and Library at Monte Cassino 1058–1105* (Cambridge, 1999).

Parkes, M. B., *Scribes, Scripts and Readers: Studies in the Communication, Presentation and Dissemination of Medieval Texts* (London, 1991).

Parkes, M. and A. G. Watson (eds.), *Medieval Scribes, Manuscripts and Libraries: Essays Presented to N. R. Ker* (Aldershot, 1978).

Petrucci, A., *Writers and Readers: Studies in the History of Written Culture*, ed. and trans. C. M. Radding (New Haven CT, 1995).

Rouse, R. H. and M. A. Rouse, *Illiterati et uxorati, Manuscripts and Their Makers: Commercial Book Producers in Medieval Paris 1200–1500*, 2 vols. (Turnhout, 2000).

Saenger, P., *Space between Words: The Origins of Silent Reading* (Stanford CA, 1997).

Scott, K. L., *Tradition and Innovation in Later Medieval English Manuscripts* (London, 2007).

Manuscripts

Beal, P., *In Praise of Scribes: Manuscripts and Their Makers in Seventeenth Century England* (Oxford, 1998).

Beal, P. and G. Ioppolo (eds.), *Elizabeth I and the Culture of Writing* (London, 2007).

Davis, T., 'The Practice of Handwriting Identification', *The Library*, VII: 8 (2007), 251–76.

Fairbank, A. and B. Dickens, *The Italic Hand in Tudor Cambridge* (Cambridge, 1962).

Fairbank, A. and R. W. Hunt, *Humanistic Script of the Fifteenth and Sixteenth Centuries* (Oxford, 1960).

Fairbank, A. and B. Wolpe, *Renaissance Handwriting: An Anthology of Italic Scripts* (London, 1960).

Hector, L. C., *The Handwriting of English Documents* (London, 1958).

Jenkinson, H., *The Later Court Hands in England, from the Fifteenth to the Seventeenth Century* (Cambridge, 1927).

Love, H., *Scribal Publication in Seventeenth Century England* (Oxford, 1993).

—, *English Clandestine Satire 1660–1702* (Oxford, 2004).

Wardrop, J., *The Script of Humanism: Some Aspects of Humanist Script 1460–1560* (Oxford, 1963).

Woudhuysen, H. R., *Sir Philip Sidney and the Circulation of Manuscripts 1580–1640* (Oxford, 1996).

Book Production, Publishing History, and Bibliographical Description

Barber, G., *Textile and Embroidered Bindings* (Oxford, 1971).

Barnard, J. and M. Bell, 'The Inventory of Henry Bynneman (1583) A Preliminary Survey', *Publishing History*, 29 (1991), 5–46.

—, *The Early Seventeenth-Century York Book Trade and John Foster's Inventory of 1616* (Leeds, 1994).

Binns, J. W., 'STC Latin Books: Evidence for Printing-House Practice', *The Library*, V: 32 (1977), 1–27.

—, 'STC Latin Books: Further Evidence for Printing-House Practice', *The Library*, VI: 1 (1979), 347–54.

Bland, M. B., 'The Appearance of the Text in Early Modern England', *TEXT*, 11 (1998), 91–154.

Blayney, P. W. M., *The Bookshops in Paul's Cross Churchyard* (London, 1990).

—, *The Stationers' Company before the Charter, 1403–1557* (London, 2003).

Bowen, K. L. and D. Imhof, *Christopher Plantin and Engraved Book Illustrations in Sixteenth Century Europe* (Cambridge, 2008).

Bowers, F. T., *Principles of Bibliographical Description* (Princeton NJ, 1949: reissued Winchester, 1986).

Carter, H., *A View of Early Typography up to about 1600* (Oxford, 1969).

—, *A History of Oxford University Press: Volume I · To the year 1780* (Oxford, 1975).

Clement, R. W., 'The Beginnings of Printing in Anglo-Saxon, 1565–1630', *PBSA*, 91 (1997), 192–244.

Foot, M. M., *Bookbinders at Work: Their Roles and Methods* (London, 2006).

Gaskell, P., 'The Lay of the Case', *Studies in Bibliography*, 22 (1969), 125–42.

Greg, W. W., *Some Aspects of London Publishing between 1550 and 1650* (Oxford, 1956).

Hammersmith, J. P., 'Frivolous Trifles and Weighty Tomes: Early Proof-reading at London, Oxford, and Cambridge', *Studies in Bibliography*, 38 (1985), 236–51.

Hellinga, L. and W. Hellinga; 'Regulations Relating to the Planning and Organization of Work by the Master Printer in the Ordinances of Christopher Plantin', *The Library*, v: 29 (1974), 52–60.

Johnson, G. D.; 'The Stationers versus the Drapers: Control of the Press in the Late Sixteenth Century', *The Library*, vi: 10 (1988), 1–17.

Krummel, D. W., *English Music Printing 1553–1700* (London, 1975).

Lucas, P. J., 'Parker, Lambarde and the Provision of Special Sorts for Printing Anglo-Saxon in the Sixteenth Century', *Journal of the Printing Historical Society*, 28 (1999), 41–69.

Mack, N. A., 'The History of the Grammar Patent, 1547–1620', *PBSA*, 87 (1993), 419–36.

McKenzie, D. F., *The Cambridge University Press 1696–1712*, 2 vols. (Cambridge, 1966).

—, 'Eight Quarto Proof Sheets of 1594 Set by Formes: *A Fruitfull Commentarie*', *The Library*, v: 28 (1973), 1–13.

—, '"Indenting the Stick" in the First Quarto of *King Lear* (1608)', *PBSA*, 67 (1973), 125–30.

McKerrow, R. B., 'The Relationship of English Printed Books to Authors' Manuscripts during the Sixteenth and Seventeenth Centuries', *Studies in Bibliography*, 53 (2000), 1–65.

McKitterick, D. J., *A History of Cambridge University Press: Volume I, Printing and the Book Trade in Cambridge 1534–1698* (Cambridge, 1992).

McMullan, B. J., 'The Origins of Press Figures in English Printing 1629–1671', *The Library*, vi: 1 (1979), 307–35.

Meynell, F. and S. A. Morison; 'Printers' Flowers and Arabesques', *The Fleuron*, 1 (1923), 1–43.

Morison, S. A., *First Principles of Typography*, 2nd edn. (Cambridge, 1967).

—, *Selected Essays on the History of Letter-Forms in Manuscript and Print*, ed. D. J. McKitterick, 2 vols. (Cambridge, 1981).

Pollard, A. W., 'Margins', *The Dolphin*, 1 (1933), 67–80.

Simpson, P., *Proof-reading in the Sixteenth, Seventeenth and Eighteenth Centuries* (Oxford, 1935).

Tanselle, G. T., *Bibliographical Analysis: A Historical Introduction* (Cambridge, 2009).

Voet, L., *The Golden Compasses: A History and Evaluation of the Printing and Publishing Activities of the Officina Plantiniana at Antwerp*, 2 vols. (Amsterdam, 1969–72).

Warde, B., 'The "Garamond" Types: A Study of XVI and XVII Century Sources', *The Fleuron*, 5 (1926), 131–79.

Woodfield, D. B., *Surreptitious Printing in England* (New York, 1973).

Material Analysis

Bland, M. B., 'Italian Paper in Early Seventeenth Century England', *Paper as a Medium of Cultural Heritage: Archaeology and Conservation*, ed. R. Graziaplena (Rome, 2004), 243–55.

Blayney, P. W. M., *The Texts of* King Lear *and Their Origins: Volume I, Nicholas Okes and the First Quarto* (Cambridge, 1982). Vol. 2 not published.

Ferguson, W. C., *Pica Roman Type in Elizabethan England* (Aldershot, 1989).

Hinman, C., *The Printing and Proof-Reading of the First Folio of Shakespeare*, 2 vols. (Oxford, 1963).

Mosser, D. W., M. Saffle, and E. W. Sullivan II (eds.), *Puzzles in Paper: Concepts in Historical Watermarks* (New Castle DE and London, 2000).

Pearson, D., *English Bookbinding Styles 1450–1800* (London, 2005).

Szirmai, J. A., *The Archaeology of Medieval Bookbinding* (Aldershot, 1999).

Weiss, A., 'Bibliographical Methods for Identifying Unknown Printers in Elizabethan/Jacobean Books', *Studies in Bibliography*, 44 (1991), 183–228.

Book History

Barker, N. J., *Form and Meaning in the History of the Book: Selected Essays* (London, 2003).

Barnard, J. and D. F. McKenzie (eds.), *The Cambridge History of the Book in Britain, Volume IV 1557–1700* (Cambridge, 2002).

Bland, M. B., '"Invisible Dangers": Censorship and the Subversion of Authority in Early Modern England', *PBSA*, 90 (1996), 154–93.

—, 'The London Book-Trade in 1600', *A Companion to Shakespeare*, ed. D. S. Kastan (Oxford, 1999), 450–63.

Bray, J., M. Handley, and A. C. Henry (eds.), *Ma'king the Text: The Presentation of Meaning on the Literary Page* (Aldershot, 2000)

Chartier, R., *The Cultural Uses of Print in Early Modern France*, trans. L. G. Cochrane (Princeton NJ, 1987).

—, *The Order of Book: Readers, Authors, and Libraries in Europe between the Fourteenth and Eighteenth Centuries*, trans. L. G. Cochrane (Oxford, 1994).

—, *Inscription and Erasure: Literature and Written Culture from the Eleventh to the Eighteenth Century*, trans. A Goldhammer (Philadelphia PA, 2007).

—, (ed.), *The Culture of Print: Power and the Uses of Print in Early Modern Europe* (Oxford, 1989).

Clegg, C. S., *Press Censorship in Elizabethan England* (Cambridge, 1997).

—, *Press Censorship in Jacobean England* (Cambridge, 2001).

—, *Press Censorship in Caroline England* (Cambridge, 2008).

Cressy, D., *Literacy and the Social Order: Reading and Writing in Tudor and Stuart England* (Cambridge, 1980).

Eliot, S. and J. Rose, *A Companion to the History of the Book* (Oxford, 2007).

Feather, J. P., 'From Rights in Copies to Copyright: The Recognition of Authors' Rights in English Law and Practice in the Sixteenth and Seventeenth Centuries', *Cardozo Law and Entertainment Law Journal*, 10 (1992), 455–73.

Fox, A., *Oral and Literate Culture in England 1500–1700* (Oxford, 2000).

Gillespie, A., Poets, Printers, and Early English *Sammelbände*', *Huntington Library Quarterly*, 67 (2004), 189–214.

—, *Print Culture and the Medieval Author: Chaucer, Lydgate, and Their Books 1473–1557* (Oxford, 2006).

Grafton, A., *Commerce with the Classics: Ancient Books and Renaissance Readers* (Ann Arbor MI, 1997).

—, *The Culture of Correction in Renaissance Europe* (London, 2011).

—, *Worlds Made by Words: Scholarship and Community in the Modern West* (Cambridge MA, 2009).

Grenby, M. O., 'Chapbooks, Children, and Children's Literature', *The Library*, VII: 8 (2007), 277–303.

Hackel, H. B., *Reading Material in Early Modern England: Print, Gender, and Literacy* (Cambridge, 2005).

Hellinga, L. and J. B. Trapp, *The Cambridge History of the Book in Britain, Volume III 1400–1557* (Cambridge, 1999).

Johnson, F. R., 'Notes on English Retail Book-Prices, 1550–1640', *The Library*, V: 5 (1950), 83–112.

Kirschbaum, L., 'Author's Copyright in England before 1640', *PBSA*, 40 (1946), 43–80.

—, 'The Copyright of Elizabethan Plays', *The Library*, V: 14 (1959), 231–50.

Maclean, I., *Scholarship, Commerce, Religion: The Learned Book in the Age of Confessions, 1560–1630* (Cambridge MA, 2012).

Mann, A. J., *The Scottish Book Trade 1500–1720* (East Linton, 2000).

Martin, H.-J., *The History and Power of Writing*, trans. L. G. Cochrane (Chicago IL, 1994).

—, *The French Book: Religion, Absolutism, and Readership, 1585–1715*, trans. P. and N. Saenger (Baltimore MD, 1996).

Martin, H.-J. and R. Chartier (eds.), *Histoire de l'édition française*, 4 vols. (Paris, 1982–6).

McKitterick, D. J., 'Ovid with a Littleton': The Cost of English Books in the Early Seventeenth Century', *TCBS*, XI: 2 (1997), 184–234.

—, et al.; *The Making of the Wren Library* (Cambridge, 1995).

Pearson, D., *Books as History: The Importance of Books beyond Texts* (London, 2008).

Pettegree, A., *The French Book and the European Book World* (Leiden, 2007).

Raven, J., *The Business of Books: Booksellers and the English Book Trade* (New Haven CT, 2007).

Sharpe, K. and S. N., Zwicker, *Reading, Society and Politics in Early Modern England* (Cambridge, 2003).

Sherman, W., *Used Books: Making Readers in Renaissance England* (Philadelphia PA, 2008).

Shuger, D., *Censorship and Cultural Sensibility: The Regulation of Language in Tudor-Stuart England* (Philadelphia PA, 2006).

Stoddard, R. E., *Marks in Books, Illustrated and Explained* (Cambridge MA, 1985).

After 1700

Allan, D., *A Nation of Readers: The Lending Library in Georgian England* (London, 2008).

Barchas, J., *Graphic Design, Print Culture, and the Eighteenth Century Novel* (Cambridge, 2003).

Barker, N. J., 'Typography and the Meaning of Words: The Revolution in the Layout of Books in the Eighteenth Century', in *Buch und Buchhandel in Europa im achtzehnten Jahrhundert*, eds. G. Barber and B. Fabian, *Wolfenbüttler Schriften zur Geschichte des Buchwesens* 4 (Hamburg, 1981), 126–65.

Bonnell, T. F., *The Most Disreputable Trade: Publishing the Classics of English Poetry 1765–1810* (Oxford, 2008).

Bronson, B. H., *Printing as an Index of Taste in Eighteenth Century England* (New York, 1958).

Fergus, J., *Provincial Readers in Eighteenth-Century England* (Oxford, 2006).

Foxon, D., *Pope and the Early Eighteenth-Century Book Trade*, rev. and ed. J. McLaverty (Oxford, 1991).

Hansen, L., *Government and the Press, 1695–1763* (Oxford, 1936).

Maslen, K. I. D., *An Early London Printing House at Work: Studies in the Bowyer Ledgers* (New York, 1993).

McKitterick, D. J., *A History of Cambridge University Press: Volume II, Scholarship and Commerce, 1698–1872* (Cambridge, 1998).

McLaverty, J., *Pope, Print and Meaning* (Oxford, 2001).

Raven, J., *Judging New Wealth: Popular Publishing and Responses to Commerce in England, 1750–1800* (Oxford, 1992).

Rivers, I. (ed.), *Books and Their Readers in Eighteenth Century England* (Leicester, 1982).

—, *Books and Their Readers in Eighteenth Century England: New Essays* (Leicester, 2001).

Suarez, M. and M. Turner (eds.), *The Cambridge History of the Book in Britain, Volume V · The Eighteenth Century* (Cambridge, forthcoming).

Libraries

Fehrenbach, R. J. and E. S. Leedham-Green (eds.), *Private Libraries in Renaissance England*, 6 vols. (Binghamton NY, 1992–2004).

Hoare, P., et al. (eds.), *The Cambridge History of Libraries in Britain and Ireland*, 3 vols. (Cambridge, 2006).

Leedham-Green, E. S. (ed.), *Books in Cambridge Inventories: Book-Lists from Vice Chancellor's Court Probate Inventories in the Tudor and Stuart Periods* (Cambridge, 1986).

McKitterick, D. J., *Cambridge University Library: A History · The Eighteenth and Nineteenth Centuries* (Cambridge, 1986).

Oates, J. C. T., *Cambridge University Library: A History · From the Beginnings to the Copyright Act of Queen Anne* (Cambridge, 1986).

Pearson, D., 'The Libraries of English Bishops, 1600–40', *The Library*, VI: 14 (1992), 221–57.

Perkin, M., *A Directory of Parochial Libraries of the Church of England and the Church in Wales* (London, 2004).

Philips, I. G., *The Bodleian Library in the Seventeenth and Eighteenth Centuries* (Oxford, 1983).

Vernet, A. (ed.), *Histoires des bibliothèques françaises*, 4 vols. (Paris, 1989).

Wormald, F. and C. E. Wright (eds.), *The English Library before 1700: Studies in Its History* (London, 1958).

Textual Criticism and Attribution

Bowers, F. T., *Bibliography and Textual Criticism* (Oxford, 1964).

—, 'Greg's "Rationale of Copy-Text" Revisited', *Studies in Bibliography*, 31 (1978), 90–161.

Bucci, R., 'Tanselle's "Editing without a Copy-text": Genesis, Issues, Prospects', *Studies in Bibliography*, 56 (2006 for 2003–4), 1–44.

Deppman, J., D. Ferrer, and M. Groden (eds.), *Genetic Criticism: Texts and Avant-Textes* (Philadelphia PA, 2004).

Greetham, D. C., *An Introduction to Textual Scholarship* (New York, 1992; 1994).

—, *Theories of the Text* (Oxford, 1999).

Love, H., *Attributing Authorship: An Introduction* (Cambridge, 2002).

McLaverty, J., 'The Concept of Authorial Intention in Textual Criticism', *The Library*, VI: 6 (1984), 121–38.

Shillingsburg, P. L., *Scholarly Editing in the Computer Age* (Ann Arbor MI, 1996).

—, *Resisting Texts: Authority and Submission in Constructions of Meaning* (Ann Arbor MI, 1997).

—, *From Gutenberg to Google: Electronic Representations of Literary Texts* (Cambridge, 2006).

Tanselle, G. T., *The Rationale of Textual Criticism* (Philadelphia PA, 1992).

—, *Literature and Artifacts* (Charlottesville VA, 1998).

Index